INDIAN LIFE

INDIAN LIFE
Transforming an American Myth

Edited and with an Introduction by

William W. Savage, Jr.

University of Oklahoma Press: Norman

By William W. Savage, Jr.

The Cherokee Strip Live Stock Association (Columbia, Missouri, 1973)

(Editor) *Cowboy Life: Reconstructing an American Myth* (Norman, 1975)

(Editor, with David Harry Miller) *The Character and Influence of the Indian Trade in Wisconsin*, by Frederick Jackson Turner (Norman, 1977)

(Editor) *Indian Life: Transforming an American Myth* (Norman, 1977)

Library of Congress Cataloging in Publication Data
Main entry under title:

Indian life.

Includes bibliographical references.
I. Indians of North America—Great Plains—Public opinion. 2. Public opinion—United States. I. Savage, William W.
E78.G73I53   301.15'43'97800497   77–9111

Copyright 1977 by the University of Oklahoma Press, Norman, Publishing Division of the University. Manufactured in the U.S.A. First edition.

To the memory of Sitting Bull

Preface

This book is a companion volume to *Cowboy Life: Reconstructing an American Myth*. Like the earlier work, it concerns the period from the end of the Civil War to the beginning of the twentieth century, and its focus is the Great Plains region. It has to do with the images of Indians developed by whites to justify white expansion into Indian domain, and thus it examines the political utility of myth. As an analysis of items in America's cultural baggage, unlike *Cowboy Life* it constitutes a pessimistic exercise.

The photographs and the narratives were again drawn from materials in the Western History Collections of the University of Oklahoma Library. I wish to thank John S. Ezell, curator of the collections, and staff members Jack D. Haley and H. Glenn Jordan, all of whom contributed generously of their time and energy to the completion of this project.

To my friend and colleague David Harry Miller, who shared with me the results of his research into ethnic stereotyping on the Roman frontier and thereby extended my own thinking about the general problem of culture contact in frontier situations, I offer special thanks.

To Shane, who helped me to understand prejudice by being so completely devoid of it, I am most grateful.

WILLIAM W. SAVAGE, JR.

Norman, Oklahoma
July 13, 1976

Contents

Preface   *page* vii

Editor's Introduction   3

RICHARD IRVING DODGE: *"He remains a savage simply from
lack of a code of morals"* (1882)   17

JACOB PIATT DUNN: *"Jack, I haven't had an Indian to eat for
a long time"* (1886)   47

JOHN F. FINERTY: *"Their music is fitter for hell than for
earth"* (1890)   91

CHARLES ALSTON MESSITER: *"Indians never spare anyone who
is in their power"* (1890)   99

RICHARD HARDING DAVIS: *"There are a great many Indians and
a great many reservations"* (1892)   111

ANDY ADAMS: *"He looked every inch a chief"* (1903)   141

EDWARD L. WHEELER: *"The great warrior straightened up like
an arrow"* (1877)   163

PRENTISS INGRAHAM: *" 'It's my Injun, boys,' he cried
exultantly"* (1881)   167

HELEN HUNT JACKSON: *"Here is a picture of a helpless
people!"* (1881)   171

JAMES WILLARD SCHULTZ: *"The squawman fought their
battles"* (1907)   209

W. FLETCHER JOHNSON: *"He was lazy and vicious, and never
told the truth when a lie would serve better"* (1891)   231

COMMISSIONER OF INDIAN AFFAIRS: *"A shot was fired and
carnage ensued"* (1891)   249

JOSEPH KOSSUTH DIXON: *"They have moved majestically down
the pathway of the ages"* (1914)   267

Illustrations

Sitting Bull   *page* 19
Sitting Bull and William F. Cody   20
Souvenir photograph of Sitting Bull   21
Quanah Parker   22
Quanah Parker in 1901   23
Geronimo skinning a buffalo   24
Jim Thorpe   26

Three Cheyenne lodges   75
Cheyennes and Arapahoes at Cantonment   76
Cantonment after a beef issue   78
Indian women butchering cattle   80
A dog feast   82
Iron Tail   115
Sioux warriors   116
Kiowa warriors   118
Cheyenne Lance Society   120
Kado, Comanche, and his wife   121
Pablino Diaz, Kiowa   122
White Swan, Crow   123
Last Horse, Sioux   124
Little Bird, Arapaho   125
Wolf Robe, Cheyenne   126
Mountain, Blackfoot   127
Ahahe, Wichita, and infant   128
Swift Dog, Sioux   129
Interpreter and entourage   130

Pawnee Bill program cover   *page* 147
Indians entering arena   148
Another grand entrance   150
101 Ranch Indian with pistol   152
Indians rehearsing wild West act   153
101 Ranch Indians   154
Cast of the 101 Ranch show   156
Bow-and-arrow demonstration   157
A sideshow attraction   158
"Realistic scenes truthfully depicted"   160
Plains Indian stereotype   162

Sioux Sun Dance   223
Indians with automobile   224
Between two worlds   226
Comanche Jack, Comanche   227
Cheyenne-Arapaho Ghost Dance   228
The dead at Wounded Knee   230

INDIAN LIFE

Editor's Introduction[*]

The Indian occupies a unique position in the American popular mind. It is not a position that is easily defined, because its historical antecedents lie in the ambiguity with which Americans have customarily contemplated Indians. Thus, "the Indian"—a myth, a conceptual monolith, a stereotypical composite of all Indians about which more will be said later—appears in American culture in a series of paired images: he is both a noble savage and a brute, a bearer of gifts and a bloodthirsty killer of women and children, a teacher without whose help survival is impossible and a ward incapable of survival without public or private assistance. Such are the renditions of Americans who have always believed that they should come to some conclusion about Indians but who have been equally uncertain how to go about it, a dilemma reflected in three hundred years of American popular culture.[1]

The first ambiguous response to Indians belonged to Christopher Columbus, their discoverer and the man who misnamed them. Struggling to define for his employers just who and what these aborigines were, he described them as being "neither black nor white." That left considerable room for speculation, as did Columbus' observation that Indians would make fine subjects for his majesties and that some could be converted to Christianity. Those who clung to idolatrous ways, he noted, would be suitable slaves.[2]

Europeans, who knew little about Indians except that they existed, craved more information. It was amply provided in extravagant and largely fictional travel narratives, accounts belonging to a literary genre designed to entertain and inform, with emphasis on

[*] Notes for the Introduction begin on page 13.

the former rather than the latter. Travel narratives fired the fantasies of Europeans for a hundred years after Columbus with tales of wild and brutish men who inhabited the New World.[3] The first English colonists, having had a steady diet of such fables and possessing no reliable information, knew at least that Indians were something with which to reckon, and so they came armed, built forts, and organized militia.[4]

On the other hand, the colonists were strangers in the Indians' environment, and, to make their way, they learned what they could of Indian survival techniques and to an extent copied Indian life styles.[5] Later, as the number of colonists grew and as European nations established patterns of expansion in North America, Indians became socially, politically, and economically expendable; thus they were systematically driven from land desired by white settlers and were confined to areas considered by whites to be uninhabitable. The mode of their secular existence was called into question, and the economic bases of their various cultures were destroyed. And, if that were not enough, their spiritual lives were deemed unacceptable to the white majority, and they were beset by missionaries of all persuasions.[6] When all other forms of exploitation had run their course, Indians were utilized by white society as entertainment, which was, after all, precisely the use to which they had been put in the travel narratives.

The history of Indian-white relations in North America, involving diverse European nationalities and equally diverse aboriginal cultures, is complex and merits more than brief consideration. But the point here is this: it is a history that has given rise to potent ideas concerning the ways in which disparate peoples view each other. From that history, or from an imperfect understanding of it, Americans acquired their mythic "Indian," their conceptual monolith—a painted horseman who dwells in tipis; wears feathers in his hair; is given to guttural speech and terrifying war cries; is crafty, wise, sly, and violent; and stands in opposition to that fixture of American popular culture the cowboy.[7] Additionally, the ways in which Americans have stereotyped Indians indicate the presence of something approaching a monumental preoccupation with Indian life. Whatever parallels one finds between the history of Indian-white relations and the patterns of culture contact on frontiers other than

North America, it is certain that nowhere else is there a comparable popular preoccupation with the details of aboriginal society and culture manifested by the dominant population. Nowhere else did numbers of whites run away to live with the aborigines, and nowhere else do the vestiges of aboriginal life enjoy such popularity.[8]

From the very beginning, Anglo-Americans ran away to the Indians. In the eighteenth century the phenomenon was sufficiently common to prompt Hector St. John de Crèvecoeur to wonder why there was no corresponding migration by Indians wishing to become "civilized Europeans" and, further, what would become of the whites who became Indians. "It will be worthy of observation," he mused,

> to see whether those who are now with the Indians will ever return and submit themselves to the yoke of European society; or whether they will carefully cherish their knowledge and industry and gather themselves on some fertile spot in the interior parts of the continent; or whether that easy, desultory life so peculiar to the Indians will attract their attention and destroy their ancient inclinations. I rather think that the latter will preponderate, for you cannot possibly conceive the singular charm, the indescribable propensity which Europeans are apt to conceive and imbibe in a very short time for this vagrant life; a life which we civilized people are apt to represent to ourselves as the most ignoble, the most irksome of any. Upon a nearer inspection 'tis far from being so disgusting.[9]

A good many Spanish conquistadores and no less a personage than Captain John Smith had discovered that a portion of the Indian population was female, and that fact accounted for some of the attraction the wilderness had for whites.[10] Longfellow's Hiawatha spoke for the nobility of it all, and James Fenimore Cooper publicized the masculine friendships that waited in the woods, rivaling, in time, the message of Nathaniel Hawthorne's Roger Chillingworth, that life among the Indians was not conducive to good mental health. Chillingworth, of course, had been captured by Indians and so represented another perspective. But if whites contemplated abandoning civilization for Indian ways, they also demonstrated an abiding interest in accounts of the lives of those forced to cohabit with aborigines. Captivity narratives—written or dictated by whites who had been captured by Indians and who subsequently were released or escaped—were enormously popular in the colonial period, and the captivity theme has endured in American popular culture to the twentieth century.[11]

Life among the Indians, whether forced or voluntary, contributed to the ambiguity of white feelings about Indians. The frontier—and the frontier was defined in terms of proximity to Indians—was at once a place to which one might flee to escape from the pressures of civilization and a place where danger lurked behind every rock and tree. There white men might find either sanctuary or death—or, for the religious, salvation in one guise or another. Conflicting images struggled for acceptance, but the contest was not confined to an intellectual plane, and when the economic realities of frontier living manifested themselves, the negative image, wherein devils and danger resided, began to dominate white thinking.

In the colonial period nations measured wealth and power by the amount of territory each controlled. The emergence of the new American nation after 1776 altered that perception only slightly. The thirteen former colonies had debts to pay—the creditors most often being their own citizens—and no money with which to pay them. To the federal and state governments land was money, and debts were paid in land, or the land was sold to private individuals or companies to generate revenue. But if whites were to occupy land, the Indians must first be removed from it, and so whites developed a series of images of Indians and Indian life useful in justifying wholesale dispossession.

The justifying images were, of course, wholly negative with regard to the portrayal of the Indian as a human being. The bloodthirsty brute of the travel narratives was resurrected and amplified in captivity narratives and journalistic pronouncements and, later, in dime novels. To justify the acquisition of territory, Anglo-Americans had to reconcile their economic motives with their ethical and moral responsibilities, a feat accomplished by recourse to law (something that Indians did not "understand") and by defining Indians as less than human. If Indians were not human—and their failure or refusal to comprehend white law proved to whites that they could not reason—then they were mere animals, and the land on which they lived was, by definition, uninhabited. God had told man, whites recalled, to subdue the earth and hold dominion over the beasts of the earth. Indians were not men but animals, and killing them was as good a way as any to hold dominion.[12] Those were widespread beliefs and, to judge from the efficiency with which whites confined, incarcerated, and slaughtered Indians, they provided the necessary philosophical underpinning for white expansion. But, widespread or not, they were not unanimously held, and the romantic myth of the noble savage survived, through one medium or another, thanks largely to the efforts of liberal reformers who opposed harsh treatment of Indians.[13]

The negative stereotype endured after it no longer had any political utility. Even before the last Indian attempt at resistance was broken at Wounded Knee in 1890, entrepreneurs found that the image of a fierce aborigine had a certain appeal to eastern and European audiences. In 1885, William F. Cody, who capitalized on his reputation as a frontiersman by exporting western characters for eastern consumption (it was he who had made a hero of the lowly cowboy), hired the storied Sitting Bull for Buffalo Bill's Wild West for $50 a week and a bonus of $125. Cody favored Sioux employees because people had heard of their tribe and because they were colorful, which is to say that they rode horses and wore feathers. Apaches, of whom people had also heard, were drab by contrast, which is to say that they managed life with few horses and fewer feathers.[14] This use of Indians as picturesque entertainment continued a long literary tradition and established patterns that would be extended yet further by the visual media of the twentieth century. Sight and sound were the Indians' stock in trade in extravaganzas like Cody's, and it is perhaps to Cody's credit that he employed the genuine articles. Motion-picture directors, after all, quickly discovered that anyone could portray an Indian if he could ride and avoid allergic reactions to paint and plumage.

The road shows of Buffalo Bill, Pawnee Bill, Colonel Frederic T. Cummins, and others were popular until well into the twentieth century, as were various traveling medicine shows featuring Indians. These spectacles originally capitalized on the image of the Indian as a teacher—in this case a specialist in the medicinal use of herbs—an image that quacks had been exploiting in America since at least the eighteenth century.[15] But at the end of the nineteenth, when the Indian acquired the status of a curiosity in the East, and in the twentieth, when nostalgia for the vanishing wilderness enjoyed the vogue that gave rise to Tarzan and the National Park Service, Indian medicine shows enjoyed something of a revival in popularity. It is axiomatic that authenticity of heritage (or anything else) was not a prerequisite for selling placebos, but, whereas Cody and the wild West show promoters had stressed the genuineness of their product, the medicine merchants made only feeble attempts at verisimilitude. There were Indians who spoke with foreign accents and Indians who claimed to be champion cowboys; and each Indian woman was a princess, each man a chief. Whether or not these people were Indians at all often seemed to be of secondary importance. It is doubtful, for example, that the audiences in the 1930's that saw Chief Sweetwater, of Harry B. Cody's Dr. Michael All-Herb and Health Institute of Chicago, cared one whit about the first item in the ballyhoo that billed him as a "full-blooded Sioux Indian, escape artist and aërial daredevil."[16] The legacy of the medicine shows to the concept of Indians-as-entertainment was that anyone who looked like an Indian could be an Indian, because anybody could act like one. Motion-picture directors would discover that, too.

Traveling shows and popular fiction kept the stereotyped Indian before the public until motion pictures could continue the tradition. But the movie Indian required time to develop, owing to the initial limitations of the film medium. The stereotype owed much to sight and sound, but in silent films the Indian could only be picturesque. Hooves could not thunder, Indians could not whoop, and victims could not scream—obvious handicaps for purveyors of popular entertainment. Still, the public wanted Indians, and it got what it wanted. Indian films were abundant in the silent era, and for the most part they marked a return to the romantic myth of the noble savage. They were melodramatic love stories set in bucolic environs, featuring Indian maidens enamored of white men, mixed-blood men enamored of white women, and vice versa, and so forth. The titles told all, as suggested by the following partial list of films with Indian themes made during 1910: *An Indian's Gratitude, Indian Blood, Indian Girl's Awakening, The Indian Girl's Romance, An Indian Maiden's Choice, Indian Pete's Gratitude, Stolen by Indians, Her Indian Mother, The Indian and the Cowgirl, His In-*

dian Bride, The Indian and the Maid, Elder Alden's Indian Ward, The Way of the Red Man, The Red Girl and the Child, Red Eagle's Love Affair, Red Wing's Constancy, White-Doe's Loves, and *Iron Arm's Remorse.* Of all the Indian films of 1910, thirteen concerned Indians who did good deeds and thereby reversed social opinion in their favor, six were all-Indian love stories, seven dealt with the love of an Indian woman for a white man, and three explored the love of an Indian man for a white woman. There was one film about Indian lust and another about white lust, and four treated the subject of intermarriage between white men and Indian women. These films far outnumbered those dealing with violent themes.[17]

The sound era, which began in 1927, changed things yet again, and the negative stereotype returned with a vengeance. Screaming savages were everywhere, burning, pillaging, raping, scalping, and generally being picturesque. They were a necessary ingredient in western action films—as necessary as horses, guns, wagons, or forts. They were, in short, props, and their function was to expire (as picturesquely as possible) as a consequence of being plugged by white soldiers, cowboys, settlers, miners, hunters, stagecoach passengers, or whatever. The Indian was to be a target, not a dramatic character, and Hollywood had every expectation that such an assignment would serve to entertain as well as enlighten white audiences. Consider for a moment Paramount's 1939 release *Geronimo,* directed by Paul H. Sloane and starring Preston Foster, Ellen Drew, and Andy Devine. The title role belonged to Cherokee actor Victor Daniels, whose stage name was Chief Thundercloud, but he received no billing under either name. He was to be a prop, not an actor, and his face was cosmetically altered to enhance whatever he could effect in the way of an evil expression. The idea was to exploit the negative stereotype, and the promotional suggestions distributed by Paramount to theater managers left no doubt about the studio's intentions. "Your community," the managers were told,

> can probably produce one or two old veterans who fought in some of the Indian wars. Find them and enlist their aid in selling "Geronimo!" Get their reactions and quote them in advance advertising. Try to plant a local [newspaper] feature story based on the experiences of the veterans and be sure to have them refer prominently to Geronimo as the most brutal savage of them all.[18]

9

Delmer Daves' *Broken Arrow*, released in 1950, has generally been acknowledged as the first modern film to portray Indians sympathetically and to suggest that Indian life was a valid alternative to existence in white society. The role of Cochise, the reasonable Apache, was played by a white, Jeff Chandler, while that of the malevolent Geronimo went to Indian actor Jay Silverheels. One is tempted to say that Hollywood's rule of thumb in westerns seemed to be, "The only bad Indian is a real Indian," but, whatever the case, it does not appear that *Broken Arrow* had much immediate impact on the ways in which Indians were portrayed in American films. A large number of Indian films concerned confrontations between aborigines and the army, and *Broken Arrow* did nothing to lessen the popularity of such fare. Between 1951 and 1970 at least eighty-six Indians-versus-army films appeared, twelve of them coming within a year of *Broken Arrow*. Titles such as *Tomahawk, Slaughter Trail, Warpath, War Paint, Massacre Canyon, War Arrow, Flaming Frontier*, and *Blood on the Arrow* continued to sell popcorn to audiences that, ironically, had forgotten the origin of that particular delicacy.[19]

And who were the movie Indians? They were actors who looked the part, which most often meant actors who could represent evil personified. Many came from the horror films (Bela Lugosi, Boris Karloff, Lon Chaney, Jr.), and many were professional cinematic heavies (Sheldon Leonard, Bruce Cabot, Claude Akins, Lee Van Cleef, Charles Bronson, Neville Brand, Anthony Caruso), while some were simply journeymen who specialized in portraying virtually every ethnic type (Akim Tamiroff, J. Carrol Naish). Others were comedians, for those occasions when funny and/or drunken Indians were required (Buddy Hackett, Joey Bishop), and still others were cowboy heroes, for those occasions when audience sympathy was a necessary ingredient (Audie Murphy, Guy Madison, John Wayne, Chuck Connors). There have been former Tarzans (Buster Crabbe, Lex Barker), part-time Lone Rangers (Clayton Moore), and pop singers (Elvis Presley). There have been Latin actors (Gilbert Roland, Ricardo Montalban), Japanese actors (Sessue Hayakawa), and black actors (Woody Strode). And there have been the women, beautiful, silent, and seductive (Nancy Kwan, Loretta Young, Katherine Ross, Debra Paget, Donna Reed,

Jennifer Jones, Cyd Charisse, Daliah Lavi, Audrey Hepburn), to say nothing of the children, who grew up to be something else (Robert Blake, Dickie Moore). The few Indian actors (Victor Daniels, Jay Silverheels, X Brands, Eddie Little Sky, Chief Yowlachie, Dan George, Will Sampson, Iron Eyes Cody) have been all but lost in that parade of wigs, contact lenses, and body paint. The real Indians remain in the background, and to that extent art imitates life.[20]

Other media have elaborated upon the Indian stereotype. Radio contributed the Lone Ranger's faithful Indian companion, Tonto. Tonto's voice belonged to John Todd, an elderly Shakespearean actor who knew the part so well that he often slept through the broadcasts, awaking only to emit guttural responses at the appropriate times.[21] And there was Straight Arrow, an articulate Indian hero of sorts who always masqueraded as a white rancher until trouble arose. The character was the brainchild of an advertising agency in search of something for Nabisco to sponsor.[22] Television cast Lebanese actor Michael Ansara as Cochise in its version of *Broken Arrow*, presented singer Ed Ames of the Ames Brothers as an educated Indian sidekick for Fess Parker in *Daniel Boone*, and aired, among other things, a contemporary series, *Hawk*, about an Indian detective in New York, with Burt Reynolds in the title role.[23]

Popular fiction continues to offer the public Navajo detectives, fierce Apaches, and ruthless squawmen.[24] Humorous novels about modern Indians waging spectacular but often ineffectual war against the federal government also have enjoyed a certain vogue,[25] but in the presentation of "funny" Indians newspaper comic strips have no equal. If films have taught that Indians are stoical, ruthless, cunning, and amoral, the western comic strips have demonstrated that these qualities and virtually every aspect of Indian culture are downright laughable. Tom K. Ryan's *Tumbleweeds* is perhaps the best known of the western strips, and Ryan's Indians are outrageous indeed.[26] Their names are Green Gills, Bucolic Buffalo, Limpid Lizard, Hulking Hawk, Fetid Fox, Vericose Viper, Squalid Squirrel, and Effervescent Elk, and they sharpen their skills each year during Sneaky Week, passing the rest of the time vying for the coveted black feather, which designates the Indian of the Month.[27] They admit to being desert dwellers, and they wear feathers and breech-cloths (the chief wears a blanket) and live in tipis, but they have no horses. In one episode they are visited by a woodlands Indian from the East who has lost his way because he had one too many for the road. They believe that the canoe he carries on his head is a hat. He has a Mohawk haircut with a feather in it, he wears an earring, and his name is Punkutunkus, son of Kookoonookus. Ryan's Indians are inept to a fault (they are forever unable to deceive Tumbleweeds, the cowboy whose name the strip carries), but they are surpassed in that by Colonel Fluster and the men of Fort Ridiculous. Thus they have at least something in their favor, although the humor they evoke succeeds largely because of the reader's awareness of, and familiarity with, Indian stereotypes; and ultimately Ryan's strip functions to confirm many of those stereotypes.

The question inevitably arises whether or not such portrayals of Indians are racially inspired. There is no thorough study of the relationship between race thinking and the history of Indian-white contact, but it seems safe to say that, while elements of racism may be present in that history, white stereotypes of Indians are cultural rather than racial responses. That race was never a significant issue is reflected in the volume of white commentary to the effect that Indians could be assimilated by the dominant population. And it is true that most observers emphasized cultural differences between Indians and whites. Although those differences often provided an excuse for white discrimination against Indians, the fact of discrimination does not in itself justify a conclusion of race prejudice. Whites who lived with Indians, or those who lived like Indians, were subject to the same discrimination. Skin color was less effective as a means of social categorization than were dietary habits, mode of dress, religious practices, and the like. Indian stereotypes developed in part because they were useful in justifying the dispossession of the aborigines, not because they were required to keep social distance between the two races. Moreover, it is doubtful that stereotypes could have functioned effectively to that end in frontier situations, particularly in view of the fact that, of the two groups, the Indians seemed most concerned about describing geographical boundaries between themselves and white populations.[28]

These, then, were the uses to which whites put their images of

Indians: First, after initial contact, the Indian was a curiosity, then an entertainment. Thereafter he was made noble by whites who required his cooperation and a beast by those secure enough to survive without his help and, beyond that, to take what he had. Then, when his numbers were diminished and he was far removed from the white population, he became again a curiosity and an entertainment. Today, his numbers replenished and his isolation ended, he is still to whites curious and entertaining, largely because, in the context afforded by the dominant society, he has no social utility—not as an Indian, not as a representative of another culture. That which is entertaining is otherwise useless, and so it was in the beginning.

The selections that follow pertain to images of the Indian that emerged at a crucial point in the history of Indian-white relations. After the Civil War, the nation turned its attention to the West as an area of economic opportunity. A transcontinental railroad, various pieces of land legislation, and an army with nothing else to do—these things, and more besides, heralded the American intention to fill out the continent. The Indian was an obstacle to that ambition and thus became the army's responsibility. There followed a series of Indian wars, justified in popular media through the presentation of adverse images of the Indian, and after that, when the deed was done, a time of contrition and talk of the plight of the vanishing Indian, wherein old myths were transformed. The selections define stereotypes and mark their transformation, and the photographs identify both the things that were and the things that were thought to be. They are neither pretty nor sentimental, nor are they offered as grist for the mills of moral judgment. They comprise an account of a meeting between technologically superior and technologically inferior peoples, a meeting that influenced the shaping of a nation, and they suggest something about what America is by examining what it has been. That they are ambiguous is surely inevitable.

NOTES TO INTRODUCTION

1. See Eleanor Burke Leacock, "Introduction," in Eleanor Burke Leacock and Nancy Oestreich Lurie (eds.), *North American Indians in Historical Perspective* (New York, Random House, 1971), 24; Sar A. Levitan and Barbara Hetrick, *Big Brother's Indian Programs—with Reservations* (New York, McGraw-Hill Book Company, 1971), 3–4; and Hazel W. Hertzberg, *The Search for an American Indian*

Identity: Modern Pan-Indian Movements (Syracuse, Syracuse University Press, 1971), 318–19. Roy Harvey Pearce, *The Savages of America: A Study of the Indian and the Idea of Civilization* (Baltimore, Johns Hopkins Press, 1953); and Richard Slotkin, *Regeneration Through Violence: The Mythology of the American Frontier, 1600–1860* (Middletown, Conn., Wesleyan University Press, 1973), contain useful background material.

2. Christopher Columbus, *Journal of First Voyage to America* (New York, Albert & Charles Boni, 1924), 25–26; Samuel Eliot Morison (trans. and ed.), *A New and Fresh English Translation of the Letter of Columbus Announcing the Discovery of America* (Madrid, Graficas Yagúes, S.L., 1959), 9–14.

3. Samuel Eliot Morison, *The European Discovery of America: The Northern Voyages, A.D. 500–1600* (New York, Oxford University Press, 1971), 106–107; and Evelyn Page, *American Genesis: Pre-colonial Writing in the North* (Boston, Gambit, 1973), 214–16. See also Percy G. Adams, *Travelers and Travel Liars, 1600–1800* (Berkeley, University of California Press, 1962), and, for a convenient abridgment, Richard Hakluyt, *Voyages and Discoveries: The Principal Navigations, Voyages, Traffiques and Discoveries of the English Nation* (ed. by Jack Beeching), Baltimore, Penguin Books, 1972).

4. William Bradford, *Of Plymouth Plantation, 1620–1647* (ed. by Samuel Eliot Morrison), (New York, Alfred A. Knopf, 1970), 25–26.

5. Carl and Roberta Bridenbaugh, *No Peace Beyond the Line: The English in the Caribbean, 1624–1690* (New York, Oxford University Press, 1972), 98–99.

6. See Wilbur R. Jacobs, *Dispossessing the American Indian: Indians and Whites on the Colonial Frontier* (New York, Charles Scribner's Sons, 1972); William Christie MacLeod, *The American Indian Frontier* (New York, Alfred A. Knopf, 1928); Angie Debo, *A History of the Indians of the United States* (Norman, University of Oklahoma Press, 1970); William T. Hagan, *American Indians* (Chicago, University of Chicago Press, 1961); and Grant Foreman, *Indian Removal: The Emigration of the Five Civilized Tribes of Indians* (new ed., Norman, University of Oklahoma Press, 1953), for an overview of Indian-white relations. For estimates of the missionary influence, see John Gilmary Shea, *History of the Catholic Missions among the Indian Tribes of the United States, 1529–1854* (New York, Edward Dunigan & Brother, 1855); Robert F. Berkhofer, Jr., *Salvation and the Savage: An Analysis of Protestant Missions and American Indian Response, 1787–1862* (Lexington, University of Kentucky Press, 1965); and Howard L. Harrod, *Mission Among the Blackfeet* (Norman, University of Oklahoma Press, 1971).

7. See John C. Ewers, "The Emergence of the Plains Indian as the Symbol of the North American Indian," in Ewers, *Indian Life on the Upper Missouri* (Norman, University of Oklahoma Press, 1968), 187–203.

8. Comparative patterns are discussed in Jacobs, *Dispossessing the American Indian*, and A. Grenfell Price, *White Settlers and Native Peoples: An Historical Study of Racial Contacts Between English-speaking Whites and Aboriginal Peoples in the United States, Canada, Australia and New Zealand* (Melbourne, Georgian House, 1950). For evidence of the contemporary preoccupation with things Indian, see Lloyd Kahn (ed.), *Shelter* (Bolinas, Calif., Shelter Publications, 1973); Steward Brand (ed.), *The Last Whole Earth Catalog* (Menlo Park, Calif., Portola Institute, 1971); and the several books by Carlos Castaneda, beginning with *The Teachings of Don Juan: A Yaqui Way of Knowledge* (Berkeley, University of California Press, 1968). Dee Brown, *Bury My Heart at Wounded Knee: An Indian History of the American West* (New York, Rinehart & Winston, Inc., 1971) was published in January, and by October, 1971, it had passed through thirteen hardcover printings. It was a selection of the Book-of-the-Month Club, the Playboy Book Club, and the Popular Science Book Club, and it was syndicated for newspaper serialization by the Des Moines Register/Tribune Syndicate. A paperback edition followed in April,

1972, and the book was thereafter abridged for young readers. On the subject of Indian art see Robert Hughes, "Tribes in the Gallery," *Time*, December 6, 1971, 78; J. J. Brody, *Indian Painters and White Patrons* (Albuquerque, University of New Mexico Press, 1971); and Fritz Scholder, *Scholder/Indians* (Flagstaff, Ariz., Northland Press, 1972).

9. St. John de Crèvecoeur, *Sketches of Eighteenth Century America: More "Letters from an American Farmer"* (ed. by Henri L. Bourdin, Ralph H. Gabriel, and Stanley T. Williams), (New York, Benjamin Blom, Inc., 1972), 194.

10. See Walter O'Meara, *Daughters of the Country: The Women of the Fur Traders and Mountain Men* (New York, Harcourt, Brace & World, Inc., 1968); and Grace Steele Woodward, *Pocahontas* (Norman, University of Oklahoma Press, 1969).

11. See, for a basic anthology, Samuel G. Drake, *Tragedies of the Wilderness; or, True and Authentic Narratives of Captives . . .* (Boston, Antiquarian Bookstore and Institute, 1841). Contemporary novels with captivity themes include Lewis B. Patten, *White Warrior* (Greenwich, Conn., Fawcett Publications, Inc., 1956); Frederick Manfred, *Scarlet Plume* (New York, Trident Press, 1964); Thomas Berger, *Little Big Man* (New York, Dial Press, 1964); and two books by Conrad Richter, *The Light in the Forest* (New York, Alfred A. Knopf, 1953), and *A Country of Strangers* (New York, Alfred A. Knopf, 1966). Captivity literature is surveyed from the anthropologist's perspective in A. Irving Hallowell, "American Indians, White and Black: The Phenomenon of Transculturation," *Current Anthropology*, Vol. 4 (December, 1963), 519–31; and within the framework of popular culture in Russel Nye, *The Unembarrassed Muse: The Popular Arts in America* (New York, Dial Press, 1970), 14–16. See also Leslie A. Fiedler, *The Return of the Vanishing American* (New York, Stein and Day, 1968); and Richard Drinnon, *White Savage: The Case of John Dunn Hunter* (New York, Schocken Books, 1972).

12. See, for example, Horace Greeley, *An Overland Journey from New York to San Francisco in the Summer of 1859* (ed. by Charles T. Duncan), (New York, Alfred A. Knopf, 1964), 119–23.

13. Theodore Roosevelt's comments on these "foolish sentimentalists" may be found in *The Winning of the West . . .* I, Vol. VIII of *The Works of Theodore Roosevelt*, National Edition (New York, Charles Scribner's Sons, 1926), 81–82. See also Robert Winston Mardock, *The Reformers and the American Indian* (Columbia, University of Missouri Press, 1971); and, for the concept of the noble savage, Hoxie Neale Fairchild, *The Noble Savage: A Study in Romantic Naturalism* (New York, Columbia University Press, 1928).

14. Don Russell, *The Wild West* (Fort Worth, Amon Carter Museum of Western Art, 1970), 22, 118.

15. See Winifred Johnston, "Medicine Show," *Southwest Review*, Vol. XXI (July, 1936), 390–99; Arrell M. Gibson, "Medicine Show," *American West*, Vol. IV (February, 1967), 35–39, 74–79; and Virgil J. Vogel, *American Indian Medicine* (Norman, University of Oklahoma Press, 1970), chap. V. *Daring Donald McKay, or, The Last War-Trail of the Modocs* (Erie, Pa., Herald Printing and Publishing Company, Ltd., 1884), an anonymous dime novel, is a splendid example of popular fiction as a vehicle for the sale of Indian medicine. The book was financed by the Oregon Indian Medicine Company of Corry, Pennsylvania, and carried several advertisements for Ka-Ton-Ka, a cure for consumption and rheumatism, and Modoc Indian Oil, a cure for everything else. It was reprinted in a facsimile edition, edited and annotated by Keith Clark and Donna Clark, by the Oregon Historical Society in 1971.

16. Johnston, "Medicine Show," *Southwest Review*, Vol. XXI (July, 1936), 393.

17. Ralph E. Friar and Natasha A. Friar, *The Only Good Indian . . . The Hollywood Gospel* (New York, Drama Book Specialists, 1972), 287ff.

18. Richard A. Maynard, *The American West on Film: Myth and Reality* (Rochelle Park, N.J., Hayden Book Company, Inc., 1974), 86.

19. Friar and Friar, *The Only Good Indian*, 322–23.

20. *Ibid.*, 281–83.

21. Raymond William Stedman, *The Serials: Suspense and Drama by Installment* (Norman, University of Oklahoma Press, 1971), 172.

22. Jim Harmon, liner notes, *Original Radio Broadcasts: Straight Arrow*, Mark 56 Records #642.

23. Television Indians are discussed in Harlan Ellison, *The Other Glass Teat: Further Essays of Opinion on Televison* (New York, Pyramid Books, 1975), 335–45.

24. See Tony Hillerman, *Dance Hall of the Dead* (New York, Harper and Row, 1973); Brian Garfield, *The Threepersons Hunt* (New York, M. Evans and Company, 1974); William M. James, *Apache: The First Death* (New York, Pinnacle Books, 1974); and Lewis Owen, *The Indian-Lover* (New York, Bantam Books, 1975).

25. See Clair Huffaker, *Nobody Loves a Drunken Indian* (New York, David McKay Co., Inc., 1967); and John Templeton, *Charlie Eagletooth's War* (New York, William Morrow and Company, 1969).

26. Many of the strips have been collected and reprinted, beginning with Tom K. Ryan, *Tumbleweeds* (Greenwich, Conn., Fawcett Publications, Inc., 1968).

27. On the subject of white rendition of Indian names, see James L. Haley, *The Buffalo War: The History of the Red River Indian Uprising of 1874* (Garden City, N.Y., Doubleday & Company, Inc., 1976), 232.

28. The dimensions of cultural differences are suggested by Lewis O. Saum, *The Fur Trader and the Indian* (Seattle, University of Washington Press, 1965); Charles L. Sanford, *The Quest for Paradise: Europe and the American Moral Imagination* (Urbana, University of Illinois Press, 1961); Ruth Miller Elson, *Guardians of Tradition: American Schoolbooks of the Nineteenth Century* (Lincoln, University of Nebraska Press, 1964); and J. Ralph Randolph, "John Wesley and the American Indian: A Study in Disllusionment," *Methodist History*, Vol. X (April, 1972), 3–11. Rev. John Heckewelder, *History, Manners, and Customs of the Indian Nations Who Once Inhabited Pennsylvania and the Neighboring States* ([1819], rev. ed., Philadelphia, Historical Society of Pennsylvania, 1876); and Henry R. Schoolcraft, *Personal Memoirs of a Residence of Thirty Years with the Indian Tribes on the American Frontiers* (Philadelphia, Lippincott, Grambo and Co., 1851), were books of wide influence that stressed cultural factors. A different view is expressed in Lewis Hanke, *Aristotle and the American Indians: A Study in Race Prejudice in the Modern World* (London, Hollis & Carter, 1959); Thomas F. Gossett, *Race: The History of an Idea in America* (Dallas, Southern Methodist University Press, 1963); and Ashley Montagu, *The Idea of Race* (Lincoln, University of Nebraska Press, 1965), but insofar as their evidence concerns cultural rather than racial matters, it does not sustain that view. The problems of distinguishing between race and culture are better defined in Roger Bastide, "Color, Racism, and Christianity," in John Hope Franklin (ed.), *Color and Race* (Boston, Houghton Mifflin Company, 1968), 34–49; and Kenneth J. Gergen, "The Significance of Skin Color in Human Relations," in *ibid.*, 112–28. That stereotypes are not synonymous with prejudice is amply demonstrated by Gordon W. Allport, *The Nature of Prejudice* (Reading, Mass., Addison-Wesley Publishing Company, 1954). Michael Banton, *Race Relations* (London, Tavistock Publications, 1967), outlines alternative approaches to the analysis of culture contact.

Richard Irving Dodge

"He remains a savage simply from lack of a code of morals"

1882

Colonel Richard Irving Dodge, once aide-de-camp to General William Tecumseh Sherman, wrote extensively on the subject of Indians and Indian life. His were popular accounts, designed to interpret things Indian for readers who possessed little or no other information. In this selection Dodge describes Indians both as natural men and as animals—intelligent people who are nevertheless primitive because they have no moral sense; and he is as critical of those who would ennoble the Indian as he is of those who would exterminate him.

Though I have served in almost every portion of our wide frontier, my largest experience has been with the "Plains Indians," those inhabiting the country between the Mississippi River and the Rocky Mountains. Among these Indians I have spent many years, much of the time in peaceful, every day intercourse.

Within the limits specified, reside at the present time not less than sixty distinct tribes, cut up into bands innumerable, comprising more than half of the whole Indian population of the United States.

Extending from the British line almost to the Gulf of Mexico, they would appear to be subjected to such climatic variation as might greatly influence their character. That this is not the case is due to the peculiarity of those great elevated plains, or steppes, high, dry, and generally destitute of trees, except along the margin of

From Richard Irving Dodge, *Our Wild Indians: Thirty-three Years' Personal Experience Among the Red Men of the Great West* (Hartford, A. D. Worthington & Co., 1882), 53–67, 204–18, 220–23.

streams. All these tribes are mounted, and all, until recently, depended upon the buffalo for all the necessaries and comforts of life.

Though distinct in language, differing somewhat in character, and each tribe, as a rule, hostile to all others, their common necessities have so assimilated their habits and modes of thought as to enable the student to group them, for description, into one general class.

These Indians I know best, and from them I have drawn most of my illustrations. In the following pages, when I speak of Indians, I mean the "Plains Indians," except when the context shows that I mean the whole race. When I wish to draw attention to the peculiarities of other Indians, as Utes, Apaches, etc., I will speak of them by name.

The ideal Indian of Cooper is a creation of his own prolific brain. No such savage as Uncas ever existed, or could exist, and no one knew this better than Cooper himself. All hostile Indians—Mingoes, Iroquois, etc.—are painted as fiends, in whom the furies themselves would have delighted.

His stories are striking and artistic, but they will not bear the test of consistent criticism. He assumed his ideal, clothed him in moral and Christian virtues, and placed him prominently in contrast with his surroundings. How he could possibly have arrived at those good qualities, when born and reared among savages without a moral code, is a question that admits of but one answer,—"no such individual could possibly have existed."

The wild Indian of to-day is the Mingo painted by Cooper, modified somewhat by time and his surroundings; a human being, in the earliest stage of development; a natural man.

Of all writers on the North American Indians, Catlin deservedly stands first. In an intercourse with Indians extending over half an ordinary lifetime, I have frequently been struck by his quickness of apprehension, and the vividness of his colorings of Indian life. But Catlin, as he himself admits, was an enthusiast. Though a poor painter, he was wrapped up in his art of painting. Give him a model suited to his taste,—a wild, free savage, adorned with all the tinsel-trappings of barbarous life,—and he immediately clothed him with all Christian virtues and knightly honors.

His pen-portraits of Indians are admirable in one sense, in an-

Sitting Bull (1831–90), Hunkpapa Sioux chief and, to whites, perhaps the best-known Indian of his day. When he toured with Buffalo Bill's Wild West, William F. Cody advertised Sitting Bull as "the warrior who killed Custer," only one of many untruths told about him. All the photographs in this book are reproduced through the courtesy of the Western History Collections, University of Oklahoma Library.

Sitting Bull and William F. Cody in a studio portrait. The two were indeed friends, and Cody gave Sitting Bull a white hat and a performing horse, both of which the chief prized highly.

Souvenir photograph of Sitting Bull.

Quanah Parker (1845–1911), last war chief of the Comanches, photographed in Indian garb. The son of a captive white woman, Cynthia Ann
Parker, Quanah led the attack on the white settlement at Adobe Walls in
the Texas Panhandle in 1874. He surrendered at Fort Sill in 1875.

Quanah Parker as he appeared in 1901. After twenty-five years, all that remained of the old Quanah, outwardly, at least, were his braids and the ring on the third finger of his left hand.

Geronimo (1829–1909), Chiricahua Apache leader, surrendered to the military in 1886 and was subsequently incarcerated in Florida and Alabama before being sent to Fort Sill, in Oklahoma Territory, in 1894. His popularity among whites led authorities to allow him to tour with Pawnee Bill's wild West extravaganza in 1908. Here, flanked by Indian performers, Geronimo demonstrates the technique for skinning buffalo. The Indian immediately behind the old man appears to be holding him.

Jim Thorpe, Sac and Fox athlete and gold medalist in the 1912 Olympics, was a dominant figure in amateur and professional sports in the early twentieth century. His success contributed much to the prevailing white notion that Indians were superior athletes. Thorpe played football for Carlisle Indian School, a Pennsylvania institution with an undeserved reputation for fielding powerful teams. Carlisle regularly defeated teams from Gettysburg College, Lebanon Valley College, and Bloomsburg Normal School, but its forays against Ivy League schools were disasters indeed. In fourteen games against Harvard, for example, Carlisle won only two, scoring 90 points to Harvard's 234.

other faulty beyond measure. Indians of whom he wrote are still living, their tribes maintaining to this day the same manners and customs which he so vividly describes. To see them now is to have seen them then, yet how different the pictures from those he drew. He could see only the natural noble qualities. To the natural ignoble qualities (inseparable from the savage state) he evinced a blindness inexplicable in a man of such perceptive faculties, except on the hypothesis of excessive enthusiasm.

Of the miserably low condition of the Crows and Blackfeet, he has not a word to say, but gives pages of eloquent writing to the beauties of their dresses and the magnificent length of their hair.

He descants on the modesty of some tribes, but tells us, in almost the same breath, that several families, consisting of men with two, three, or more wives, and children of all ages and sexes, occupy, for all purposes, one single lodge of twelve or fifteen feet in diameter.

His whole attention is occupied with externals,—dress, dances, religious and other ceremonies. Nowhere does he give us a close insight into their inner life, their religion, social and domestic habits and customs. Had he written of these things, his characters must have assumed other shadings than those his "fancy painted."

Here and there throughout his works are evidences that he does see these things, but is determined to say nothing about them. He evidently regarded the Indian as doomed to speedy extinction, and in so far, already dead. He constitutes himself his biographer, and closely adheres to the Roman maxim, *"nil de mortuis nisi bonum,"* (say nothing but good of the dead).

Writing of the Indian of forty years ago, Catlin says, "In his native state, he is an honest, hospitable, brave, warlike, cruel, revengeful, relentless, yet honorable, contemplative, and religious being." To these epithets, which are yet true in a certain sense, as I shall show hereafter, I add, that he is vain, crafty, deceitful, ungrateful, treacherous, grasping, and utterly selfish. He is lecherous, without honor or mercy; filthy in his ideas and speech, and inconceivably dirty in person and manners. He is affectionate, patient, self-reliant, and enduring. He has a marvellous instinct in travelling, and a memory of apparently unimportant landmarks simply wonderful. In short, he has the ordinary good and bad qualities of the mere animal, modified to some extent by reason.

Primitive man is an animal differing from other animals in but one single quailty, the greater development of the reasoning faculties. The condition of the races of mankind is simply the greater or less progression of each from that starting-point. The Indian, though so far behind in this race of progress as to be still a savage, is yet far ahead of many tribes and people. The grand difference between the North American Indian and the civilized people of the same continent comes not from degrees of intelligence, or forms of religion, but from what we call morality. The intellect of an Indian may be as acute as that of a congressman, and his religion as austere as that of a bishop, yet he remains a savage simply from lack of a code of morals.

People of enlightened countries, particularly moral and Christian people of our own land, will have difficulty in understanding this lack.

Religion is the disposition of man to recognize some power superior to, and hidden from, himself. It is innate, a part of the constitution of man, common alike to "savage and to sage." It is doubtful if there be a race of mankind so low as to be without a religion.

Morality recognizes and inculcates the rights and duties of individuals in their relation to their social life. It is above religion, and its possession by a people is indicative of great strides in advance of the primitive condition.

The Jewish code, the ten commandments, mingled the two in one common law, and the embodiment of these into two simple commandments by Christ (himself a Jew) nearly nineteen hundred years ago, have forever, to all Christian people, so welded together religion and morality that the one cannot exist without the other.

We are taught in childhood, at our mother's knee, that certain things are right, others wrong. The morality is inculcated with the religion, and we with difficulty separate the one from the other.

As will be seen further on, the Indian has a religion, as firmly seated in his belief as Christianity in the faith of the Christian; but that religion has no added moral code. It teaches no duty or obligation either to God or man.

Right and wrong, as abstract terms, have no meaning whatever to the Indian. All is right that he wishes to do, all is wrong that opposes him. It is simply impossible for him to grasp the abstract idea that anything is wrong in itself. He has no word, or set of words, by which the ideas of moral right and wrong can be conveyed to him; his nearest synonyms are the words good and bad.

He will tell you that it is wrong (bad) to steal from a man of his own band, not that theft is wrong, but because he will be beaten and kicked out of the band if detected. There is no abstract wrong in the murder of a white man, or Indian of another tribe; it is wrong (bad) simply because punishment may follow.

The Indian is absolutely without what we call conscience, that inward monitor which comes of education, but which our religious teachers would persuade us is the voice of God.

He is already as religious as the most devout Christian, and if our good missionaries would let him alone in his religion, cease their efforts to proselyte him to their particular sect, and simply strive to supply him with a code of morals, his subsequent conversion might be easy and his future improvement assured.

In his manner and bearing, the Indian is habitually grave and dignified, and in the presence of strangers he is reserved and silent. These peculiarities have been ascribed by writers on Indian character to stoicism, and the general impression seems to be that the Indian, wrapped in his blanket and impenetrable mystery, and with a face of gloom, stalks through life unmindful of pleasure or pain. Nothing can be farther from the truth. The dignity, the reserve, the silence, are put on just as a New York swell puts on his swallow-tailed coat and white choker for a dinner-party, because it is his custom. In his own camp, away from strangers, the Indian is a noisy, jolly, rollicking, mischief-loving braggadocio, brimful of practical jokes and rough fun of any kind, making the welkin ring with his laughter, and rousing the midnight echoes by song and dance, whoops and yells.

He is really as excitable as a Frenchman, and as fond of pleasure as a Sybarite. He will talk himself wild with excitement, vaunting his exploits in love, war, or the chase, and will commit all sorts of extravagances while telling or listening to an exciting story. In their every-day life Indians are vivacious, chatty, fond of telling and hearing stories. Their nights are spent in song and dance, and for the number of persons engaged, a permanent Indian camp (safe from all danger of enemies) is at night the noisiest place that can be found.

One of the strongest traits of Indian character is curiosity, a positive craving to know all that is going on about him. He must know the meaning of every mark on the ground; he must know all the camp tattle. A stranger arrives in the village and goes into a lodge. In a few moments half the inhabitants of the village are in or about that lodge standing on tiptoe, straining eyes and ears, and crowding each other and the stranger, with as little compunction as if the whole thing were a ward primary meeting.

Whether or not he evinces surprise at anything depends on his surroundings, and somewhat on the nature of the thing itself. In a formal assemblage, or when in the presence of strangers, it would be the height of bad manners to show surprise, however much might be felt. Uneducated people of our own race feel no surprise at the rising and setting of the sun, the changes of season, the flash of lightning or the roll of thunder. They accept them as facts without explanation, and though beyond their comprehension, without surprise. One shows surprise at something out of the ordinary range of his experience. It is an act of comparison.

The Indian has actual and common experience of many articles of civilized manufacture, the simplest of which is as entirely beyond his comprehension as the most complicated. He would be a simple exclamation point, did he show surprise at everything new to him, or which he does not understand. He goes to the other extreme, and rarely shows, because he does not feel, surprise at anything.

He visits the States, looks unmoved at the steamboat and locomotive. People call it stoicism. They forget that to his ignorance the production of the commonest glass bottle is as inscrutable as the sound of the thunder. The whirl and clatter of innumerable spindles are as far beyond his power of comprehension as that the summer's heat should be succeeded by the winter's snows; and a common mirror is as perfect a miracle as the birth of a child in his lodge. He knows nothing of the comparative difficulties of invention and manufacture, and to him, the mechanism of a locomotive is not in any way more a cause for surprise than that of a wheel-barrow.

When things, in their own daily experience, are performed in what to them is a remarkable way, they feel and express the most profound astonishment. I have seen several hundred Indians—men, women, and children—eager and excited, following from one telegraph pole to another, a repairer whose legs were encased in climbing-boots. When he walked easily, foot over foot, up the pole, their surprise and delight found vent in the most vociferous expression of applause and admiration.

I once rode into a large Indian village, accompanied by a beautiful lady, an accomplished horsewoman. The horse, not liking his surroundings, brought out by his plunges and curvetings, all her grace and skill. Had she been astride, as is customary with Indian women, no notice whatever would have been taken of her, but, being perched on a side-saddle, in what to the Indian was an almost impossible position, she was soon surrounded by a crowd of all ages and sexes, evincing in every possible way their extremity of surprise and delight.

Surprise in an Indian sometimes takes very comical forms. An officer, now on the retired list, who having lost a leg in service, had had it skilfully replaced by one of light hollow wood, with open slits, was one day visiting the lodge of a distinguished Sioux chief (now dead). After some rather abortive attempts at conversation, the officer took a knitting-needle from the hand of the old wife of the chief, and passed it through his leg. This at once attracted the notice of all. The chief made signs asking to see the leg. Stripping up his pantaloons the officer managed to show the artificial limb, but concealing its connection with the leg proper. After a long and minute examination the chief asked if the other leg was the same. The amused officer could not resist a little lie, and nodded yes, whereupon the chief took him by the shoulders and thrust him out of the lodge as "bad medicine."

The excitability of the Indian results in another peculiarity, generally overlooked by his historians. Though undoubtedly brave, and performing feats and taking chances almost incredible, he is, when surprised, more easily and thoroughly stampeded than any other race of people of which I have any knowledge.

The Indian's endurance of pain and suffering of any and every kind, is his "patent of manhood." Custom and Indian public opinion have made endurance the exponent of every manly virtue; and he who can subject himself, without a look or expression of pain, to the greatest amount of excruciating torture, is the best man, whatever may be his other qualities.

Another most admirable quality he possesses in an eminent degree. This is patience. Endurance and patience would seem to be naturally allied, and to a close observer they appear to be the warp and woof of Indian character. Every manly quality possessed by the Indian is the outgrowth of one or the other of these traits. His skill and success as warrior, or thief, or hunter; his avoidance of quarrels or conflicts with his associates; his submission to wrongs, outrages and starvation, all come from his endurance and his patience. Even his disposition to torture his enemies is, to some extent, but the reflex of the conscious pride which would enable him to bear those tortures without flinching.

Modesty, as we understand the term, is totally lacking in the Indian character. The chief or warrior who put a low estimate on his qualities or achievements would be taken at his word and nothing thought of. There are no reporters, no newspapers, to herald the praises of a skilful warrior. He must blow his own trumpet, and he does it with magnificent success. Self-praise is no disgrace to him, and half the talk of warriors to each other is made up of exaggerated boasts of what they have done, and most extraordinary assertions as to what they intend to do.

The ordinary conversations, at home or in company, are broad even to indecency. In some of the tribes the women are retiring and modest in manners, because custom requires it, but they listen with delight to the story-teller's most filthy recitals, and receive with great applause indecent jests and proposals in the sign-dance.

Clothing is for ornament, not for decency. Ordinarily, even among the wildest tribes, men and women wear some covering (very frequently the men only the breech-clout), but I have seen entirely naked men stalking about a village, or joining in a dance, without exciting surprise, comment, or objection from others. Although most gayly bedecked on occasions of ceremony, the ordinary covering of the male Indian is not what would be regarded as decent among civilized people. The women are more decently clothed habitually, but men and women, even young girls, think nothing of bathing together in "puris naturalibus," and it is not at all unusual to see boys and girls, even up to ten years of age, running around the camp in the same condition.

There is a curious difference of opinion among writers as to the honesty of the Indian, some asserting that he is an arrant thief, others insisting that he is exceptionally honest. Catlin says that the Indian is "honest and honorable," and that he "never stole a shilling's worthy of property" from him. The fact is, that all these authors are both right and wrong.

In their own bands, Indians are perfectly honest. In all my intercourse with them, I have heard of not over half a dozen cases· of such theft. It is the sole unpardonable crime among Indians. There being no bolts nor bars, no locks nor safes, and each Indian having by common custom the right to enter into any lodge of the band, at any and at all hours, the property of no one would be safe for a moment but for the most rigid infliction of the severest punishments on the perpetrator of this solitary Indian crime.

The value of the article stolen is not considered. The crime is the theft. A man found guilty of stealing even the most trifling article from a member of his own band, is whipped almost to death (every individual of the band having the disposition, as well as the right, to take part in the amusement, and there being no limit, except his own will, to the amount of punishment inflicted by each), his horses are confiscated, his lodge, robes, blankets, and other property destroyed or divided among the band, and, naked and disgraced, he is, with his wives and children, unceremoniously kicked out of the band, to starve, or live as best they can. A woman caught stealing is beaten and kicked out of the band, but her husband and children are not included in the punishment.

Children detected in thefts are thrashed most unmercifully, not only by the person from whom they stole, but by the father, who is also obliged to pay damages.

But this wonderfully exceptional honesty extends no further than to the members of his immediate band. To all outside of it, the Indian is not only one of the most arrant thieves in the world, but this quality or faculty is held in the highest estimation, the expert thief standing in honor, and in the estimation of the tribe almost, if not quite, on the same plane as the brave and skilful warrior.

The earliest lessons of the youthful brave are in stealing. The love-sick youngster can only be sure of winning his mistress by stealing enough horses to pay for her. Indians are not very successful breeders of horses, and every man of the tribe expects to keep himself in stock by stealing.

Even different bands of the same tribe (when not in one general encampment) do not hesitate to steal from each other. A most flagrant case came under my personal observation. In the winter of 1867–8, I was stationed at North Platte, Nebraska, in charge of Spotted Tail's band of Brulé Sioux. A party of six Minneconjou Sioux came into Spotted Tail's camp on a visit. They were stalwart, good-looking youngsters, beautifully dressed, well armed and mounted, and claimed to have been in the Phil. Kearny massacre of the year before. They were received as most distinguished guests, with all hospitality and honor. Feasted and honored by day, danced with, ogled and made love to at night, the happy visitors, fascinated with their surroundings, apparently thought only of pleasure; but early on the morning of the fourth or fifth day after their arrival, I was waked up by an Indian who informed me that the Minneconjous had gotten away in the night with over one hundred of their entertainers' ponies. A war party was promptly organized for pursuit, but returned unsuccessful, after running the fugitives for over a hundred miles.

The Indian, as a rule, is honorable after a fashion of his own. Hide anything from him and he will find and steal it. Place it formally in his possession, or under his charge for safe keeping, and it will in all probability be returned intact, with, however, a demand for a present as reward for his honesty.

I apply the term "wild" to a class of Indians to distinguish it from another class inhabiting the Indian Territory, or living within the boundaries of some of the States, and which has made some progress in civilization and moral knowledge. With these exceptions, the vast numbers of Indians in the territory of the United States are "wild." Sioux, Cheyennes, Arrapahoes, Comanches, Apaches, Utes, Shoshones, Chippewas, and the almost numberless small tribes and fragments scattered through the vast region west of the Mississippi, or collected at agencies, or on reservations, all furnish material and shading for the picture I give of them. Here and there a small tribe— as the Nez Percés—show a slight advance in morality, due to the efforts of Roman Catholic priests so many years ago that their traditions but vaguely fix the time. Here and there, also, even among the wild tribes, are found men who give some evidence of moral perception, probably due to the influence of missionaries and teachers. These cases are, however, individual. The mass of the wild tribes are as depicted.

A large class of most excellent people conscientiously believe that the Indian is a supernatural hero, with a thousand excellent qualities, so admirably woven and dove-tailed into his nature that even civilization and Christianity could not improve him. To such persons I have nothing to say. Their opinions are simply sentimental prejudice, without foundation in knowledge or reason, and could not be changed, "though one rose from the dead."

There is another class of excellent people who firmly believe that it is impossible to civilize the Indian, and who argue that humanity and policy alike point to his extermination as the most prompt and effectual way of solving our Indian problem. These are also wrong. The Indian has never had a fair chance, and he is entitled to a full and fair trial. That, with his miserable opportunities, he has been at least partially civilized, as shown by the exceptions before noted, and by the condition of the more advanced of the Cherokees, is ample evidence of capacity for a further improvement. . . .

The life of an Indian woman is a round of wearisome labor. Her marriage is only an exchange of masters, and an exchange for the worse, for the duties devolved upon a girl in the parental lodge are generally of the lightest kind. She may be required to assist in the cooking, in making or repairing the lodge, to make and mend clothing, and most of the elaborate ornamental bead and feather work comes from her hand. All her labors, however, are in or near the family lodge, and where she is immediately under the eyes of her parents. For an unmarried girl to be found away from her lodge alone, is to invite outrage, consequently she is never sent out to cut and bring wood, nor to take care of the stock. She may sometimes be required to go with her mother on these errands and duties, or to work with her in the fields, but as a rule all the hard out-door work devolves on the married women.

The pride of the good wife is in permitting her husband to do nothing for himself. She cooks his food, makes and mends his lodge and his clothing, dresses skins, butchers the game, dries the meat, goes after and saddles his horse.

When making a journey she strikes the lodge, packs the animals, cares for all the babies, and superintends the march, her lord and master, who left camp long before her, being far off in front or flank looking after game.

On arriving at the camping-place, she unpacks the animals, pitches the lodge, makes the beds, brings wood and water, and does everything that is to be done, and when her husband returns from his hunt, is ready to take and unsaddle his horse.

What she gets in exchange for all this devotion it is impossible to say, but whether from ignorance of any better fate, or from constant occupation, it is absolutely certain that a happier, more light-hearted, more contented woman cannot be found.

The husband owns his wife entirely. He may abuse her, beat her, even kill her without question. She is more absolutely a slave than any negro before the war of the rebellion, for not only may herself, but her person be sold or given away by her husband at his pleasure and without her consent.

In spite of all this the women are not without their weight and influence, not only in their own household, but in all the affairs of the tribe, and though not permitted even to enter the council lodge, they are very frequently "the power behind the throne," directing and guiding almost without knowing it themselves.

The custom in the Plains tribes which makes every man in the tribe a possible suitor for the hand of every woman, though either or both may be already married, is so at variance with all established ideas of what savages regard as "the rights of woman" is so entirely unparalleled among other savage races of mankind, that I have devoted unusual time and care to its study, more especially from the fact that the custom is not mentioned, so far as I know, by any writer on the North American Indians.

This custom gives to every married woman of the tribes the absolute right to leave her husband and become the wife of any other man, the sole condition being that the new husband must have the means to pay for her.

How the savage Indian with his utter lack of any sense of justice to woman, his mere slave, could have permitted such an act to grow into a custom, is one of the curiosities of mental progression.

We may naturally suppose that it arose at first from the tendency of the chiefs to take to their bosoms the handsome wives of the commoners of the tribes. They probably paid for them liberally, and the bereaved husband was obliged to be satisfied. The new wives did not lose, but gained standing and position.

The example of chiefs was followed, and thus, what at first were mere acts of rapine, became firmly engrafted on the tribes by custom.

However it may have originated, it is certain that this custom exerts a most beneficial influence in ameliorating the condition of the women. Abject slave as the wife is, she has, if moderately good-looking or having a fair reputation as a worker, a sure remedy against all conjugal ills, in being able to leave her husband for any other man who will take her and pay for her.

The transfer of devotion and allegiance of women to other men than their rightful owners, is not an unusual occurrence among the Plains Indians. It may come from ill treatment on the part of the husband, or from what our civilization would term "an affinity," an ordinary love affair.

A woman is ill treated by, or lives unhappily with her husband. She secures the services of some friendly and cautious old woman of the tribe, secrecy being most essential, the husband having a perfect right to kill the wife should he suspect what is going on. The old woman sounds the warriors, and finding one willing to take and pay for the woman, the affair is accomplished.

Or a man has taken a fancy to another man's wife. He makes his advances, is met by encouragement, and, after a siege more or less protracted, wins her.

In either case, the husband wakes up some morning to find his wife gone. He searches for her through the encampment and finds her in another man's lodge, doing the ordinary work as if she belonged there, and he is informed that she has become the wife of that man.

Etiquette and custom prevent his saying a word to the new husband, or to upbraid or injure the woman. He has but one recourse. He immediately proceeds to the chief and states his grievance. One or two prominent old warriors are summoned. They and the chief examine into the case and assess the damages, somewhat in accordance with the actual market value of the woman, but more usually by simply considering the relative wealth of the two men. If a rich man takes a poor man's wife he would probably be heavily assessed; while the poor man who took the rich man's wife would get off with a comparatively small bill of costs.

There is no appeal from the decision, and whatever forfeit is declared must be paid at once. This done, the affair is over. There is no wrangling or fighting, and in every case, forfeit or none, the woman has the right to remain with the man of her choice.

Should the wife of a chief change her allegiance, nothing, as a rule, is said or done about it. The chief is too great a man, too high and mighty, too far removed from the common feelings of humanity, to waste a moment's time or thought on so insignificant a thing as a woman.

His runaway wife may be in the same camp, in the very next lodge; he may pass her every day, or even chat with her when she comes to his lodge to see her children, but no look or word from him will ever show that he is aware that she has changed her allegiance.

With a custom giving her the absolute right to change her husband at will, and with the temptation arising from the constant approaches of all other Indian men,—who, animal like, approach a female only to make love to her,—it is very remarkable that so many are chaste, and that these exchanges of husbands are the exception and not the rule. The concession of the right to change takes from most of them the temptation to avail themselves of it.

The new husband must be prepared to pay at once for the runaway woman whatever price is assessed by the chief and old men. This rule is imperative, and a failure to comply with this sole condition may lead to most disastrous consequences, the abandoned husband having the right to inflict death on the absconding wife.

A young girl had become the third or fourth wife of a man at least fifty years old. As was perhaps natural, she became enamoured of a young warrior who, not having the means to pay for her, persuaded her to run away with him.

The elopement was successfully accomplished and the young couple arrived at the encampment of another band of the same tribe, where they set up housekeeping as man and wife.

Some five or six months after the whole tribe was called together for the "Medicine Dance." The old man found his runaway wife and demanded either that he be paid for her or that she be turned over to him for punishment. The young man could pay nothing and the girl was, by order of the chief, delivered to her first husband. Seating her on the ground he crossed her feet so that the instep of one was directly over that of the other, and deliberately fired a rifle ball through the two. He then formally presented her to the young man, grimly remarking,—

"You need not fear that she will run away with any other man."

Custom has given to the unmarried girls of the tribes a somewhat similar right of self-protection against arbitrary sale by their fathers. The girl is sold. If, after two or three days, the husband's entreaties have failed to make her his, she may return to her father's lodge, who in this case, however, is obliged to return to the purchaser the price he paid for her.

I have known but few such cases, the reward given the girl by her father in the shape of a most outrageous whipping having the effect to discourage such perverseness. Besides this, she knows that after marriage, she can leave her husband almost at will, and it ministers to her vanity to know that her father got an exceptionally good price for her.

I have been at pains to show that the Indian has not only no moral code, but that he has not the faintest conception of an idea of moral obligation. This is exemplified not only in their general customs, but in their individual every-day life.

For the man there is no such word, no such idea, as continence. He has as little control over his passions as any wild beast, and is held to as little accountability for their indiscriminate gratification. Of all the tribes that I know of, Indian men are the same.

No tribe visits any punishment on the lover. Every man's right is to importune, to win, if possible; and the attempt of one on the virtue of another's wife is not at all incompatible with the closest and most intimate friendship between the men. And what is more singular, the friend may make the most violent love to the wife, with every protestation of passion, and every promise of love, devotion, constancy, and kind treatment, in the immediate presence and hearing of the husband, who, whatever he may feel, is debarred by custom from noticing it in any way.

There is no single point in which tribes differ so greatly as in the average chastity of their women. The Cheyenne and Arrapahoe tribes occupy the same territory, live together in the same camps, and are constantly and intimately associated. The men of the two tribes are identical in their habits of personal incontinence, but differ entirely in their ideas of family government, and in the management of their women.

Among the Arrapahoes infidelities are not specially reprobated, even by the husband. Among the Cheyennes a discovery of such conduct would entail most serious consequences, possibly death to the woman.

The result is remarkable. The Cheyenne women are retiring and modest, and for chastity will compare favorably with the women of any nation or people. The Arrapahoe women, on the contrary, are loose almost without exception.

Under tribal government the Plains tribes differed very greatly in the punishment meted out to unfaithful wives, that is those who entered into a "liaison" while yet living with the husband, or those who by neglect of some rule become culpable. In all tribes the husband absolutely owns the wife, and may put her to death, which, as before stated, was sometimes, though rarely, done by the Cheyennes. The Comanches split their noses, while the Apaches and Navahoes frequently cut that organ off entirely.

Since the almost utter impoverishment of the tribes by the benignant action of the government, punishment of the woman for infidelity is extremely rare. The bereaved husband, whatever may be his feelings, cannot afford the loss of so much valuable property. He, therefore, sends the wife back to her father, and gathers in from the lover whatever spoil he can lay his hands on, the interference of the chief to assess damages not in this case being necessary. The woman, though living in her father's lodge, is now the property of the lover, and though he may not take her to wife, she is obliged by custom to remain faithful to him. He, therefore, keeps a close watch on her, and should he discover her in a liaison with another man, he proceeds to levy damages from that man equal to those taken from himself by the rightful husband. The ownership of the woman and duty of watching her now devolve on the latest lover. I have known several instances where a loose but good-looking woman has thus passed through half a dozen different ownerships, though all the time living in the lodge of her father.

It must be understood that the women here spoken of are those who enter into liaisons while yet living with and presumably faithful to their husbands. It is rare that the successful lover takes such an one to wife, he naturally fearing that one lapse from fidelity may be followed by another.

The exchange of husbands, as heretofore described, is in no sense a violation of the rules of the strictest chastity. It is customary, legitimate, and proper. It is the woman's protection against tyranny. The Cheyenne woman, being of a spirited, high-strung race, is quick to resent the ill treatment or neglect of one husband by taking another.

The Cheyennes and Arrapahoes have a curious custom which also obtains, though to a limited extent, among other of the Plains tribes. No unmarried woman considers herself dressed to meet her beau at night, to go to a dance, or other gathering, unless she has tied her lower limbs with a rope, in such a way, however, as not to interfere with her powers of locomotion; and every married woman does the same before going to bed when her husband is absent. Custom has made this an almost perfect protection against the brutality of the men. Without it, she would not be safe an instant, and even with it, an unmarried girl is not safe if found alone, away from the immediate protection of her lodge.

A Cheyenne woman, either married or single, is never seen alone. Though any man has the right to assault her, she is required to protect herself, and this can only be done by always having some one with her.

The sale of a wife is not unusual, though becoming less so every year. The Indians are very fond of children, and anxious to have as many as possible. Should the wife not bear a child in a reasonable time, she is liable to be sold, and very likely with her own full consent.

Should a husband sell a wife, by whom he has children, which is now extremely rare, he generally keeps the children, though I have heard of cases where wife and children were sold together. The possibility of separation from her children helps to keep the wife in proper subjection, though neither her sale, nor her voluntary abandonment of her husband for another, as already described, prevents her visiting or receiving visits from her children at pleasure.

It is regarded as effeminate in a man to show any special affection for his wife in public. A very notable exception to their habit in this particular is "Powder Face," a prominent chief of the Arrapahoes, a desperate and dangerous man, covered with scars, and celebrated for the number of scalps he has taken, and the risks he has run. His wife is a woman of average good looks, and of some thirty years of age. They have been married about fifteen years, and have no children. In spite of this, no two people could be more devoted and apparently happy. Contrary to custom he has but one wife, and she goes with him everywhere, his most devoted and willing slave. He will sit for hours before his lodge door combing her hair, painting her face, petting and fondling her; conduct which would disgrace a less determined or well-known warrior.

"Powder Face" has some other peculiarities somewhat inconsistent with Indian custom. When talking to him one day about the Indian habit of making love to each other's wives, I asked, "What would you do if another Indian made love to your wife?" He made no answer in words, but putting his hands to his belt he seized the sheath of his knife, and turned the handle towards me, putting on at the same time a scowl of malignant determination that completed the pantomime, and assured me that it would be very unhealthy for any Indian to devote himself to that woman.

Indians are gregarious, even the chief preferring to have one or more families, besides his own, in his lodge. These are generally relatives, or poor dependants.

The ordinary estimate of the inhabitants of an Indian village is three fighting men, or from twelve to fifteen individuals to the lodge. When it is recollected that even the very largest lodge is scarcely over more than eighteen feet in diameter, and contains but one room, some idea may be formed, not only of its crowded condition, but of the utter lack of privacy of the inmates, and consequently their entire lack of modesty and delicacy, either in word or act.

The husband of one wife brings home another and another. Each wife has a bed, in which she sleeps with her smaller children, the husband generally keeping the latest favorite to himself. I have never heard of any serious difficulty or trouble between the wives on that account, and the sentiment of jealousy seems to be nearly wanting in the woman. The devotion of a man to a new wife, or his infidelity to them all, seems not to awaken the slightest feeling or idea of resistance to so universal a custom. In their sexual and marital relations, the Indians are scarcely above the beasts of the field. They marry very young; the youth as soon as he is fortunate enough to steal horses enough to pay for a wife, or can persuade his father to buy one for him.

About a year previous to this writing, the seventeen year old son of a prominent and wealthy chief having been initiated as warrior, informed his father that he wished to marry.

The fond and proud father immediately presented him with quite a number of ponies, and told him to look around and choose his wife. He went directly to the father of a pretty girl, to whom he had already been paying his addresses, after Indian fashion.

After some haggling, the price of the girl was agreed upon, the youngster, however, making the unusual condition that the affair must be kept a profound secret until a certain day, when he would bring the ponies, and take away the girl. He then went to the father of another girl and closed a bargain with him. A third bargain was also consummated, all on the same terms.

The parents of the youth were informed that he would be married on a certain day, but were kept in profound ignorance as to the intended wife. However, a new and large teepee was provided by his loving mother, and all arrangements made for a grand marriage feast.

The day arrived. The precocious young rascal drove up his herd of ponies, and proceeding to the teepee of one of the fathers with whom he had bargained, paid over a number of them and carried off the girl. Then going to the teepee of the second and the third he paid their prices, and returned to his bridal teepee, minus ponies, but bringing with him the three prettiest girls in the village.

The affair caused the greatest sensation, all applauding his ingenuity and cunning. He became the hero of the hour, and the old father was so tickled that he gave him another supply of ponies, to enable him to begin his married life in style suitable to his birth and talents.

Girls generally marry very soon after the age of puberty, the father as a rule being anxious to realize her value, and the girl, with true feminine instinct in these matters, wishing to be a woman and have a husband as soon as possible.

Sometimes a father gets "hard up" and has to sell his girls while they are yet mere children. These are bought up cheap by well-to-do bucks, who give them, even while mere children, all the rights and privileges as wives.

San-a-co, a Comanche chief, and the best Indian from our standpoint I have ever known, had as wife a pretty little maid of ten years, of whom he was very fond.

In March, 1880, "Red Pipe," a Cheyenne, sold his little unformed daughter of eleven years, to be the wife of a man old enough to be her grandfather; and I have known several other warriors who have mere children as their third or fourth wives.

Either from lack of suitable food, or the constant drudgery of her hard life, the Indian woman, though perfectly healthy, is not prolific. The mother of even four children is very rare, and many women are barren. The average in most bands is scarcely more than two children to each woman; while some lodges, even where there are several wives, are childless.

The widows and orphans of a tribe are cared for after a fashion by the "dog-soldiers," who, in the general division of meat and skins, set aside a portion for their maintenance. This, when buffalo were plenty, was sufficient for their wants; but the present scarcity of game and scanty issues of the Indian Department cause no little suffering among this class.

Among the Plains tribes a woman, on the death of her husband, becomes not only herself free, but the owner of her female children as property, provided that no man has gained a lien on them by marrying the oldest daughter. The sons are independent, but are obliged to support the mother and sisters, if old enough, or if they have no families of their own.

The widows are like their white sisters in their aversion to the sweets of single blessedness, and, if at all young and good-looking, are soon married again. The old and ugly, who have no sons to support them, not unfrequently purchase for themselves a husband by giving over to him the ownership of their daughters, not as wives, but as so much saleable property. The life of an Indian woman, who has a husband to provide for and take care of her, is so much more secure from insult and outrage, so much freer from the chance of hunger and want, that every woman greatly prefers even the annoyance of a bad husband to the precarious hazards of widowhood.

A grave trouble to the Indians, and one of which I have heard many complaints, is the number of widows and orphans left on their hands by white men. The Indians have this whole matter in their own hands, having but to prohibit their women from marrying white men. But this is not at all to their taste. A father can get for his daughter possibly twise as much from a white man as an Indian would pay, and he sells at the highest price. To prohibit his selling his own property would be regarded as an invasion of his most sacred and vested rights. Having sold and got his price, he feels himself relieved of all responsibility regarding her. She should henceforth be supported by the husband; and the father regards it as a hardship, an outrage, a real cause of complaint, to be obliged, even partially, to assist in the support of a woman, his own daughter, sacrificed by his cupidity to a man whom he knew would abandon her sooner or later.

At the very important council at North Platte in 1867, one of the chiefs spoke feelingly on this subject. He said that his tribe was poor and could not support the widows and orphans left on their hands by white men, and begged that special provision might be made by the Government for them.

In looking for a wife the man is careful to select one who has no blood relationship to himself. A man who would marry a whole lodge full of sisters will not think for an instant of marrying his own cousin, even though twice removed. The relationship of first cousin is regarded as almost the same as brother and sister, and the affection of these close relationships is very warm and tender.

It is a very remarkable fact, as showing the utter want of chivalrous feeling among Indians, that though the brother may love his sister most tenderly, he never, under any circumstances, interferes to protect her from insult, or to avenge her outrage by other bucks.

There are very few madmen or idiots among the Indians. They are never confined or maltreated, but, being looked upon as directly under the malevolent influence of the Bad God, are rather avoided.

Some years ago a gentleman, now a prominent scientist, was in pursuit of knowledge on the Upper Missouri. In spite of the remonstrances of his friends and the captain, he insisted on being put off the steamboat, that he might walk across a great bend which it would take the boat some days to go around.

In a country full of hostile Sioux, without a blanket or mouthful to eat, he started alone, armed only with his butterfly net and loaded only with his pack for carrying specimens. One day, when busily occupied, he suddenly found himself surrounded by Indians. He showed no fear, and was carried to the village. His pack was found loaded with insects, bugs, and loathsome reptiles. The Indians decided that a white man who would come alone into that country unarmed, without food or bedding, for the accumulation of such things, must be crazy; so, the pack having been destroyed as "bad medicine," the doctor was carefully led out of camp and turned loose.

Jacob Piatt Dunn

"Jack, I haven't had an Indian to eat for a long time"

1886

At the end of the nineteenth century Colonel Dodge and Jacob Piatt Dunn were considered to be among the most reliable chroniclers of Indian history and life. Theodore Roosevelt endorsed their work and said that Americans were fortunate to have it. Dunn was trained in law and worked at various times as a historian, a librarian, a journalist, and a politician. The following account of Colonel John M. Chivington's attack on the Cheyennes and Arapahos at Sand Creek in 1864, written when Dunn was secretary of the Indiana Historical Society, emphasizes Indian brutality and examines the attack in a context rather more moral and ethical than historical.

On the night of November 28, 1864, about seven hundred and fifty men, cavalry and artillery, were marching eastward across the plains below Fort Lyon. There was a bitter, determined look on their hardset features that betokened ill for some one. For five days they had been marching, from Bijou Basin, about one hundred and fifty miles to the northwest, as the crow flies, but some fifty miles farther by their route. When they started the snow was two to three feet deep on the ground, but, as they progressed, it had become lighter, and now the ground was clear. The night was bitter cold; Jim Beckwith, the old trapper who had been guiding them, had become so stiffened that he was unable longer to distinguish the course, and they were obliged to rely on a half-breed Indian. About one third of the men

From J. P. Dunn, *Massacres of the Mountains :A History of the Indian Wars of the Far West* (New York, Harper & Brothers, 1886), 396–446.

had the appearance of soldiers who had seen service; the remainder had a diversity of arms and equipments as well as of uniforms, and marched with the air of raw recruits. About half a mile in advance were three men, the half-breed guide and two officers, one of the latter of such gigantic proportions that the others seemed pygmies beside him. Near daybreak the half-breed turned to the white men and said: "Wolf he howl. Injun dog he hear wolf, he howl too. Injun he hear dog and listen; hear something, and run off." The big man tapped the butt of his revolver in an ominous way, and replied: "Jack, I haven't had an Indian to eat for a long time. If you fool with me, and don't lead us to that camp, I'll have you for breakfast." They found the camp. There were one hundred and twenty Cheyenne and eight Arapahoe lodges in it, stretched along the bank of a shallow stream, which crept sluggishly down a broad bed of sand. On each side of the camp, ranging out perhaps a mile, was a herd of ponies, the two numbering about eleven hundred. It was between daybreak and sunrise; the Indians were just beginning to move. A squaw heard the noise of the approaching horses, and reported that a herd of buffalo was coming. Others ran out, who quickly discovered that the rumbling was the tread of horses, and that a large body of troops was approaching. In a moment all was confusion. Men, women, and children ran here and there, getting their arms in readiness or preparing for flight. The principal Cheyenne chief hastily ran up an American flag over his teepee, with a white flag above it. A white trader, who was in one of the teepees, came out and hastened towards the soldiers. At the same time two detachments of cavalry were galloping towards the herds, and some of the Indians were running in the same directions.

Firing began between these parties. The white trader seemed confused, and stopped. A cavalryman said: "Let me bring him in, major," and, starting from the ranks, galloped towards him, but a bullet from the camp tumbled him from his horse, and the trader turned and ran back. The herd of ponies on the farther side of the camp became alarmed and ran towards the camp, the soldiers cutting off only about half of them. The main body of troops pressed forward, firing as they came, led by their giant commander, who rode through the ranks, calling out: "Remember our wives and children, murdered on the Platte and the Arkansas." The Indians were beginning to fall rapidly under the deadly fire. Part of them caught the straggling ponies which had reached the camp, and fled. The remainder, warriors and squaws, with some children, retired slowly up the creek, fighting as they went. They continued thus for about three quarters of a mile, to a point where the banks rose from three to ten feet, on either side of a level expanse of sand, some three hundred yards wide. Along the banks the Indians made their stand, protected by them on one side, and on the other by heaps of loose sand which they had scraped up. Most of the troops were now in confusion, each doing about as he liked. About one half of them were firing on the line of Indians in the creek bed, and squads were riding about, killing stragglers, scalping the dead, and pursuing the flying. No prisoners were being taken, and no one was allowed to escape if escape could be prevented. A child of about three years, perfectly naked, was toddling along over the trail where the Indians had fled. A soldier saw it, fired at about seventy-five yards distance, and missed it. Another dismounted and said: "Let me try the little —— ——; I can hit him." He missed too, but a third dismounted, with a similar remark, and at his shot the child fell. At the creek bed the fight was at long range and stubborn. A private was firing at an Indian who climbed up on the bank from time to time, and made derisive gestures at the soldier's fruitless efforts. "Let me take that gun of yours for a minute, colonel," said the soldier. The colonel handed him his rifle, an elegant silver-mounted one, presented him by the citizens of Denver; the Indian showed himself again; the rifle cracked and he dropped dead. The squaws were fighting along with the men. One had just wounded a soldier with an arrow, and a comrade put his rifle in rest, remarking, "If that squaw shows her head above the bank again, I'll blow the whole top of it off." An officer, standing by him, said: "I wouldn't make a heathen of myself by shooting a woman." The words had hardly dropped from his lips when the same squaw sent an arrow through the officer's arm, and his philanthropic remark changed to a howl of "Shoot the —— ——," and the soldier did it. The Indians could not be dislodged by the small arms, but towards noon two howitzers were brought into action and they broke the line. The Indians fell back from one position to another, the combat becoming gradually a running fight, which was kept up for five miles or more, and abandoned by the pursuers a short time before dusk. The soldiers then gathered at the Indian camp, where they remained until the second day following. Most of the corpses were scalped, and a number were mutilated as bodies are usually mutilated by Indians, with all that implies. Near evening, on the day after the battle, Jack Smith, the half-breed who had guided the soldiers to the camp, and a son of the white trader who was in the camp, was shot by one of the men. He had tried to run away during the fight, but had been brought back. The colonel commanding was warned that he would probably be killed if the men were not ordered to let him live. He replied: "I have given my orders, and have no further instructions to give." There were, at the time, seven other prisoners in the camp, two squaws and five children, who were taken to Fort Lyon and left there. They were the only prisoners taken. When the camp was broken, the buffalo-robes were confiscated for the sick, the soldiers took what they wanted for trophies, and the remainder was burned. The Indians lost three hundred, all killed, of whom about one half were warriors and the remainder women and children. The whites lost seven killed and forty-seven wounded, of whom seven afterwards died.

This was "the massacre of the friendly Cheyenne Indians at Sand Creek, by the Colorado troops, under Colonel John M. Chivington," or "the battle on the Big Sandy, with the hostile Cheyennes and Arapahoes," as you may be pleased to consider it. That is to say, it is a statement of what occurred there, as nearly as the truth can be arrived at, without favor or reservation. It is but just to add that the great majority of the troops who participated in it say it was not so bad as here represented, and that the witnesses of the action and events connected with it, who subsequently denounced it, make it no worse, notwithstanding the fact that many, who knew nothing of the facts in the case, have added much to the statement above given. The number killed was the point most in controversy in the investigations of the matter, ranging from about seventy, in Major Wynkoop's estimate, to six hundred, in Colonel Chivington's original report. The Indians conceded a loss of one hundred and forty, of whom sixty were warriors, and the testimony of all who counted bodies, after the battle, indicates the number stated above. Concerning this affair there has been much of exaggeration, much of invective, much of misunderstanding, and much of wholly unfounded statement. Indeed, so much has been said in regard to it that the controversy is far more extensive than the original trouble, and the historical shape that it has assumed is the creation of the controversy, not the fight. Now that twenty years have passed away —that the Indian is only a memory where he then roamed—that a new generation has taken the place of the old—let us try calmly to unravel the thread of truth from the fantastic fabric which has so long concealed it; and to do this we must first know something of the actors on that field.

Who was Colonel Chivington? In 1840 he was a rough, uncouth, profound child of nature, just stepped across the threshold of manhood. He lived in Warren County, Ohio, about two miles south of the line of Clinton. At a log-rolling in the neighborhood a good old Methodist brother reproved him, one day, for profanity, and the sturdy youth answered defiantly: "I will swear when I please and where I please." But he brooded over the rebuke, and a few days later he went to his reprover's house, determined to swear there, before his family. He did not do as he intended. Some unknown power beat down his resolution, and the curse died trembling on his tongue. He went away, but the mysterious influence followed him; his eyes were turned inward on his guilty soul; he could not rest. He struggled against it, but in vain, and soon he sought at the altar the pardon for his sins. Scoffers may smile at the change of heart by divine grace, but sure it was there was a change in him. He became an industrious, orderly man; he joined the Methodist Church and lived consistently with its discipline; he apprenticed himself to a carpenter and thoroughly learned the trade. Towards 1850 he determined to move West and enter the ministry, and this he did, working meantime at his trade. At the end of the second year of his clerical service he was transferred to the Missouri Conference and continued his labors there. It was a troubled field for him, for he was peculiarly a Northern man. Mobs collected at various times to hinder his preaching, but his apparent abundance of "muscular Christianity" kept him from serious trouble, and his intended disturbers often remained to hear him preach.

His kindly nature helped him to preserve peaceful relations, also. One day he met an old planter, hauling logs, with his team mired down. Chivington dismounted, tied his horse, waded into the mud, and helped him out. The planter desired to know to whom he was indebted, and on being told, exclaimed: "Come right home with me. A preacher that will get off in the mud to help a stranger won't steal niggers." They were good friends thereafter. A few years later Chivington was in Kansas, taking an active part with Lane and his friends in the border war. After the Kansas troubles were settled, we find him serving acceptably, for two years, as a missionary to the Wyandot Indians, and afterwards, as interpreter and guide, traveling through the West with the Methodist bishops who were establishing missions among the Indian tribes. Soon after the beginning of the war he went to a quarterly meeting at Denver, being then a Presiding Elder in Western Kansas and Colorado, and, while there, preached to the soldiers at their barracks. They liked his style and urged him to stay with them. Governor Gilpin offered him a chaplaincy, but he said that if he went with the soldiers he wanted to fight, so he was made a major instead. There is one point in his character that must not be lost sight of, if his history is to be understood. He was, like other Kansas free-soilers, an uncompromising Union man, and had no use for a rebel, white or red. His dislike to anything savoring of treason got him into trouble time and again, but he never held back on that account. On one occasion, after the war, he seriously disturbed his domestic peace by peremptorily shutting off some reminiscences from his brother-in-law, an ex-confederate.

And what of the Colorado troops? They included men from all ranks and classes in life; many of them are prominent and respected citizens of Colorado now. About two thirds of those at Sand Creek were one-hundred-days' men, of the 3d regiment; the remainder were veterans, mostly of the 1st regiment. These last had established a military reputation beyond all cavil, and, without referring to other services, a brief sketch of their work in New Mexico will satisfy the reader that no equal body of men ever did greater or more gallant service for the Union. In the early part of 1862 General Sibley invaded New Mexico with an army of twenty-five hundred, including a large number of Texan Rangers, having evidently in view the conquest of the entire mountain country. Our government had been paying little or no attention to the Far West; its hands were full in the East. Even the official communications in some departments had not been replied to in a year past. The Confederacy was more watchful. Full information of the situation in the West had been given to its leaders by officials, civil and military, who had been located at various Western points, and had hastened to the South as soon as the war opened. The United States troops in the country were few in number. The Indians were ready for war whenever an opportunity presented itself. The Mexicans were supposed to be friendly to the South, and the lower classes were known to be ready for rapine and pillage, at any time and against anybody. The Mormons were in ecstasy over the apparent fulfillment of their late Prophet's war prophecy, and were willing to help on the "Kilkenny-cat fight." Besides, they were still sore over the troubles of 1857, and had no love for the national government. The Secession element in California was quite strong, especially in the southern part, which was to have been a slave state under the Calhoun plan. These facts at once determined the policy of the South, and the invasion was begun. If it had been successful—what an awful possibility!—the South would have had a coast-line impossible of blockade, the entire line of Mexico for external communication, the mines to fill her depleted treasury, and an extensive country which could have been reconquered only at immense cost of life and money. The Texans entered New Mexico from the south. They took Fort Fillmore without resistance, and marched up the Rio Grande unchecked, until they reached Fort Craig, where General Canby awaited them. They decided not to attack the fort, and were flanking it, to go forward, when Canby came out and attacked them at Valverde. They rather worsted him, and he retired to the fort, while they pursued their march up the river. They occupied Santa Fé, and found that the Mexicans were not nearly so glad to see them as they had anticipated; still, little discouraged, they pushed on towards Fort Union, some sixty-five miles northeast, on the edge of the plains, the arsenal and supply depot for that section.

Governor Gilpin, all this time, had been moving in the mining camps of Colorado, and, on February 22, the 1st Colorado regiment, under Colonel Slough, left Denver through snow a foot deep. They reached Fort Union on March 11, after a journey of great hardship, and were there armed and equipped. They pressed forward, and, on the 23d, reached the mouth of Apaché Cañon, the location of

"Pigeon's Ranch," or, more properly, the ranch of M. Alexandre Vallé; the Texans had by this time reached the opposite end of the cañon. In this cañon, where Armijo had failed to meet Kearney, the Greek miner met the Greek cowboy. It was a contest the like of which never occurred elsewhere. The Southerners had adopted as their favorite name, "Baylor's Babes;" the Coloradoans gloried in their chosen title of "Pet Lambs"—grim satires these, as well on the plainsmen who charged McRae's Battery with revolvers and bowie-knives, as on the mountaineers who never learned what it was to be whipped. On the 26th the advance of the Texans met two hundred and ten cavalry and one hundred and eighty infantry under Major Chivington, and, in the words of a local writer, it "was more like the shock of lightning than of battalions." Said M. Vallé, who witnessed the fight, "Zat Chivington, he poot down 'is 'ead, and foight loike mahd bull." Both detachments reeled back from this hard bump, and on the 28th, the main forces having arrived, they went at it again. The Texans surprised the Coloradoans' camp, but the Lambs stood their ground, and, after a desperate fight, the Babes were forced to retire, and they retired to a little surprise-party at home. While they had been making their attack, Chivington had led a force of one hundred men up the precipitous side of the cañon, along a rugged and dangerous path, and down on the Texan rear-guard of some six hundred men. It was a desperate charge to make, but it resulted in a brilliant success, and the Texan train of sixty-four wagons and two hundred mules, with all their supplies and ammunition, were destroyed. The Texan invasion was ruined. Sibley began his retreat, and Slough fell back on Fort Union for his supplies, but only for a breathing space. On April 13 the Coloradoans had joined General Canby and begun a pursuit of the retiring Texans, which was kept up for one hundred and fifty miles; a pursuit so disastrous to the pursued that one half of their original force was left behind, dead, wounded, and prisoners, together with all their stores, public and private. So much for the Colorado troops.

The Cheyennes we know something of already. The village attacked was that of Black Kettle (Moke-ta-ve-to), the principal chief of the southern Cheyennes, and the few lodges of Arapahoes were under Left Hand (Na-watk), second in rank of the southern chiefs. There had been trouble in these tribes ever since the treaty of Fort

Wise, in 1861. The warriors denounced the chiefs for making the treaty, and were particularly opposed to the construction of the Kansas Pacific Railroad through their lands, as they knew it would drive away the buffalo. The chiefs were threatened with death if they undertook to carry out its provisions, and so the intense desire of the Cheyennes and Arapahoes for an agricultural life, which is recited as the cause of the treaty, had to go ungratified. The first serious troubles, after Sumner's campaign, occurred after this treaty was made, and all the succeeding troubles grew out of it. The Cheyennes began committing minor offences in 1861, and, as they were unpunished, they gradually grew bolder, until, in 1863, Agent Lorey reported that the Cheyennes were dissatisfied, and that the Sioux were urging them to open war. In other words, the war feeling had grown so strong that it was necessary to treat with them anew. Governor Evans went out, by agreement, to treat with them, on the head-waters of the Republican, but they failed to come as agreed. The governor sent his guide, a squaw-man named Elbridge Gerry (a grandson of the signer of the Declaration of Independence, of the same name), in search of them. He returned after an absence of two weeks, and reported that they had held a council and decided not to treat. One chief, Bull Bear (O-to-ah-nac-co), the leader of the "Dog-soldiers," had offered to come in, but his warriors would not allow him to do so. The Cheyennes afterwards confirmed this statement fully; they said they were going to remain at peace, but would make no treaty that they had to sign; that they were going to have their lands; and even if a railroad was built through their country, they would not allow any one to settle along it. The chiefs who had signed the treaty of Fort Wise said they were obliged to repudiate it or their warriors would kill them. Minor depredations were committed during the remainder of 1863 and the early part of 1864, and, during the winter, word was received, from spies among them, that a coalition was being formed among all the plains tribes, to drive the whites out of the country. This information proved true, for in the spring and summer of 1864, the Sioux, Comanches, Kiowas, Cheyennes, and Arapahoes were engaged in active hostilities. The reader will note here, that no one has ever pretended that any of the eighteen hundred Southern Cheyennes, except the six hundred at Sand Creek, were not open enemies at the time.

The effect of this warfare on the whites was distressing. Nearly every stage was attacked, emigrants were cut off, and the settlements were raided continually. The overland trains, on which the entire settlements depended for supplies, were deterred from moving by fear of attack. On June 14 Governor Evans applied for authority to call the militia into the United States service, or to call out one-hundred-days' men, which was not granted. Matters became worse. All the settlements from the Purgatoire to the Cache la Poudre, and for two hundred miles on the Platte, were in consternation. The settlers left their crops and built block-houses for mutual protection. Those near Denver fled to that place. The governor was besieged with petitions for arms and authority to organize for protection. On August 8 all the stage lines were attacked. On August 11 Governor Evans issued a proclamation, calling the people to organize for self-protection, and under this several companies were formed which were considered sufficient for the defence of the settlements. But they could not protect the settlements from famine. On August 18 Governor Evans despatched Secretary Stanton: "Extensive Indian depredations, with murder of families, occurred yesterday thirty miles south of Denver. Our lines of communication are cut, and our crops, our sole dependence, are all in exposed localities, and cannot be gathered by our scattered population. Large bodies of Indians are undoubtedly near to Denver, and we are in danger of destruction both from the attack of Indians and starvation. I earnestly request that Colonel Ford's regiment of 2d Colorado Volunteers be immediately sent to our relief. It is impossible to exaggerate our danger. We are doing all we can for our defence." There was no favorable answer received to this, and on September 7, a second despatch followed: "Pray give positive orders for our 2d Colorado Cavalry to come out. Have notice published that they will come in detachments to escort trains up the Platte on certain days. Unless escorts are sent thus we will inevitably have a famine in addition to this gigantic Indian war. Flour is forty-five dollars a barrel, and the supply growing scarce, with none on the way. Through spies we got knowledge of the plan of about one thousand warriors in camp to strike our frontier settlements, in small bands, simultaneously in the night, for an extent of three hundred miles. It was frustrated at the time, but we have to fear another such attempt soon. Pray give the order for our troops to come, as requested, at once, or it will be too late for trains to come this season." The troops were not sent, but, in the mean time, authority had been given by the War Department to raise a regiment of one-hundred-days' men, and the 3d Colorado was organized and impatiently waiting for arms and equipments, which they did not get until a short time before their march to Sand Creek.

But were the Cheyennes responsible for all this? Quite as much so as any of the tribes. They began stealing stock early in the spring, and, on April 13, a herdsman for Irving, Jackmann, & Co. reported that the Cheyennes and Arapahoes had run off sixty head of oxen and a dozen mules and horses from their camp, thirty miles south of Denver. Lieutenant Clark Dunn was sent after them with a small party of soldiers. He overtook them as they were crossing the Platte, during a heavy snow-storm. A parley was commenced, but was interrupted by part of the Indians running off the stock, and the soldiers attempting to disarm the others. A fight ensued, in which the soldiers, who were greatly outnumbered, were defeated, with a loss of four men, the Indians still holding the cattle. After this fight, there was not a word nor an act from any member of the Southern Cheyennes indicative of peace, until the 1st of September, when the Indian agent at Fort Lyon received the following:

"CHEYENNE VILLAGE, *Aug.* 29, 1864.
"MAJOR COLLEY,—We received a letter from Bent, wishing us to make peace. We held a council in regard to it. All come to the conclusion to make peace with you, providing you make peace with the Kiowas, Comanches, Arapahoes, Apaches, and Sioux. We are going to send a messenger to the Kiowas and to the other nations about our going to make peace with you. We heard that you have some [Indian prisoners] in Denver. We have seven prisoners of yours which we are willing to give up, providing you give up yours. There are three war-parties out yet, and two of Arapahoes. They have been out for some time, and are expected in soon. When we held this council there were few Arapahoes and Sioux present. We want true news from you in return. That is a letter.
"BLACK KETTLE, *and other chiefs.*"

This letter was written for the chiefs by Edmond Guerrier and George Bent, Cheyenne half-breeds. Black Kettle was head chief of all the Southern Cheyennes, and conceded by all to be the most friendly of the chiefs towards the whites, with, possibly, the exception of Bull Bear. Yet, by this letter, he and the other chiefs admit fully that they were hostiles; that three Cheyenne war-parties were then out; that they were in coalition with the other tribes, and would consult them before treating; that they would treat only if all the other tribes treated. Indeed, why should the Cheyennes deny that they were hostile? They had been raiding in every direction; had run off stock repeatedly; had attacked stages and emigrant trains; had killed settlers; had carried off women and children; had fought the troops under Major Downing; had defeated those under Lieutenant Dunn and Lieutenant Ayres; and had been evading other bodies of troops all summer. They attacked the settlements on the Little Blue, and, after killing the men, they carried off Mrs. Ewbanks, Miss Roper, and three children. It was almost certainly they who killed Mr. and Mrs. Hungate and their two babies at Running Creek. They carried off Mrs. Martin and a little boy from a ranch on Plum Creek. General Curtis prepared two or three times to march against them, but was diverted from his purpose by rebel raiders from Arkansas. He sent General Blunt after them, and they ambushed his advance-guard at Pawnee Fork and almost annihilated it. On November 12, after Black Kettle had gone to Sand Creek, a party of Cheyennes and Arapahoes approached a government train on Walnut Creek, east of Fort Larned, and, after protesting friendship and shaking hands, suddenly fell upon the teamsters and killed fourteen of them, the only person who escaped alive being a boy who was scalped and left for dead. He recovered, but became imbecile, and died from the effects of the injury.

The Cheyennes never denied that they were hostiles; that they were was a discovery of the Indian ring, perpetuated by Indian worshippers. When they sent in the letter quoted above Major Wynkoop went out to them, and brought in Black Kettle, his brother White Antelope, and Bull Bear, of the Cheyennes, and Neva and other Arapahoes, representing Left Hand, for a talk with Governor Evans. They said then: "It was like going through a strong fire or blast for Major Wynkoop's men to come to our camp; it was the same for us to come to see you." From this talk I quote the following: "Gov. EVANS. 'Who committed the murder of the Hungate family on Running Creek?' NEVA. 'The Arapahoes; a party of the northern band who were passing north. It was Medicine Man or Roman Nose and three others. I am satisfied, from the time he left a certain camp for the North, that it was this party of four persons.' AGENT WHITELY. 'That cannot be true.' Gov. E. Where is Roman Nose?' NEVA. 'You ought to know better than me; you have been nearer to him.' Gov. E. 'Who killed the man and the boy at the head of Cherry Creek?' NEVA (after consultation). 'Kiowas and Comanches.' Gov. E. 'Who stole soldiers' horses and mules from Jimmy's camp twenty-seven days ago?' NEVA. 'Fourteen Cheyennes and Arapahoes together.' Gov. E. 'What were their names?' NEVA. 'Powder Face and Whirlwind, who are now in our camp, were the leaders.' COL. SHOUP. 'I counted twenty Indians on that occasion.' Gov. E. 'Who stole Charley Autobee's horses?' NEVA. 'Raven's son.' Gov. E. 'Who took the stock from Fremont's orchard and had the first fight with the soldiers this spring north of there?' WHITE ANTELOPE. 'Before answering this question I would like for you to know that this was the beginning of the war, and I should like to know what it was for. A soldier fired first.' Gov. E. 'The Indians had stolen about forty horses; the soldiers went to recover them, and the Indians fired a volley into their ranks.' WHITE ANTELOPE. 'That is all a mistake; they were coming down the Bijou and found one horse and one mule. They returned one horse, before they got to Gerry's, to a man, then went to Gerry's expecting to turn the other one over to some one. They then heard that the soldiers and Indians were fighting somewhere down the Platte; then they took fright and all fled.' Gov. E. 'Who were the Indians who had the fight?' WHITE ANTELOPE. 'They were headed by the Fool Badger's son, a young man, one of the greatest of the Cheyenne warriors, who was wounded, and though still alive he will never recover.' NEVA. 'I want to say something; it makes me feel bad to be talking about these things and opening old sores. . . . The Comanches, Kiowas, and Sioux have done much more injury than we have. We will tell what we know, but cannot speak for others.' Gov. E. 'I suppose you acknowledge the depredations on the Little Blue, as you have the prisoners then taken in your possession.' WHITE ANTELOPE. 'We [the Cheyennes] took two prisoners west of Fort Kearney, and destroyed the trains.' . . . NEVA. 'I know the value of the presents which we receive from Washington; we cannot live without them. That is why I try so hard to keep peace with the whites.' Gov. E. 'I cannot say anything about those things now.' NEVA. 'I can speak for all the

Arapahoes under Left Hand. Raven has sent no one here to speak for him; Raven has fought the whites.'" Little Raven (Oh-has-tee) was head chief of the Southern Arapahoes, and was notoriously hostile. Even Major Wynkoop conceded that he had, during the summer, killed three men and carried off a woman.

But even if most of the Cheyennes had been hostile, were not the Indians at Sand Creek friendly? It is usually difficult to disprove an Indian's protestations of friendship in a satisfactory way, but if ever it was done it was here. Black Kettle had admitted his hostility, as shown above. So had his brother, White Antelope. War Bonnet, a chief who was killed there, was identified as one of the most active hostiles in the attack on General Blunt at Pawnee Fork. The testimony shows, without contradiction, that there were at least two hundred warriors in the camp, and it would be very difficult to point out a Cheyenne warrior who had been friendly. It had been the plea of the chiefs, all along, that they desired to carry out the treaty of Fort Wise, but were deterred by fear of their warriors. But more satisfactory than the established reputation of these Indians was the testimony of scalps, women's and children's dresses, and stolen goods, which were found in profusion in the teepees. Perhaps medical testimony will be most convincing as to the condition of the scalps. Dr. Caleb S. Birtsell, Assistant Surgeon, testified: "While in one of the lodges dressing wounded soldiers a soldier came to the opening of the lodge and called my attention to some white scalps he held in his hand; my impression, after examination, was that two or three of them were quite fresh; I saw, in the hands of soldiers, silk dresses and other garments belonging to women." Major Anthony, commanding at Fort Lyon, considered that there were three Indians in the camp who were friendly, Black Kettle, Left Hand, and One Eye, and these he desired to be spared. Black Kettle escaped unhurt; Left Hand received a wound from the effect of which he afterwards died; and One Eye was killed. He was in the camp as a spy; placed there, on a salary of $125 per month and a ration, by Major Wynkoop, to watch these "friendly" Cheyennes, and continued in the same position by Major Anthony.

And this brings us to another equally serious question. Although these Cheyennes at Sand Creek had been hostile, were they not at Sand Creek under a promise of protection by the military? To this the testimony answers clearly, "No." That is a rather startling statement to one who is familiar only with the current version of Sand Creek, but it is true, nevertheless. Both the congressional and departmental investigations were peculiar. The former was conducted by a committee of men whose minds were made up before they began; the style of their questions, the inaccuracy of their findings, and the fact that they condemned every one for prevarication who differed from what they expected in testimony, prove this. The latter was conducted by Major Wynkoop, who had been displaced by Major Anthony at Fort Lyon but a short time previous to the fight, who was one of the leading prosecuting witnesses, and who was, immediately after the investigation, appointed to the Agency, a position which is very rarely forced on men against their wishes. There was also a military commission appointed, which took testimony at Denver and Fort Lyon; it was presided over by Colonel Tappan, of the 1st Colorado Cavalry, who was recognized as a personal enemy of Chivington. This was the only one of the tribunals before which Chivington appeared and was given opportunity to cross-examine or produce witnesses. The reports of the other investigations were made without any knowledge of its proceedings; in fact, its proceedings were not published for two years after the reports were made. In the testimony at both of the earlier investigations, scheming and jealousy crop out at many points. The prosecuting witnesses who were out of office charged the prosecuting witnesses who were in office with stealing from the Indians, and selling them their own goods. The fullest latitude was given to hearsay, and expressions of opinion were courted. But the most striking thing in all that testimony was the adroit manner in which several witnesses confused the relations of Black Kettle's Cheyennes, to Fort Lyon, with those of Little Raven's Arapahoes. Their real relations were explained to the Committee on the Conduct of the War, clearly enough to have been understood by men who were not blinded by prejudice, but the committee only carried on to perfection the work which the witnesses had begun. The testimony of all the witnesses, taken together, shows that the Indians who came to the fort and were subsisted by Major Wynkoop were six hundred and fifty-two of the Southern Arapahoes, under their head chief, Little Raven. That this chief had been hostile is not questioned;

Major Wynkoop himself blames him and his warriors for all the depredations committed by the Arapahoes. On November 2 Major Anthony arrived and assumed command; he found these Arapahoes camped two miles from Fort Lyon, with all their arms, and coming daily to the fort for provisions; he told them they must surrender their arms, and they gave up a lot of old and worn-out weapons, which, they said, were all they had. After ten days he concluded that he was exceeding his authority in this, returned their arms to them, and told them to go away. They went; Major Wynkoop says that Little Raven's band went to Camp Wynkoop, and Left Hand's joined the Cheyennes. The Arapahoes who went with Left Hand numbered about forty.

The most satisfactory evidence in regard to this is not in the testimony of any one, but in the official report of Major Anthony, made at the time, when there was no "Sand Creek" to attack or defend. On November 6, in a letter to headquarters, after recounting his disarming the Arapahoes, he says: "Nine Cheyenne Indians to-day sent in, wishing to see me. They state that six hundred of that tribe are now thirty-five miles north of here, coming towards the post, and two thousand about seventy-five miles away, waiting for better weather to enable them to come in. I shall not permit them to come in, even as prisoners, for the reason that if I do I shall have to subsist them upon a prisoner's rations. I shall, however, demand their arms, all stolen stock, and the perpetrators of all depredations. I am of the opinion that they will not accept this proposition, but that they will return to the Smoky Hill. They pretend that they want peace, and I think they do now, as they cannot fight during the winter, except where a small band of them can find an unprotected train or frontier settlement. I do not think it is policy to make peace with them now, until all perpetrators of depredations are surrendered up, to be dealt with as we may propose." This, then, was the true state of affairs; on November 6 there was not a Cheyenne at Fort Lyon; there were six hundred and fifty-two Arapahoes under the hostile chief Little Raven, who was then playing friend; there were six hundred Cheyennes under Black Kettle, thirty-five miles north, proposing to come in. And what was done in regard to the Cheyennes? They came on down after some further parleying; they were not allowed to come into the fort at all, or camp in the vicinity of the post. They were told that they might go over on Sand Creek, forty miles away, and camp, and if the commandant received any authority to treat with them he would let them know. They were not in the camp two miles from Fort Lyon at any time; they were never disarmed; and they were never held as prisoners.

Neither did these Indians have any promise of immunity from Governor Evans or Colonel Chivington, as is intimated by the committee. They met but once, at the council in Denver, on September 28. It has been stated over and over that the Cheyennes came to Sand Creek, in response to Governor Evans's circular, calling on the friendly Indians to take refuge at the forts—friendly Cheyennes and Arapahoes at Fort Lyon. This statement is absolutely and unqualifiedly untrue. The circular was dated June 27. Three months later the chiefs appeared in Denver to talk peace, in consequence of the circular, but were plainly told it was too late for any treaty. Governor Evans said to them: "Whatever peace they make must be with the soldiers, and not with me;" and the entire talk was on that basis. I quote again: "WHITE ANTELOPE. 'How can we be protected from the soldiers on the plains?' Gov. E. 'You must make that arrangement with the military chief.' WHITE ANTELOPE. 'I fear that these new soldiers who have gone out may kill some of my people while I am here.' Gov. E. 'There is great danger of it.'" Again, Governor Evans said: "I hand you over to the military, one of the chiefs of which is here to-day, and can speak for himself to them if he chooses." The chief referred to was Colonel Chivington, Commander of the District—it should be noted, however, that Fort Lyon was not in Chivington's district. He said: "I am not a big war chief, but all the soldiers in this country are at my command. My rule of fighting white men or Indians is to fight them until they lay down their arms and submit to military authority. They are nearer Major Wynkoop than any one else, and they can go to him when they get ready to do that." If any one can torture those utterances into promises of immunity he is welcome to do so.

Some five weeks later the messengers of the Cheyennes arrived at Fort Lyon and were turned away, as above stated. They did not arrive there until after Major Wynkoop was superseded by Major Anthony. They did not make any arrangement with Major Wynkoop; it was impossible for them to do so, as he was not in command.

More than that, Major Wynkoop never, at any time, had any authority to make any treaty with them, and the Indians knew it. White Antelope said, in the council: "When Major Wynkoop came, we proposed to make peace. He said he had no power to make a peace, except to bring them here and return them safe." The Cheyennes went over to Sand Creek and camped, not anticipating any trouble, because there were no soldiers near them, except the garrison, and it was too small to risk an attack. Indeed, they were ready for an attack from it, and sent word that, "If that little —— —— red-eyed chief wants a fight, we will give him all he wants." The chief referred to was Major Anthony, who was afflicted with sore eyes at the time. The Indians were not allowed to visit the fort, and none of their friends or supposed allies, except on first being blindfolded. This was under general orders which were adopted a few weeks previously, after a Sunday-morning performance by friendly Indians at Fort Larned. On that occasion the Indians had drawn supplies for the week, and some squaws were executing a dance for the edification of a part of the officers and men, when the braves stampeded the cattle belonging to the post, with all the horses and mules, and succeeded in getting away with them. At the first whoop of the stampede the dancers jumped on their ponies and scampered away, demonstrating that the affair had been planned in cold blood. Major Anthony testified that he had no friendly relations with these Cheyennes; that he should have attacked them before Chivington came if his force had not been too small; that he told Chivington it was only a question of policy whether they should be attacked or not, as it would probably cause an attack by the large band, which was not far distant. So far as the propriety of attacking these Indians was concerned, there is not the least question but that Chivington was justified in his attack, under all the rules of civilized warfare. They were hostiles, and there was no truce with them. There is another matter—it seems almost absurd to mention it, but it were well to prevent any further misunderstanding—and that is the display of flags by Black Kettle, which some persons have seemed to lay much stress upon. The uniform testimony of the soldiers was that they saw nothing of the kind, but that is immaterial. No one of common understanding would profess that the display of a flag of any kind was cause for stopping troops in the midst of a charge, and especially in the midst of a surprise of an enemy's camp.

Having now shown the propriety of the attack, we arrive at the question of the propriety of the manner in which it was made, a question much more difficult of solution. One point is certain—every one in authority felt that the Indians ought to be punished. Major Wynkoop testifies that Governor Evans at first objected to seeing the chiefs at all, but finally consented to hold the council which has been mentioned. His feelings on the subject were exposed to the Indians at the council in these words: "The time when you can make war best is in the summer time; when I can make war best is in the winter. You, so far, have had the advantage; my time is just coming." He told them, as before stated, that they would have to talk to the military authorities, and his action was approved by the Indian Bureau. The military had no desire for peace at the time. It is quite true that the field orders of General Curtis directed hostilities only against hostile Indians, and expressly stated that "women and children must be spared," but "hostile Indians" meant Indians who had been hostile, and neither he nor any other commander in the West was in favor of treating till the Indians had been punished. On the day of Governor Evans's council with the chiefs, General Curtis telegraphed the District Commander: "I fear agent of the Interior Department will be ready to make presents too soon. It is better to chastise before giving anything but a little tobacco to talk over. No peace must be made without my directions." The last telegram Chivington received from him, before marching, was: "Pursue everywhere and punish the Cheyennes and Arapahoes; pay no attention to district lines. No presents must be made and no peace concluded without my consent." The reader will observe that General Curtis is not by these directions made responsible for killing the women and children, or deciding that the Sand Creek camp was hostile, but his desire to punish the Indians was clear and decided. And it was so all through the West. A few weeks later, when Colonel Ford wanted to make peace with the Kiowas and Comanches, General Dodge, his Department Commander, telegraphed him: "The military have no authority to treat with Indians. Our duty is to make them keep the peace by punishing them for their hostility. Keep posted as to their location, so that as soon as ready we can strike them." So, in New Mexico, General Carleton had instructed Colonel Kit Carson: "If the Indians send in a flag and desire to treat for peace, say to the bearer that when the people of New Mexico were attacked by the Texans, the Mescaleros broke their treaty of peace, and murdered innocent people, and ran off their stock; that now our hands are untied, and you have been sent to punish them for their treachery and their crimes; that you have no power to make peace; that you are there to kill them wherever you can find them; that if they beg for peace, their chiefs and twenty of their principal men must come to Santa Fé to have a talk here; but tell them fairly and frankly that you will keep after their people and slay them until you receive orders to desist from these head-quarters." On September 19 Curtis writes to Carleton: "General Blunt is at or near Fort Larned looking out for Indians, and may co-operate with you in crushing out some of the vile hordes that now harass our lines of communication." On October 22 Carleton writes to Blunt, hoping he will effect a union with Carson, "so that a blow may be struck which those two treacherous tribes will remember." On January 30, 1865, Curtis writes to Governor Evans: "I protest my desire to pursue and punish the enemy everywhere, in his lodges especially; but I do not believe in killing women and children who can be taken."

It is equally certain that the desire of punishing these Indians was increased, with loyal people, by the belief that their hostility was produced will never be definitely known, but there was reason for the belief, without doubt. Soon after the beginning of the war the insurgents had occupied Indian territory and enrolled many Indians in Confederate regiments. The loyal Indians tried to resist, but, after two or three engagements, about seven thousand of them were driven into Kansas. From the men among them three regiments were organized, and the women and children were subsisted out of the annuities of the hostiles. In the latter part of 1862, John Ross, head chief of the Cherokees, announced officially that the Cherokee nation had treated with the Confederate States, and, as is well known, there were several regiments of Indians in the regular Confederate service, besides numbers in irregular relations, among whom were Cherokees, Creeks, Choctaws, Chickasaws, Osages, Seminoles, Senecas, Shawnees, Quapaws, Comanches, Wachitas,

Kiowas, and Pottawattamies, and none of them regained friendly relations with the United States until the treaty of September 21, 1865. On the south of Colorado the Comanches and Kiowas were at war, with Southern sympathies. The Mescaleros had taken the war-path on the advance of the Texans. To the north it was the same. The Sioux troubles all originated in Minnesota, and concerning them our Consul-general in Canada, Mr. Giddings, wrote at the time: "There is little doubt that the recent outbreak in the Northwest has resulted from the efforts of secession agents operating through Canadian Indians and fur-traders." The war feeling was so strong among the Sioux that the friendly Yanktons, in 1862, refused to receive their annuities unless a force of soldiers was brought, to protect them from the other Sioux, who insisted on their becoming hostile. As the Minnesota Sioux were driven west the feeling spread everywhere, and in the winter of 1863–64 ripened into the coalition "to clean out all this country," while the government had its hands full with the South. With the Indians on all sides of them moved to war by Southern emissaries, the natural supposition is that the Cheyennes and Arapahoes were at war from the same reason, and especially as the Sioux, Comanches, Kiowas, and Apaches were their friends and allies, while the Pawnees, Kaws, and Osages, their hereditary enemies, were in the service of the United States. It was certain that the South had hopes of opening hostility in this region, for, in 1863, nineteen rebel officers were killed by friendly Osages, and on their persons were found papers authorizing them to organize the sympathetic in Colorado and Dakota. White Wolf, a friendly Arapahoe, informed Agent Whitely, in the latter part of August, that the Cheyennes had "declared their intention to take all the forts on the Arkansas when joined by the Texan soldiers," and this indicated that some one had told them a move in that direction was contemplated. Finally, George Bent, half-breed Cheyenne, son of Colonel Bent, had served under Price in Missouri, had been captured, and, after being paroled, had joined the Cheyennes. He had taken part in their depredations, and helped write their letter to Colley, and was reported and believed to be a rebel emissary to them. Chivington spoke of them as "red rebels" in official correspondence, long before the Sand Creek fight, and to men of his feelings there was just this one crime of treason that could add anything to the atrocity of Indian warfare.

There are two reasons given for killing women and children, and for mutilation, which are worthy of consideration. First, as a matter of policy, it is believed by frontiersmen that Indians should be fought just as they fight. They look contemptuously on the policy of treating them according to the rules of civilized warfare. They believe that the only way to make Indians sign a treaty which they will keep is, when at war with them, to kill them at every opportunity, destroy their property, and make their homes desolate; in short, to make them suffer. The plains Indians have given more cause for this belief than other tribes. They have repeatedly shown a disposition to go to war in the spring, when their ponies were getting fat, and subsistence was easily had, but as winter came on, and hardship began, they were ready to treat. They have had cause, too, to laugh at the silly whites, who bought their friendship with presents, while the blood of slaughtered innocents was hardly dried. They took advantage of the white man by killing his helpless people, while, for the safety of their own, they relied on the white man's ideas of warfare. Their women took advantage of him by fighting, as they did at Sand Creek, Ash Hollow, and many other places, along with the men, and, when the battle went against them, proclaiming their sex and claiming immunity. There is not a bit of doubt that killing women and children has a very dampening effect on the ardor of the Indian. In this very case of Sand Creek they said "they had always heard that the whites did not kill women and children, but now they had lost all confidence in them." Their "loss of confidence" grows a trifle amusing, when it is remembered that they had been killing women and children all summer themselves. Scalping and mutilation also strike terror to the Indian heart. Their religious belief is that the spirit in the next world has the same injuries that are inflicted on the body here. For this reason they almost invariably mutilate corpses, besides taking the scalp, which is almost an essential for entrance to the happy hunting-grounds. The greatest acts of daring ever shown by plains Indians have been in carrying off the bodies of their dead to prevent these misfortunes. That the Sand Creek affair inspired them with terror is beyond question. The Cheyennes and Arapahoes got over into Kansas and Indian Territory as quickly as possible, and stayed there. A party of Sioux raided down into Colorado once afterwards, but when they heard that the Colorado troops were after them they scampered off as though the evil spirit were at their heels.

Secondly, is the matter of vengeance. There is a certain amount of justice in the theory of meting to a man in his own measure, and the people of Colorado had old scores to pay in the accounts of murder, robbery, and rape. The treatment of women, by any Indians, is usually bad, but by the plains Indians especially so. When a woman is captured by a war-party she is the common property of all of them, each night, till they reach their village, when she becomes the special property of her individual captor, who may sell or gamble her away when he likes. If she resists she is "staked out," that is to say, four pegs are driven into the ground and a hand or foot tied to each, to prevent struggling. She is also beaten, mutilated, or even killed, for resistance. If a woman gives out under this treatment, she is either tied so as to prevent escape, or maimed so as to insure death in case of rescue, and left to die slowly. That there may be no question of the guilt of these Sand Creek Cheyennes, I quote the statement of Mrs. Ewbanks, who was captured at the same time as the prisoners surrendered by them, as taken down by Lieutenant Triggs, of the 7th Cavalry, and Judge-advocate Zabriskie, of the 1st Nevada Cavalry. "Mrs. Lucinda Ewbanks states that she was born in Pennsylvania; is twenty-four years of age; she resided on the Little Blue, at or near the Narrows. She says that on the 8th day of August, 1864, the house was attacked, robbed, burned, and herself and two children, with her nephew and Miss Roper, were captured by Cheyenne Indians. Her eldest child, at the time, was three years old; her youngest was one year old; her nephew was six years old. When taken from her home was, by the Indians, taken south across the Republican, and west to a creek, the name of which she does not remember. Here, for a short time, was their village or camping-place. They were traveling all winter. When first taken by the Cheyennes she was taken to the lodge of an old chief, whose name she does not remember. He forced me, by the most terrible threats and menaces, to yield my person to him. He treated me as his wife. He then traded me to Two Face, a Sioux, who did not treat me as a wife, but forced me to do all menial labor done by squaws, and he beat me terribly. Two Face traded me to Black Foot (a Sioux) who treated me as his wife, and because I resisted him his squaws abused and ill-used me. Black Foot also beat me unmercifully, and the Indians generally treated me as though I was a dog, on account of my showing so much detestation towards Black Foot. Two Face traded for me again. I then received a little better treatment. I was better treated among the Sioux than the Cheyennes; that is, the Sioux gave me more to eat. When with the Cheyennes I was often hungry. Her purchase from the Cheyennes was made early last fall (1864), and she remained with them (the Sioux) until May, 1865. During the winter the Cheyennes came to buy me and the child, for the purpose of burning us, but Two Face would not let them have me. During the winter we were on the North Platte the Indians were killing the whites all the time and running off their stock. They would bring in the scalps of the whites and show them to me and laugh about it. They ordered me frequently to wean my baby, but I always refused; for I felt convinced if he was weaned they would take him from me, and I should never see him again."

Mrs. Ewbanks's daughter died in Denver, from injuries received among the Indians, before her mother was released. Her nephew also died from his injuries, at the same place. Miss Roper, who was surrendered with the children, had experienced the same treatment that no white woman was ever known to escape at the hands of the plains Indians. Mrs. Martin, another prisoner surrendered by them, was taken by the Cheyennes on Plum Creek, "west of Kearney," as testified by herself and admitted by White Antelope in the council. Mrs. Snyder, another captive, had grown weary of the friendship of these Cheyennes, and hung herself before Major Wynkoop arrived. These things were known to the people of Colorado, and two thirds of the troops who went there were citizen-soldiers, raised for the express purpose of fighting Indians. Be it known, also, that these offenses were committed without any provocation from settlers, beyond occupying the lands which the chiefs of the Cheyennes had relinquished in treaty. There is absolutely not on record, from any source, a single charge, let alone an instance, of aggression or injury to any Cheyenne or Arapahoe, by any settler of Colorado, prior to Sand Creek. The sole troubles had been with the soldiers in chastising the Indians for past offences. The people of

Colorado did want revenge, and these men, who had been cooped up all summer in towns and blockhouses, whose crops were ruined, whose stock had been run off, whose houses had been burned, who had been eating bread made of forty-five-dollar flour, who had buried the mutilated bodies of their neighbors, in helpless wrath, who had heard the stories of the women captives—these men marched to Sand Creek, with the fire of vengeance in their hearts, and quenched it in blood.

Let us now look for a moment at the report of the Joint Committee on the Conduct of the War. It states, first, that these Indians wished "to deliver up some white captives they had purchased of other Indians." The Indians did not pretend to have purchased them. They admitted in the council that they had captured them, and the captives themselves testified to the same, as shown above. It states that after the council these Indians went to Fort Lyon, where they "were treated somewhat as prisoners of war, receiving rations and being obliged to remain within certain bounds." As has been shown, the Cheyennes were never treated as prisoners of war, received no rations, and did not remain within any bounds. The Indians who did so were Little Raven's Arapahoes, who were hostile, by the declarations of the Arapahoe chiefs in the council, and the testimony of Major Wynkoop. These Indians went away before the Cheyennes came, but eight lodges of them, under Left Hand, who was friendly, went to the Cheyennes and camped with them at Sand Creek. This wrongful and unjust confusion is kept up all through the report. It states that "all the testimony goes to show that the Indians under the immediate control of Black Kettle and White Antelope, of the Cheyennes, and Left Hand, of the Arapahoes, were and had been friendly to the whites, and had not been guilty of any acts of hostility or depredation." Not only does the testimony show the opposite to be true, but also there is no testimony whatever to that effect. There was testimony to the friendly character of these chiefs, but not to that of their Indians, and, in fact, no Indians could be separated out as theirs, for at the time of their letter, and the council, and afterwards, the Cheyennes were all together, and all under their "immediate control." Even when the party at Sand Creek came in ahead, it was reported by them that the remainder of the tribe was a short distance back, waiting for good weather.

It states that "a northern band of the Cheyennes, known as the Dog Soldiers, had been guilty of acts of hostility; but all the testimony goes to prove that they had no connection with Black Kettle's band," and that "Black Kettle and his band denied all connection with or responsibility for the Dog Soldiers." As shown in a former chapter, the Dog Soldiers were not a separate band, but were a department in the tribal government. Black Kettle and his band did not deny connection with them or responsibility for them; many of the band at Sand Creek were Dog Soldiers. Bull Bear, the leader of the Dog Soldiers, was at the council in Denver as one of Black Kettle's sub-chiefs. The only time that any of the Indians had an opportunity to make a statement which could go to the committee, was at the council in Denver, and there the Dog Soldiers were mentioned but once, and in this passage: "BLACK KETTLE. 'We will return with Major Wynkoop to Fort Lyon; we will then proceed to our village and take back word to my young men, every word you say. I cannot answer for all of them, but think there will be but little difficulty in getting them to assent to help the soldiers.' MAJOR WYNKOOP. 'Did not the Dog Soldiers agree, when I had my council with you, to do whatever you said, after you had been here?' BLACK KETTLE. 'Yes.'" The committee is far more kind to Black Kettle than he is to himself. It had determined that he should not be connected with them. Senator Doolittle pressed this question on John S. Smith, one of the most bitter of the prosecuting witnesses: "Is the northern band the same that are commonly called the Dog Soldiers?" Smith, who had been among them twenty-seven years, answered: "No. sir; the Dog Soldiers are mixed up promiscuously; this is a band that has preferred the North Platte and north of the North Platte, and lives over in what is called the bad land, *mauvais terre.*" The same fact was shown by Major Wynkoop in his cross-examination, by Chivington, before the Military Commission, as follows: "Q. Will you explain what the Dog Soldiers are and how they are controlled? A. I understand that the Dog Soldiers are a portion of the warriors of the Cheyenne tribe, and presume that they are controlled by the head men."

It states that "these Indians, at the suggestion of Governor Evans and Colonel Chivington, repaired to Fort Lyon and placed themselves under the protection of Major Wynkoop." Enough of the council proceedings has been quoted to show the falsity of this. They told the Indians that they could not treat with them, but that they must go to the military, and when they got ready to lay down their arms and surrender as prisoners of war they might go to Major Wynkoop. But, in fact, the Cheyennes did not even send in their messengers until after Major Wynkoop was suspended. They were never under his protection at all. It states that Jack Smith, the half-breed son of John S. Smith, was in Black Kettle's camp, at the time of the attack, as a spy, employed by the government. As shown above, he guided the troops to the camp to make the attack. This man was the only prisoner killed after the fight, and it was in evidence before the committee that he had led an attack on a stage a short time previously. That he was present he did not deny, but said he approached the stage for some information, and, on being fired on, fired back in self-defence. But it is not necessary to particularize further. The report abuses every one who, in telling the truth, happened to differ from the preconceived judgment of the committee; it distorts and colors every matter of fact involved so as to injure Chivington and his men; it omits or glosses over all the injuries to the people of Colorado; and, having arrived at a proper pitch of indignation and misrepresentation, it assails Colonel Chivington in a gush of sanguinary rhetoric, that reads more like the reputed address of Spartacus to the gladiators than the impartial judgment of rational men.

But, outrageous as was the report of the committee, it was dignified, just, and proper by the side of the ornamental misrepresentation that outsiders have added. It has been said that Sand Creek "brought on the general war of 1865, which cost the government $35,000,000 and much loss of life," and this statement has become a part of the "history" of the affair. Sand Creek brought on that war just about as much as the battle of Gettysburg brought on the late civil war. It was an event in the war, and no amount of misrepresentation can make it anything else. Leaving the Cheyennes out of consideration altogether, the general war had been in progress since the early spring of 1864. But, as a matter of fact, it did not even aggravate the war. It has already been shown that the Cheyennes had been at war all summer, and no other tribe went to war on account of it. On January 12, 1865, on receipt of orders to investigate

Chivington's action, General Curtis despatched to Washington: "Although the colonel may have transgressed my field orders concerning Indian warfare, and otherwise acted very much against my views of propriety in his assault at Sand Creek, still it is not true, as Indian agents and Indian traders are representing, that such extra severity is increasing Indian war. On the contrary, it tends to reduce their numbers and bring them to terms. . . . I will be glad to save the few honest and kindly disposed, and protest against the slaughter of women and children; although, since General Harney's attack of the Sioux many years ago at Ash Hollow, the popular cry of settlers and soldiers on the frontier favors an indiscriminate slaughter which is very difficult to restrain. I abhor this style, but so it goes, from Minnesota to Texas. . . . There is no doubt a portion of this tribe assembled were occupied in making assaults on our stages and trains, and the tribes well know that we have to hold the whole community responsible for acts they could restrain, if they would properly exert their efforts in that way." Again, on January 30, he wrote to Governor Evans: "Let me say, too, that I see nothing new in all this Indian movement since the Chivington affair, except that Indians are more frightened and keep farther away. By pushing them hard this next month, before grass recruits their ponies, they will be better satisfied with making war and robbery a business." On the same day he wrote Major-general Halleck: "There is no new feature in these Indian troubles except that Indians seem more frightened." General Curtis commanded the department; he had all the information as to the state of the hostilities that could be had; he evidently was not inclined to defend Chivington; and therefore his testimony on this point ought to be conclusive.

Said Hon. Mr. Loughridge to the House of Representatives: "Some of the few captured children, after they had been carried many miles by the troops, were taken from the wagons and their brains dashed out. I gather this from the records and official reports, and blush to say that its truth cannot be questioned." Mr. Loughridge might well blush for other reasons. There is not one word in all the testimony, records, and official reports, to substantiate this statement. The nearest and only approach to it, in the report of the Joint Committee, is this statement by Lieutenant Cannon, who accompanied the expedition: "I heard of one instance of a child, a few

Three Cheyenne lodges in western Oklahoma, photographed in the 1890's. A child plays with a wagon near the entrance to the lodge in the foreground. A partly covered plow is visible at the far left.

Cheyennes and Arapahoes waiting for a beef issue at Cantonment, in western Oklahoma, in 1890. The penned cattle in the foreground were released, pursued, killed, and butchered by individual families. The cattle,

provided by the government, replaced the buffalo, but in the manner of
their distribution the Plains Indians tried to preserve at least something
of their old way of life.

The scene at Cantonment after the beef issue. To some observers, such as Richard Harding Davis, the slaughtering was "not a pretty thing to watch," but within two decades Upton Sinclair's exposé of the meat pack-

ing industry would reveal that white slaughtering procedures were neither more attractive nor more sanitary.

Indian women butchering cattle while camp dogs wait for scraps. The white men in the photograph probably killed the cattle as the unarmed Indians looked on.

Stages in the preparation of a dog feast. Dogs were clubbed and thrown on the fire to roast without evisceration. In the bottom photograph the man at the far left holds a dead puppy. Despite their practicality when other food was in short supply, such dietary habits revolted whites and reinforced cultural prejudices.

months old, being thrown into the feed-box of a wagon, and, after being carried some distance, left on the ground to perish." In the testimony taken by the Military Commission, Lieutenant Cramer and Private Louderback give similar hearsay evidence, in almost the same words. Only one witness was examined, at any time, who professed to have personal knowledge of this abandonment, and that was Sergeant Lucian Palmer, who was introduced by the prosecution, before the Military Commission. He said: "They [the two squaws] took care of it [the pappoose in question] the first day after we left Sand Creek; they had it in bed with them the night we stopped this side of Sand Creek; they left it themselves, as no one else had anything to do with it, to my knowledge." Thus the prosecution disposed of the feed-box story, and left Mr. Loughridge without even that faint support for his slander. It was distinctly testified, by every witness who was questioned on the subject, that no one was killed after the fight except Jack Smith. It was also established, without contradiction, that the two squaws (wives of white men) and five children, who were said, by every witness except those mentioned, to have been the only prisoners taken, were conveyed to Fort Lyon and left there. These are but samples that show the extraordinary extent to which this delusion has been carried. The wealth of epithets and invectives that has been gathered to damn the reputation of this man Chivington, by people who have, at best, but superficially examined his case, constitutes a veritable treasury of vituperation. If everything that was said against him by the witnesses were true, and much of it, on its face, was not, he is still the colossal martyr to misrepresentation of this century.

The sequel to Sand Creek throws some valuable light on the character of the case. On October 14, 1865, a treaty was made with the Cheyenne chiefs on the Little Arkansas, on which occasion John S. Smith and Major Wynkoop were figuring prominently. The treaty, in its original draft, went out of the way to attack Chivington and the troops, and this feature the Senate omitted by amendment. The treaty was made on behalf of the entire tribe, but the majority of the Dog Soldiers were not present and never formally accepted its provisions. The most striking feature of it is that, while they were assigned a reservation with the privilege of roaming over their original territory, these friendly Indians were prohibited from camping within ten miles of a main travelled road, night or day, and were pledged not to go to any town or post without permission of the authorities there. Special remuneration was given to every one who had lost relatives or property at Sand Creek, and annuities of goods and money to the tribe in general, to the amount of $56,000 annually until they moved to the reservation, and $112,000 annually afterwards. Thefts, murders, and other offences were perpetrated by Indians in the following summer, and, so far as could be learned, they were committed by a party of Dog Soldiers, numbering some two hundred lodges, who had joined with about one hundred lodges of Sioux, under the chief Pawnee Killer. In the spring of 1867 General Hancock started with an expedition into the plains with the intent of making a peaceful demonstration of power, which would induce all doubtful and hostile Indians to go on reservations. Agents of the Indian bureau were invited to accompany the expedition, to assist in talks with the Indians, and did so.

They found the band of Dog Soldiers and Sioux on Pawnee Fork, about thirty miles above Fort Larned. After negotiating, and making several appointments for councils, which they did not keep, the Indians slipped away one dark night with all their property that they could carry. Spring was not their season for treating. The next heard of them was that they had burned several stage stations on the Smoky Hill route and killed, after torturing, three station keepers at Lookout Station, near Fort Hays. On receipt of information of this, General Hancock destroyed what was left of their village, and troops were kept in search of the Indians all summer, under command of General Custer. There were a number of engagements between them, and considerable loss of life, with no material advantage to either side. At the same time a severe pen-and-ink contest was being waged between war people and peace people in the East, and the peace people got the upper hand. The result of it all was that at the end of the season Custer was under arrest on a charge of leaving Fort Wallace without orders, while the Indians, who had had no opportunity to lay in supplies for the winter, made another treaty, in which the whole tribe, Dog Soldiers included, joined. This time they took a reservation wholly within Indian Territory, a triangular tract bounded by the Kansas line and the Cimarron and Arkansas rivers. They were to receive a suit of clothes for each Indian, and

$20,000 annually, besides teachers, physicians, farmers, millers, carpenters, blacksmiths, and other guides to civilization. It was not agreed that they were to be given any arms or ammunition, and this the reader will remember. They agreed not to molest any coach or wagon, carry off any white woman or child, nor kill or scalp any white man; to surrender any wrong-doer for punishment, and not to interfere in any way with the building of the Kansas Pacific Railroad.

In the spring of 1868 it was learned that arms and ammunition were being issued to Indians, and a military order was made prohibiting it. The agents raised a cry that the Indians could not hunt the buffalo without arms and ammunition (they prefer the bow and arrow for this, and seldom used anything else); the peace people joined in the chorus that the Indians were being starved, and the order was revoked. On August 1 the Arapahoes received 100 pistols, 80 Lancaster rifles, 12 kegs of powder, a keg and a half of lead, and 15,000 caps. On August 10 Colonel Wynkoop, our old acquaintance, who had been promoted, and appointed Indian Agent after the investigations, wrote: "I yesterday made the whole issue of annuity goods, arms, and ammunition to the Cheyenne chiefs and people of their nation; they were delighted at receiving the goods, particularly the arms and ammunition, and never before have I known them to be better satisfied, and express themselves as being so well contented previous to the issue. . . . They have now left for their hunting-grounds, and I am perfectly satisfied that there will be no trouble with them this season." What hunting-grounds had they left for? On September 10, just thirty days later, Colonel Wynkoop, in explaining that the Indians had gone to war because "their arms and ammunition" had not been issued promptly, writes: "But a short time before the issue was made a war-party had started north from the Cheyenne village, on the war-path against the Pawnees; and they, not knowing of the issue, and smarting under their supposed wrongs, committed the outrages on the Saline River which have led to the present unfortunate aspect of affairs." It was rather unfortunate. The inference from his letter is that it was all right for them to use their weapons, furnished for the purpose of hunting, in making war on the Pawnees, who had been, for several years, our most valuable allies and friends on the plains; but that they should attack the whites was unfortunate. Two hundred Cheyenne, four Arapahoe, and twenty Sioux warriors raided down the Saline and the Solomon, killing, ravishing, burning, and torturing. They carried off two young women, who were afterwards recovered from Black Kettle's band, if he can be said to have had any particular band, by threatening to hang some of their principal chiefs, who were captives. Much of the plundered property was found in Black Kettle's camp.

Wynkoop then proposed to locate the friendly Indians near Fort Larned, in order to separate the good ones from the bad ones, Larned being about as near to the seat of war as they could be placed; but General Sherman would have nothing of that kind. He said the Indians who were peaceable should stay on their reservation, where they belonged. Never was a better opportunity for friendly Indians to separate themselves from the bad ones and let themselves be known: and they did it. After some hard fighting in the summer and fall, notably the eight days' fight between General Forsyth's party and four hundred and fifty Cheyennes, aided by Sioux and Arapahoes, on the Arickaree fork of the Republican, the bad Indians went into winter quarters, and a winter expedition was sent against them under Custer, who was reinstated for the occasion. The reservation was vacant. The good Cheyennes were not visible. The entire southern tribe was camped away south on the Wachita, on lands where they had not even the right to hunt, with the hostile Kiowas, Arapahoes, Comanches, and Apaches, forming an almost continuous camp for twelve miles. Custer followed the trail of a returning war-party into Black Kettle's camp, and, in the early dawn of November 27, surprised the Indians, while they were sleeping off the effects of the previous night's celebration over fresh scalps and plunder. Here, as at Sand Creek and Ash Hollow, women fought with the men, and a number of them were killed, but their fighting did no good. 103 Indians were killed, and 53 squaws and children were captured, together with 875 ponies, 1123 robes, 535 pounds of powder, 4000 arrows, and arms and goods of all descriptions, constituting all their possessions. What could be advantageously kept was retained, and the remainder, including 700 ponies, was destroyed. The entire Indian force attacked Custer, but he succeeded in getting his troops and captives safely away. And what did the irrepressible Wynkoop after this affair? He affirmed that the Cheyennes were martyrs ever, and that on this occasion they were peaceably on their way to Fort Cobb to receive their annuities when attacked! He also resigned his position as Indian Agent, feeling, probably, that it would be forced on him again. But Hancock and Custer were bigger game than poor Chivington. Their brother officers and officials examined their cases more carefully than they did that of the volunteer colonel, and Custer himself ventilated the matter in a series of articles in the *Galaxy* that made some people open their eyes.

After the war, Chivington returned to his old home in Ohio and settled on a small farm. A few years later his house was burned, and he afterwards moved to Blanchester, Clinton County, where he purchased the *Press*, and edited it for two or three years. In 1883 he was nominated on the Republican ticket for Representative to the legislature, and in the campaign "Sand Creek" was used for all it was worth. It began in the contest for the nomination and was continued until Chivington withdraw from the race. It was believed, and still is, by good judges of politics, that he would have been elected by a majority of five hundred or more, but there was a large Quaker population in Clinton, and, as is well known, the Society of Friends considers itself the special guardian of the Indian. He had an up-hill fight on his hands, and the opposition was very bitter. I can but think another thing influenced his determination. While this fight was being pressed upon him, he received an urgent letter from Colorado, asking him to attend and address a meeting of old settlers, on the twenty-fifth anniversary of the settlement of the state. There he would find old friends, who knew the true history of Sand Creek, and felt as he did. He went. There were hearty welcomes given to distinguished pioneers by the people assembled in Jewell Park on that day, but none so demonstrative as Colonel Chivington's. The chairman introduced him with these words: "We all remember the Indian wars of 1864 and '65, and with what joy we received the news that some of them at least had met the reward due to their treachery and cruelty. The man who can tell you all about those wars, who can tell you all you want to know of the Indians, and who can give you the true story of Sand Creek, is here. I have the honor, ladies and gentlemen, to introduce Colonel Chivington, one of Colorado's 'Pet Lambs.'"

He began his speech amid enthusiastic cheers, but as he proceeded the attention grew breathless. He told his story in a simple, straightforward way, and nods of assent and approval, from all parts of the pavilion, silently indicated that he need not prove the truth of his statements to the people gathered there. He did not reply to the thousand charges made against him, nor did he assume an argumentative style until he closed in these words: "But were not these Indians peaceable? Oh, yes, peaceable! Well, a few hundred of them have been peaceable for almost nineteen years, and none of them have been so troublesome as they were before Sand Creek. What are the facts? How about that treaty that Governor John Evans did not make with them in the summer of 1863? He, with Major Lorey and Major Whiteley, two of his Indian Agents, and the usual corps of attachés, under escort, went out to the Kiowa to treat. When he got there, they had gone a day's march farther out on the plains and would not meet him there, and so on, day after day, they moved out as he approached, until, wearied out, and suspicious of treachery, he returned without succeeding in his mission of peace. He told them by message that he had presents for them, but it was not peace and presents they wanted, but war and plunder. What of the peaceableness of their attack on General Blunt's advance-guard, north of Fort Larned, almost annihilating the advance before succor could reach them? What of the dove-like peace of their attack on the government train on Walnut Creek, east of Fort Larned, under the guise of friendship, till the drivers and attachés of the train were in their power, and at a signal struck down at once every man, only a boy of thirteen years barely escaping, and he, with the loss of his scalp, taken to his ears, finally died. What of the trains captured from Walnut Creek to Sand Creek on the Arkansas route, and from the Little Blue to the Kiowa on the Platte route, of supplies and wagons burned and carried off, and of the men killed? What of the Hungate family? Alas!! what of the stock of articles of merchandise, fine silk dresses, infants' and youths' apparel, the embroidered nightgowns and chemises? Ay, what of the scalps of white men, women, and children, several of which they had not had time to dry and tan since taken? These, all these, and more were taken from the belts of dead warriors on the battle-field of Sand Creek, and from their teepees which fell into our hands on the 29th day of November, 1864. What of the Indian blanket that was captured, fringed with white-women's scalps? What says the dust of the two hundred and eight men, women, and children, ranchers, emigrants, herders, and soldiers, who lost their lives at the hands of these Indians? Peaceable? Now we are peaceably disposed, but decline giving such testimonials of our peaceful proclivities, and I say here as I said in my own town, in the Quaker county of Clinton, State of Ohio, one night last week, I stand by Sand Creek."

Said the *Rocky Mountain News*, of the following day, "Colonel Chivington's speech was received with an applause from every pioneer which indicated that they, to a man, heartily approved the course of the colonel twenty years ago, in the famous affair in which many of them took part, and the man who applied the scalpel to the ulcer which bid fair to destroy the life of the new colony, in those critical times, was beyond a doubt the hero of the hour." This is the simple truth. Colorado stands by Sand Creek, and Colonel Chivington soon afterwards brought his family to the Queen City of the Plains, where his remaining days may be passed in peace.

What an eventful history! And how, through it all, his sturdy manhood has been manifest in every action. Through all the denunciation of that Indian fight, he has never wavered or trembled. Others have dodged and apologized and crawled, but Chivington never. He has not laid the blame upon superior officers, as he might do. He has not complained of misinformation from inferior officers, as he might do. He has not said that the soldiers committed excesses there which were in no manner directed by him, as he might do. He has simply stood up under a rain of abuse, heavier than the shower of missiles that fell on Coeur de Leon before the castle of Front de Boeuf, and answered back: "I stand by Sand Creek." And was it wrong? To the abstract question, whether or not it is right to kill women and children, there can be but one answer. But as a matter of retaliation, and a matter of policy, whether these people were justified in killing women and children at Sand Creek is a question to which the answer does not come so glibly. Just after the massacre at Fort Fetterman, General Sherman despatched to General Grant: "We must act with vindictive earnestness against the Sioux, even to their extermination, men, women, and children. Nothing less will reach the root of the case." Was it right for the English to shoot back the Sepoy ambassador from their cannon? Was it right for the North to refuse to exchange prisoners while our boys were dying by inches in Libby and Andersonville? I do not undertake to answer these questions, but I do say that Sand Creek is far from being "the climax of American outrages on the Indian," as it has been called. Lay not that flattering unction to your souls, people of the East, while the names of the Pequods and the Conestoga Indians exist in your books; nor you of the Mississippi Valley, while the blood of Logan's family and the Moravian Indians of the Muskingum stain your records; nor you of the South, while a Cherokee or a Seminole remains to tell the wrongs of his fathers; nor yet you of the Pacific slope, while the murdered family of Spencer or the victims of Bloody Point and Nome Cult have a place in the memory of men—your ancestors and predecessors were guilty of worse things than the Sand Creek massacre.

John F. Finerty

"Their music is fitter for hell than for earth"

1890

John F. Finerty was a war correspondent assigned by the *Chicago Times* to accompany General George Crook on his campaign against the Sioux in 1876. Called by Crook's men the "Fighting Irish Pencil Pusher," Finerty was as given to strong opinions as he was to strong drink, and his biases were readily apparent. To Finerty, Custer was a "dashing hero" and a man of "brilliant deeds," while Indians, as this selection reveals, were generally "mysterious, untamable, barbaric, unreasonable, childish, superstitious, treacherous, thievish, murderous" people. And Finerty so informed his readers.

Just as we began to give up all hope of ever seeing our scouts or hearing from our Indian allies, Frank Gruard and Louis Richard, accompanied by a gigantic Crow chief, came into camp at noon on the 14th, and, amid the cheers of the soldiers, rode direct to the General's headquarters. I proceeded there at once and had an interview with the celebrated scout, Gruard, who is half a Frenchman and half a Sandwich Islander. He was brought to this country from Honolulu when a mere boy; ran the mail for the government on the Pacific coast for some years, and, when only nineteen years old, was captured by Crazy Horse's band of Sioux. The chief spared the young man's life, and he lived in the Indian village, having espoused a handsome squaw, for some years. A misunderstanding with his wife's relatives made the village too hot for him, and, being allowed

From John F. Finerty, *War-Path and Bivouac, or The Conquest of the Sioux* (Chicago, M. A. Donohue & Co., 1890), 99–109.

comparative liberty, he took the very earliest opportunity of taking "French leave." He was then about twenty-eight years of age, was familiar with every inch of the country, could speak nearly every Indian dialect, and was invaluable to General Crook, who would rather have lost a third of his command, it is said, than be deprived of Frank Gruard. The scout told the writer that he and his companions had had a hard time of it since they left Fort Reno to search for the Crows. A band of Sioux got sight of them the second day out, and chased them into the mountains. They eluded their pursuers, and, after four days' hard riding, reached the Big Horn river, which they had to swim with their horses. A few miles from that stream they saw an Indian village, full of women and warriors. The latter to the number of about 300, charged down upon them, mounted on ponies. The scouts had a river between them and the Indians—a small river, but sufficient to insure their safe retreat. The red men fired upon them without effect, and then Gruard, by their large, bushy heads, entirely different from the trimmer Sioux, recognized the Crows. He immediately shouted to them in their own language, and very soon the three scouts were in their midst, saluted by a storm of "Hows!" Then they learned that five Crow scouts had started to find our camp. It was this party that attempted to speak to us from Tongue river bluffs previously, but when Arnold spoke Sioux they became alarmed, suspecting a trap, and retreated. They would have come in only that Gruard told them we were going to camp on Goose creek. They saw us leave Fort Phil. Kearney, but when we took the Tongue river road they concluded we were not the party they were looking for, and turned back. Gruard soon set matters right, and before many hours had nearly 200 warriors ready for the road.

They were, he said, within ten miles of our camp, but, with true Indian caution, declined to come in until perfectly assured that it would be a safe proceeding. Baptiste Pourier had remained behind with the Indians to give them confidence. Five Snake, or Sho-sho-ne, scouts, sent from their tribe at Sweetwater valley to notify the Crows that they were coming to help us and should be treated as friends, were with the party. Louis Richard, the Indian scout, and Major Burt went back for the Crows. We waited impatiently for their arrival. At six o'clock a picket galloped into camp to notify Crook that his allies were in sight.

Then we saw a grove of spears and a crowd of ponies upon the northern heights, and there broke upon the air a fierce, savage whoop. The Crows had come in sight of our camp, and this was their mode of announcing their satisfaction. We went down to the creek to meet them, and a picturesque tribe they were. Their horses— nearly every man had an extra pony—were little beauties, and neighed shrilly at their American brethren, who, unused to Indians, kicked, plunged and reared in a manner that threatened a general stampede. "How! How!" the Crows shouted to us, one by one, as they filed past. When near enough, they extended their hands and gave ours a hearty shaking. Most of them were young men, many of whom were handsomer than some white people I have met. Three squaws were there on horseback—wives of the chiefs.

The head sachems were "Old Crow," "Medicine Crow," "Feather Head," and "Good Heart," all deadly enemies of the Sioux. Each man wore a gaily colored mantle, handsome leggings, eagle feathers, and elaborately worked moccasins. In addition to their carbines and spears, they carried the primeval bow and arrow. Their hair was long, but gracefully tied up and gorgeously plumed. Their features, as a rule were aquiline, and the Crows have the least prom- inent cheek bones of any Indians that I have yet encountered. The squaws wore a kind of half-petticoat and parted their hair in the middle, the only means of guessing at their sex. Quick as lightning they gained the center of our camp, dismounted, watered and lariated their ponies, constructed their "tepees," or "lodges," and, like magic, the Indian village arose in our midst. Fires were lighted without delay, and the Crows were soon devouring their evening meal of dried bear's meat and black-tailed deer. In the middle of this repast, we saw several warriors raise their heads and say "Ugh, ugh! Sho-sho-ne." They pointed southward, and, coming down the bluffs in that direction, we saw a line of horsemen, brilliantly attired, riding at whirlwind speed. Crook sent a scout to meet them. Hardly had he time to start forward when the new-comers crossed the creek, and, in column of twos, like a company of regular cavalry, rode in among us. They carried two beautiful American flags, and each warrior bore a pennon. They looked like Cossacks of the Don, but were splendidly armed with government rifles and revolvers. Nearly all wore magnificent war bonnets and scarlet mantles. They were not as large as the Crow Indians, nor as good-looking, but they appeared to be hardy and resolute. The meeting between them and the Crows was boisterous and exciting. Demoniacal yells rang through the camp, and then this wild cavalry galloped down to headquarters, rode around Crook and his staff, saluted, and, following the example of the Crows, were soon bivouacked and deep in their rough-and-ready suppers. Tom Cosgrove, chief of souts in the Wind River valley, accompanied them. His lieutenant was Nelson Yurnell, and his interpreter, a young half-breed, called Ulah Clair. The Indian chiefs of the Snakes present were Wesha and Nawkee, with the two sons of old Washakie.

That night an immense fire was kindled near Crook's tents, and there all the chiefs of both tribes, together with our commanding officers, held "a big talk." Louis Richard acted as interpreter, and had a hard time of it, having to translate in three or four languages. A quarter of an hour intervened between each sentence. The chiefs squatted on their heels according to their ancient custom, and passed the long pipe from man to man. Crook stood in the circle, with his hands in his pockets, looking half bored, half happy. Major Randall, chief of scouts, and other members of the staff were with him. The Indians were quite jolly, and laughed heartily whenever the interpreter made any kind of blunder. The Snakes retired from the council first. They said very little. "Old Crow," the greatest chief of the Crow nation, made the only consecutive speech of the night, and it was a short one. Translated, it was as follows: "The great white chief will hear his Indian brother. These are our lands by inheritance. The Great Spirit gave them to our fathers, but the Sioux stole them from us. They hunt upon our mountains. They fish in our streams. They have stolen our horses. They have murdered our squaws, our children. What white man has done these things to us? The face of the Sioux is red, but his heart is black. But the heart of the pale face has ever been red to the Crow. ['Ugh!' 'Ugh!' 'Hey!'] The scalp of no white man hangs in our lodges. They are thick as grass in the wigwams of the Sioux. ['Ugh!!'] The great white chief will lead us against no other tribe of red men. Our war is with the Sioux and only them. We want back our lands. We want their women for our slaves—to work for us as our women have had to work for them. We want their horses for our young men, and their mules for our squaws. The Sioux have trampled upon our hearts. We shall spit upon their scalps. ['Ugh!' 'Hey!' and terrific yelling.] The great white chief sees that my young men have come to fight. No Sioux shall see their backs. Where the white warrior goes there shall we be also. It is good. Is my brother content?"

The chief and Crook shook hands amid a storm of "Ughs" and yells.

All the red men then left the council fire and went to their villages, where they put on their war-paint and made night hideous with a war-dance and barbarous music. They imitated in succession every beast and bird of the North American forests. Now they roared like a bison bull. Then they mimicked a wildcat. All at once they broke out with the near, fierce howling of a pack of wolves; gradually the sound would die away until you might imagine that the animals were miles off, when, all of a sudden, the howling would rise within a few yards, and in the darkness you would try to discern the foul "coyotes"—next to the Indians the pest of the plains. All night long, despite the incredible fatigue they must have endured in coming to join us, the savages continued their infernal orgies. Their music is fitter for hell than for earth. And yet these were not the worst red men existing. These were "the truly good" Indians. Our young soldiers appeared to relish the yelling business immensely, and made abortive attempts to imitate the Indians, greatly to the amusement of those grotesque savages. I fell asleep dreaming of "roistering devils" and lakes of brimstone.

Crook was bristling for a fight. The Sioux were said to be encamped on the Rosebud, near the Yellowstone river, holding Gibbon at bay. "They are numerous as grass," was the definite Crow manner of stating the strength of the enemy.

Some of the officers, who had had charge of different tribes of Indians at their respective agencies, were fond of discussing at the evening camp-fires the characteristics of the various Indian bands or "nations." From what may be termed the consensus of military opinion I learned what follows:

Nearly every Indian, of any note whatever, possessed at that

time two equines—one, a pony for pack work, the other, a horse for
war and the chase. The latter can go like a meteor, and has wonderful endurance. Mounted upon him, the Indian warrior could secure
a retreat from the *Chasseurs d'Afrique* of Macmahon, with all their
Arab horses.

The Indian war-horse is not as beautiful a beast as the Arabian,
but he has more toughness than an ordinary mule. These combined
qualities of strength, speed and "hold out" made him the main stay
of the red man of the plains, whether he was Sioux, Cheyenne or
Snake. Where the breed came from, or of what blood compounded,
nobody seems to know. It is not a mustang, neither is it an Arabian—
perhaps a combination of both. It may be for aught we know, in-
digenous to this continent—a theory sustained by the fact that the
Indians can get more work out of such a horse than any other race
of men, white, black or yellow.

When Indians kill game on the hunt, they cut out the tongue,
liver and heart, and unless very hungry, leave the carcass to rot upon
the prairie. They don't want to load their horses much unless when
near their villages, where the squaws can dry the meat, for the
average Indian is still unchanged—still the same mysterious, untamable, barbaric, unreasonable, childish, superstitious, treacherous,
thievish, murderous creature, with rare exceptions, that he has been
since first Columbus set eyes upon him at San Salvador. Whether
friendly or hostile, the average Indian is a plunderer. He will first
steal from his enemy. If he cannot get enough that way, he steals
from his friends. While the warriors are fat, tall and good-looking,
except in a few cases, the squaws are squatty, yellow, ugly and
greasy looking. Hard work disfigures them, for their lazy brutes of
sons, husbands and brothers will do no work, and the unfortunate
women are used as so many pack mules. Treated with common
fairness, the squaws might grow tolerably comely; their figures being
generally worse than their faces. It is acknowledged by all that the
Sioux women are better treated and handsomer than those of all
other tribes. Also they are more virtuous, and the gayest white
Adonises confess that the girls of that race seldom yield to the
seducer.

The Sioux abhor harlots, and treat them in a most inhuman
manner—even as they treat white captive women—when they are

detected. If they do not kill them outright, they injure them for life and then drive them from the tribe. Among the married, such as their marriage is—for polygamy is a recognized institution in the tribe— adultery generally means death to the female concerned if she is discovered, while among the interested "braves" it begets a feud that only blood can extinguish. The Sioux hold it a sin against nature —according to their ideas of sin and nature—for a woman to remain unmarried, and they sometimes punish her, if she continues obstinate, in a very cruel and indelicate fashion. Fortunately for the Sioux women, they, for the most part, believe in matrimony and are spared all trouble on the score of their prolonged virginity.

Imagine all the old maids in America being punished because the men of their generation did not have the good taste to woo and marry them!! The Sioux will not have any old maids hanging around their wigwams. This is a truly patriarchal way of providing husbands for the fair sex.

The other Indian tribes are more lax in their ideas of female propriety, and care much less whether a woman is married or the reverse. Taken all in all, the Sioux must be descendants of Cain, and are veritable children of the devil. The rest are a very little behind them, except in point of personal appearance and daring, in which the Sioux excel nearly all other Indians. Most of them are greedy, greasy, gassy, lazy and knavish.

In connection with the subject of female Sioux virtue, I am reminded of a story which caused great amusement in military circles several years ago. A certain handsome and dashing cavalry officer, now deceased, was badly smitten with the really pretty daughter of a leading Sioux chief, whose village was situated quite close to the post. Lieutenant ——— paid some attentions to the girl, in order to while away the tedious summer hours, and, one day, remarked casually to a half-breed interpreter that he would like to own the savage princess and take her East as a living curiosity. The half-breed, taking the matter seriously, informed the maiden's warlike sire. The latter took the matter in good faith also, and resolved to make the "giving away" of his daughter in marriage, for that was how he understood it, memorable. The gay lieutenant was then acting adjutant of his battalion, and at the evening parade, just as he had "set his battle in array," heard a most infernal tumult in the direction of the Indian village. The major in command looked both annoyed and astonished and asked for an explanation. The adjutant could give none, but, by order of his superior, rode in the direction of the disturbance to find out, if possible, its meaning. As he approached the village he saw a great cavalcade moving toward him at full speed, with the old chief and his daughter heading the procession. A horrible suspicion dawned upon the mind of the unlucky adjutant, and this was confirmed a moment later, when the half-breed interpreter, and author of all the mischief, rode forward to inform the officer that Spotted Elk was coming up to the post in due order to surrender his daughter into the keeping of Lieutenant ——— as his wife—or one of his wives. Uttering a most heart-felt malediction on the chief, the girl, the interpreter and the whole Indian generation, Lieutenant ——— spurred back to the parade, requested to be relieved on the ground of sudden illness, wrote a note of explanation to his commanding officer, obtained temporary leave of absence, which was afterwards extended, and bade an eternal farewell to the post, and the village and the Indian princess.

Long afterwards, I met the hero of the foregoing adventure, and found him one of the most winning and gifted officers of the army, who, although an American, had all of "an Irishman's heart for the ladies," and all the Hibernian's fondness for getting into love scrapes. Poor ———! He died in the flower of his years—died, too, plainly and unromantically, in his bed, and not as he would wish to have died, on the broad field and at the head of charging squadrons.

Charles Alston Messiter

"Indians never spare anyone who is in their power"

1890

Charles Alston Messiter was one of the hundreds of British travelers who visited the post–Civil War West. While most were content with the thought of having an opportunity to shoot a buffalo, Messiter appears to have gone west with the idea of killing an Indian and taking his scalp for a trophy. In this selection from his *Sport and Adventures Among the North-American Indians*, Messiter described a running battle with a Comanche war party and his acquisition of an Indian scalp. Here the image of the Indian was exported for foreign consumption.

At Fort Belknap we found four companies of cavalry, under the command of General Sturgess; and here we remained several days, and were allowed to replenish our stores from the commissariat. At the Post were a number of Tonkaway Indians, some of them being employed as scouts; they were the remnant of a tribe which had been very much thinned by small-pox, and the day after our arrival they sent us an invitation to a buffalo dance, which is a ceremony to insure success in hunting. On going to their camp we found about sixty Indians collected, besides twice that number of women and children, and the festivities commenced with a talk, in which they said they had heard that we came from the land of the "Great White Queen," and that we were very welcome to their country, all in it being at our service, and then hinting that anything coming from us

From Charles Alston Messiter, *Sport and Adventures Among the North-American Indians* (London, R. H. Porter, 1890), 211–27.

would be very much valued: on which we said a few words through an interpreter of the pleasure it gave us to see a tribe of which we had heard so much; that we thanked them for their welcome, and hoped they would accept some tobacco and beads, which we handed round.

After this the dance began—two old Indians playing on the "tom tom," and chanting a very hideous accompaniment. The men and women danced together—a thing I had never seen before among Indians—forming a circle, and going through some shuffling steps, repeating a prayer to the Great Spirit for success in their next hunt, and for protection against their enemies the Comanches. This was kept up for about an hour, some sitting down and others taking their places, even the elder children joining in. We were asked to take part in the dance, but the partners were not sufficiently tempting so we contented ourselves with looking on. One old fellow whom I sat near had a necklace made of the finger-and toe-joints of a Comanche he had killed some years before; and he was evidently very proud of it, refusing to sell it to me, though I offered what to him was a long price. Killing a Comanche seemed a very rare event, for they had divided the man amongst them—one having the scalp, another the ears, which he had dried and hung round his neck.

These Indians never trust themselves far from a fort, except when acting as scouts, dreading the Comanches and being despised by them. We tried to get one of them to act as our guide, but no offer would tempt them when they heard that we were only seven in number. One of the soldiers told us that there was a Comanche chief at the Post who might go with us. He had, it seemed, quarrelled with his brother "Queen-a-ha-be," the war chief of the Comanches, and had to leave the tribe in consequence. We sent for him, and found him to be an immense man, standing six feet four and broad in proportion, with a very ill-tempered and treacherous face, the hair growing close down to the eyebrows. He seemed very willing to go, saying that he knew the country well nearly to Denver, and should we meet any of his tribe he thought that he could protect us from them, and that he would fight for us if necessary. It was at last agreed that we should take him, and he was to receive on our getting through safely two horses, a rifle and ammunition for it, a revolver, and twenty-five dollars in money. At first he wished payment in advance; but this we positively refused, giving him a pair of blankets and some ammunition only. We left Belknap on the eighth day, and our next point was old Fort Cobb—a deserted post, about a hundred and forty miles further on.

As we had now one more man it made the guards at night much easier, each of us getting three clear nights in bed. It took some time to make A-sa-ha-be understand how long he was to remain on guard; but he soon got into it, and used to measure his two hours pretty correctly. We had been out about six days when one of the men told us that he had gone out of the tent during A-sa-ha-be's guard, and had found him absent, so we spoke to him about it, when he replied that having seen some suspicious sign that day, he had gone during his guard to see what it meant. Now this was highly improbable; for as the nights were very dark just then, he could not possibly follow a trail, nor would he have had time to go very far during his two-hour watch. So we told him that we allowed no one to leave the camp during the night, and that he must do his scouting in the daytime, when one of us would go with him.

We had mistrusted him from the first, and now were almost sure that he meant to betray us; but it was nearly impossible to get proof, or we would have shot him at once. As he only knew a few words of English, it was difficult to explain anything to him, the only other means being by signs, which he was wonderfully quick at understanding.

Things went smoothly for two days, when one night F——, who was on guard, woke me to say that A-sa-ha-be had just left the waggon, under which he slept, and had gone towards his horse.

Getting my rifle, F—— and I followed him very cautiously, keeping under the shelter of some bushes which grew round camp, and we saw him go to his horse, put on the saddle, and prepare to mount. We then ran forward and called to him to stop, on which he sprang on the horse and rode off at full speed. Being convinced then that he meant treachery, we both fired at him; but the night was dark, and we missed him. The shots roused the men, and we held a consultation as to the best thing to do. To turn back was what we thought wisest; but this neither of us proposed, hoping that some other plan might be devised. If we had been travelling with pack-animals we could have pushed on quickly, having probably a good many hours' start;

but with a waggon this was of no use—four miles an hour being as much as we could manage. In any case we had to move at once to a better position, as our present camp was on a flat plain covered with bushes, affording capital cover to Indians creeping up to fire at us; so we hitched up at once and moved on to a ridge, about a mile further on, where we remained till morning, carrying up water in every vessel that would hold it, in case the Indians should come sooner than we expected.

Morning came, and no sign of the Indians; so we had another talk, and all the men being for an immediate return to Fort Arbuckle, we were at last compelled to agree to it; so we put the mules in and started about eight o'clock. We calculated that we were about seventy-five miles from the Post, and that, unless hindered by the Comanches, we could do it in two days and a half, throwing away some of our load if necessary. About ten o'clock F———, who was acting rear-guard, called to us that they were coming; and on looking back we saw about forty Indians on some high ground to our right. We kept on as fast as we could go, pulling up when on a bare hill a short distance further on, as it was a good place for a fight if we were to have one. We had nine Winchester repeating-rifles with us and three thousand rounds of ammunition for them, having bought five hundred rounds per man in case we had any fighting; then we had four double rifles and several hundred rounds of ammunition for them; and, lastly, we had a double eight-bore duck-gun, which loaded with about two ounces of buckshot in each barrel would be grand at close quarters.

The Indians galloped up to within two hundred yards of us, when we waved them back, A-sa-ha-be advancing alone, with a branch in his hand as a flag of truce. On his arrival at the waggon he dismounted and calmly seated himself, made signs that we should do the same quite with the air of a superior addressing his inferiors. We, however, sat down, A-sa-ha-be beginning the talk by saying that he had not betrayed us, but that finding signs of a party of his tribe being near us, he had ridden away in the night to find out their intentions and to do the best he could for us, and this he was still willing to do, in spite of our having fired at him. He said that he had found about forty of his tribe camped a few miles away, and that he had made the best possible terms for us, which were as follows:—

That we should give up our waggon and outfit, all horses but one apiece, and that then we should be given a rifle to kill game with, and be allowed to return to Fort Arbuckle, or go in any direction we wished. Now there was not the smallest doubt that if we did as he wished we should all be dead men within the hour, as Indians never spare anyone who is in their power, as they thought we were; so we replied at once that we should give up nothing, but that as the country we were in belonged to his tribe, we were willing to purchase permission to pass through it at a moderate price. As-sa-ha-be answered that the terms he had mentioned were the only ones which would be accepted, and put on a very insolent air as he said it; so we told him we would give him two minutes to leave our camp, and that if he was not gone by that time we would shoot him, and would not miss him a second time, and that if his tribe wanted our outfit, they must come and take it, but that so long as we had a cartridge left they should have nothing. He jumped up in a furious rage, waited till we had finished speaking, and then mounted and rode off, shaking his fist at us; and we could see that on rejoining his companions he was making the most of what we had said, to rouse them, as otherwise forty Indians might hesitate to attack six well-armed white men. I am speaking of twenty years ago, when a rifle was very seldom seen in an Indian's hands, and when the few they had were of a very old pattern, and the supply of ammunition for those was scanty.

In the meantime we started again, throwing out of the waggon several sacks of flour to lighten the load, the Indians remaining where they were for nearly an hour, two messengers being sent away at full speed, we feared for reinforcements. About one o'clock, when we were thinking of halting to rest the animals, the Indians appeared again, coming at a gallop and, passing us at a distance of about four hundred yards, fired as they passed, and several balls came unpleasantly near, one of them going through the side of the waggon. On this we gave them three or four volleys from the Winchesters, the result being the wounding of a horse, which bolted, and was only stopped after going about a mile, when the rider dismounted and got up behind one of his companions. This seemed to show them the range of our rifles and the rapidity with which they could be fired (a Winchester rifle firing its fourteen cartridges in less than as many seconds if in good hands), and for some hours they contented themselves with keeping us in sight. We drove on till nearly dark, filling buckets and kettles at a pond we passed and watering all the animals, so that we might camp in the middle of a prairie, where there was no cover of any kind to hide a crawling man. Here we had supper, and arranged that one half should keep guard while the other half slept.

The Indians let us know that they were near by firing now and then, the bullets going far overhead, but they did not try to attack us, and at daylight, after a very hasty breakfast, we were off again. We had a number of creeks to cross that day, and always rode ahead to find out whether they were lying in wait for us, but saw nothing of the Comanches, except in the distnce, till we came to a stream having very heavy timber and bushes on both banks, when F——, H——, and I rode along, about a hundred yards from the timber, going at full speed, and lying, Indian fashion, on the side of our horses, having one elbow in a noose round the horse's neck and one foot on the saddle, and we had not gone more than a few hundred yards when five or six shots were fired at us, all of them going wide. We immediately turned and rode in for the creek, hearing the Indians making their way through the bushes but seeing none of them; till one, thinking he was concealed, came out on the opposite side and ran along in the open, loading as he went. We all jumped off and waited till he passed an open space, when we fired together, and over he went, seeming to die at once.

We now beckoned to the waggon and got it across, not far from where the Indian lay ,and on going to see how he had been killed, we found that a bullet had passed through the shoulder and a no. 12 Metford shell had burst low down in his back, making a hole almost as large as the crown of a hat, and nearly cutting him in two. We had all said that if we shot an Indian and could get at the body we would scalp him and think nothing of it; but when the time came to do it, each one tried to get out of it, till the driver of our waggon came up and, asking why we made such a fuss about such a trifle, took it off at once, removing merely the scalplock and the skin under it, about the size of, and in the same position as, the tonsure of a priest.

When Indians have plenty of time, they like to take the whole skin of the head, beginning behind, skinning the head and the whole face, including the ears; and the scalp when thus taken presents a ghastly appearance when stretched. Soon after we left the stream we could hear the Indians howling over the body of the man we had scalped, and they came by a few minutes later, yelling their war-whoop, and placing their closed fists against their foreheads and then opening and shutting them, which means "war to the knife." As they passed we fired a good many shots, and three horses went down, their riders getting bad falls, though it was impossible to tell whether any of them were hit, as when a man has fallen and seems hurt, two of them will at once gallop by him, one on either side, reaching down and catching a limb, when they swing him on to the saddle in front of one of them and ride off.

The scalping of their companion had evidently made them frantic, as it is their belief that a scalped warrior has to act as servant to the others in the happy hunting-grounds; and they, in consequence, came much nearer, several times gathering as if for a rush, and then giving up the idea on our firing a volley at them. Towards evening a large party of Indians suddenly appeared and joined the others, making their number up to about two hundred. They all met and had a short consultation, we in the meantime camping, as we were in a capital place to receive them—a clump of timber standing on a rise about two hundred yards from a stream, and there was no other cover near but a few small bushes, which we at once cut down. We drove the waggon in among the trees, and all set to work to cut down some of the smallest of these to make a breastwork.

Our stopping seemed to disconcert them, as they did not care to attack a fortified position; so they began to taunt us, and made insulting gestures, and fired a number of shots, one of which killed one of the mules, the poor brute being hit through the stomach, so we had to shoot him. We had a very quiet night, and were off by day-break, keeping as much as possible in open ground, even when we had to make a detour to do so. We calculated that we must have done nearly half the distance, and as yet no one was hurt, our loss being one mule; and as we put a horse in his place, this did not much matter.

That day the Indians were bolder than ever, coming within two hundred yards, and losing five horses during the day, besides one man, whom we were sure of, as we shot him as he ran away when his horse was killed. We had offered a reward of fifty dollars to our men if they could shoot A-sa-ha-be; but he would not come within range, galloping by on a fine black stallion at a distance of five or six hundred yards. That day, however, he suddenly turned his horse, and lying over so that we could see only one elbow and a foot, he passed within two hundred yards, firing as he did so. We all ran forward as he came near, and, kneeling down, gave him a volley, the black horse being killed almost instantly, and turning a summersault, giving his rider so rough a tumble that he lay where he fell, and we made a rush for the body. The Indians, however, seeing their chief in such danger, closed in from all sides; and as we dared not risk a hand-to-hand fight we had to retreat, but we did so firing as we went, and four more horses fell, causing great confusion, some of the men whose horses were shot crawling away, as they did not dare to rise and run. The Indians drew off, and we were left in peace for some hours, when about three in the afternoon we saw them all galloping to one point, apparently in chase of something; and in a few minutes later we made out, with the glasses, three men making straight for us at full speed, closely followed by the Comanches. On their reaching us, we found them to be three Caddo Indians, speaking English very fairly, and they told us that, being on a hunt from Fort Arbuckle and hearing the firing, they had come to see what it meant, and finding that it was their enemies the Comanches, and knowing from our waggon that we must be whites, they had ridden through to see if they could help us in any way. We camped at once and held a consultation, and it was at length decided that one of them should take "Polly," and try to get through the Comanches and bring us help from Arbuckle.

The distance was, they thought, eleven miles, and the only question was, could the mare do it? The Caddos were all of them small men and very light, but some of the Comanches seemed well mounted, though A-sa-ha-be's stallion—the animal we most feared—was now dead. We promised a very large reward should help arrive in time, and all three of the Caddos were willing to go, so we chose the one who seemed the lightest.

He prepared himself by taking off everything but a shirt, a breech-clout, and moccasins; and, provided with a raw-hide whip and holding a green branch in his right hand, he started, riding slowly, so as to give the Comanches time to collect at one point. This we saw them doing, thinking, no doubt, that he was commissioned to treat for peace. On getting to what seemed to us to be about a hundred yards, he threw away the bough and struck off to the left, and we could see that he had passed them; but so near, that every moment we expected to see the mare fall, struck by one of the bullets which were being fired at her. A few seconds after this, the Comanches shut him out from us, and an anxious time began. Would he succeed in distancing them, and could the mare hold out, thin as she was, and having had nothing but grass for so long?

We hitched up and went on again, all the Indians being out of sight, and must have made three miles, when we saw some of them coming back, the slow pace at which they came making us feel sure that our messenger had got through, and very soon they were all collected together, apparently consulting, about half a mile from us. We knew that they would now do their best to get us, as they could pretty well calculate how long it would be before the arrival of the troops; so we made all preparations for a rush, loading every weapon we had and laying ammunition handy.

The country here was alternately wood and small prairies, the former being open and not affording much cover, and we were passing round one of these small woods when the Comanches made a rush at us, coming on in a double line and yelling their war-whoop. Our men were excited and fired wildly, not a man dropping, till they were within about a hundred yards of us, when the horses fell fast and the Indians wavered. Our magazines were empty, but just at this moment the cook gave them six ounces of buckshot, which, as they were pretty close together, told well on the horses, many becoming quite unmanageable, and the whole party turned and galloped off into the timber, leaving seven horses and two men on the ground. As they opened fire upon us from cover, we turned and drove for some thick bushes on our left, losing another mule and two horses before reaching them, one of the latter being my bay horse. He was wounded in the side, and breaking the rope with which he was fastened to the waggon, he galloped off, falling after going a few hundred yards.

Our casualties were as follows:—One of the Caddos had a groove cut in his left arm by a bullet, and the other was hit in the left arm below the elbow, but the arm was not broken. One of the men was very slightly wounded in the calf of the leg; another (Brown) got a bullet through the side, six inches above the hip, and although we did all we could for him, and laid him in the waggon, he died just as we got into Arbuckle, and everything in the waggon was saturated with blood. F—— got an arrow in the back, but not making a serious wound; and I got a bullet in the right shoulder, which F—— that evening cut out with a razor, and an arrow under the knee.

But to return: we soon got out of shot of where the Indians had posted themselves, and they seemed to have had a lesson and left us alone. We now put one of F——'s ponies and the Sheridan horse in harness, and got on slowly, the going being very bad. The country, too, began to be more heavily wooded, so that it was difficult to keep a straight course. Our two Caddos had behaved bravely in the fight, standing well out in front, and using their Spencer carbines with great effect, and they were now very useful in showing us the road to the fort. When within about four miles of it they left, riding to meet the soldiers, to show them where we were; and shortly afterwards we decided to camp, so we drove in among some scattered trees and began to make a barricade, when it suddenly occurred to us that we were a man short, Halliday having disappeared. It seemed impossible that he could have been left behind without our knowing it, and we were on the point of trying to ride back to the spot where the rush had been made, when the cook, who was standing at the back of the waggon, beckoned to me, and on going up and looking into the waggon I saw a pair of boots, with the soles towards me, standing upon their toes—an impossible position for boots which had not feet in them; and the same thought occurring to each of us, we suddenly caught hold of a foot each, and pulled Halliday—all covered with flour—from under some sacks, bedding, &c., jerking him over the tail-board of the waggon and letting him fall on the ground. He at once shammed ill, calling us inhuman wretches for treating a sick man in that way; but a look at him was enough to let us know what his illness was—the man was simply shaking with fear. It came out now that he must have been there some time, no one having seen him when the rush took place, and the other men said that he had been of no use all through, giving out that he felt very unwell. We made him work at the barricade, and it was wonderful how soon his illness passed off.

About six o'clock P.M. two companies of cavalry rode up, the Indians still remaining within sight, as they knew that the cavalry horses could not catch them; for these large eastern horses when sent west and living on grass and half rations of corn, beside being constantly on scout duty, where they hardly get any, soon fall away to nothing and can hardly carry themselves. About two hours' travelling took us into the Post, where we arrived nearly worn out, having been fighting for three days, with very little food and less sleep. The young Caddo returned with the troops, but left the mare at the Post, as she well deserved a rest. She had behaved splendidly, having run away from the Comanches in the first two or three miles; so that most of them had turned back, and only three or four had followed nearly to the fort.

Richard Harding Davis

"There are a great many Indians and a great many reservations"

1892

Richard Harding Davis paid less attention to Indians than did other journalists who toured the West. The managing editor of *Harper's Weekly* was at least candid about his cursory examination of Indian life, admitting that he wrote of the Indian only as "a picturesque figure of the West." His description of Indian reservations in Oklahoma in the early 1890's is of interest because it reflects an easterner's bias (Davis had a low opinion of the West and most of what was in it) and because it was widely read.

The American Indian may be considered either seriously or lightly, according to one's inclination and opportunities. He may be taken seriously, like the Irish question, by politicians and philanthropists; or lightly, as a picturesque and historic relic of the past, as one regards the beef-eaters, the Tower, or the fishwives at Scheveningen. There are a great many Indians and a great many reservations, and some are partly civilized and others are not, and the different tribes differ in speech and manner of life as widely as in the South the clay-eater of Alabama differs from a gentleman of one of the first families of Virginia. Any one who wishes to speak with authority on the American Indian must learn much more concerning him than the names of the tribes and the agencies.

The Indian will only be considered here lightly and as a picturesque figure of the West.

From Richard Harding Davis, *The West from a Car-Window* (New York, Harper & Brothers, 1892), 151–81.

111

Many years ago the people of the East took their idea of the Indian from Cooper's novels and "Hiawatha," and pictured him shooting arrows into herds of buffalo, and sitting in his wigwam with many scalp-locks drying on his shield in the sun outside. But they know better than that now. Travellers from the West have told them that this picture belongs to the past, and they have been taught to look upon the Indian as a "problem," and to consider him as either a national nuisance or as a much-cheated and ill-used brother. They think of him, if they think of him at all, as one who has fallen from his high estate, and who is a dirty individual hanging around agencies in a high hat and a red shirt with a whiskey-bottle under his arm, waiting a chance to beg or steal. The Indian I saw was not at all like this, but was still picturesque, not only in what he wore, but in what he did and said, and was full of a dignity that came up at unexpected moments, and was as suspicious or trustful as a child.

It is impossible when one sees a blanket Indian walking haughtily about in his buckskin, with his face painted in many colors and with feathers in his hair, not to think that he has dressed for the occasion, or goes thus equipped because his forefathers did so, and not because he finds it comfortable. When you have seen a particular national costume only in pictures and photographs, it is always something of a surprise to find people wearing it with every-day matter-of-course ease, as though they really preferred kilts or sabots or moccasins to the gear to which we are accustomed at home. And the Indians in their fantastic mixture of colors and beads and red flannel and feathers seemed so theatrical at first that I could not understand why the army officers did not look back over their shoulders when one of these young braves rode by. The first Indians I saw were at Fort Reno, where there is an agency for the Cheyennes and Arapahoes. This reservation is in the Oklahoma Territory, but the Government has bought it from the Indians for a half-dollar an acre, and it is to be opened to white settlers. The country is very beautiful, and the tall grass of the prairie, which hides a pony, and shows only the red blanketed figure on his back, and over which in the clear places the little prairie-dogs scamper, and where the red buttes stand out against the sky, and show an edge as sharp and curving as the prow of a man-of-war, gives one a view of a West one seems to have visited and known intimately through the illustrated papers.

I had gone to Fort Reno to see the beef issue which takes place there every two weeks, when the steers and the other things which make up the Indian's rations are distributed by the agent. I missed the issue by four hours, and had to push on to Anadarko, where another beef issue was to come off three days later, which was trying, as I had met few men more interesting and delightful than the officers at the post-trader's mess. But I was fortunate, in the short time in which I was at Fort Reno, in stumbling upon an Indian council. Two lieutenants and a surgeon and I had ridden over to the Indian agency, and although they allow no beer on an Indian reservation, the surgeon had hopes. It had been a long ride—partly through water, partly over a dusty trail—and it was hot. But if the agent had a private store for visitors, he was not in a position to offer it, for his room was crowded with chiefs of renown and high degree. They sat in a circle around his desk on the floor, or stood against the wall smoking solemnly. When they approved of what the speaker said, they grunted; and though that is the only word for it, they somehow made that form of "hear, hear," impressive. Those chiefs who spoke talked in a spitting, guttural fashion, far down the throat, and without gestures; and the son of one of them, a boy from Carlisle, in a gray ready-made suit and sombrero, translated a five-minutes' speech, which had all the dignity of Salvini's address to the Senators, by: "And Red Wolf he says he thinks it isn't right." Cloud-Shield rose and said the chiefs were glad to see that the officers from the fort were in the room, as that meant that the Indian would have fair treatment, and that the officers were always the Indians' best friends, and were respected in times of peace as friends, and in times of war as enemies. After which, the officers, considering guiltily the real object of their visit, and feeling properly abashed, took off their hats and tried to look as though they deserved it, which, as a rule, they do. It may be of interest, in view of an Indian outbreak, to know that this council of the chiefs was to protest against the cutting down of the rations of the Cheyennes and the Arapahoes. Last year it cost the Government one hundred and thirteen thousand dollars to feed them, and this year Commissioner Martin, with a fine spirit of economy, proposes to reduce this by just one-half. This means hunger and illness, and in some cases death.

"He says," translated the boy interpreter, gazing at the ceiling, "that they would like to speak to the people at Washington about this thing, for it is not good."

The agent traced figures over his desk with his pen.

"Well, I can't do anything," he said, at last. "All I can do is to let the people at Washington know what they say. But to send a commission all the way to Washington will take a great deal of money, and the cost of it will have to come out of their allowance. Tell them that. Tell them I'll write on about it. That's all I can do."

That night the chiefs came solemnly across parade, and said "How!" grimly to the orderly in front of the colonel's headquarters.

"You see," said the officers, "they have come to complain, but the colonel cannot help them. If Martin wants a war, he is going just the best way in the world to get it, and then we shall have to go out and shoot them, poor devils!" . . .

Anadarko is a town of six stores, three or four frame houses, the Indian agent's store and office, and the City Hotel. Seven houses in the West make a city. I said I thought this was the worst hotel in the Indian Territory, but the officers at Fort Sill, who have travelled more than I, think it is the worst in the United States. It is possible that they are right. There are bluffs and bunches of timber around Anadarko, but the prairie stretches towards the west, and on it is the pen from which the cattle are issued. The tepees and camp-fires sprang up overnight, and when we came out the next morning the prairie was crowded with them, and more Indians were driving in every minute, with the family in the wagon and the dogs under it, as the country people in the East flock into town for the circus. The men galloped off to the cattle-pen, and the women gathered in a long line in front of the agent's store to wait their turn for the rations. It was a curious line, with very young girls in it, very proud of the little babies in beaded knapsacks on their backs—dirty, bright-eyed babies that looked like mummies suddenly come to life again at the period of their first childhood—and wrinkled, bent old squaws, even more like mummies, with coarse white hair, and hands worn almost out of shape with work. Each of these had a tag, such as those that the express companies use, on which was printed the number in each family, and the amount of grain, flour, baking-powder, and soap to which the family was entitled. They passed in at one door and in

Iron Tail, a Sioux, was one of sculptor James Earle Fraser's three models for the buffalo nickel. Fraser used three models—a Kiowa and a Cheyenne joined Iron Tail—because they had "combined features of the hardy, virile types of Great Plains Indian."

Sioux warriors with coup sticks and various firearms.

Kiowa warriors with lances and rifles. The Indian standing at right appears to be wearing a breechcloth made from an American flag. Next to him, mounted, is Pablino Diaz, whose portrait appears later in this book.

Members of the Cheyenne Lance Society.

Kado, Comanche, and his wife in a studio portrait.

Pablino Diaz, Kiowa.

White Swan, Crow, with a six-shooter.

Last Horse, Sioux.

Little Bird, Arapaho, with a crucifix, a watch chain, and a campaign button.

Wolf Robe, Cheyenne.

Mountain, Blackfoot.

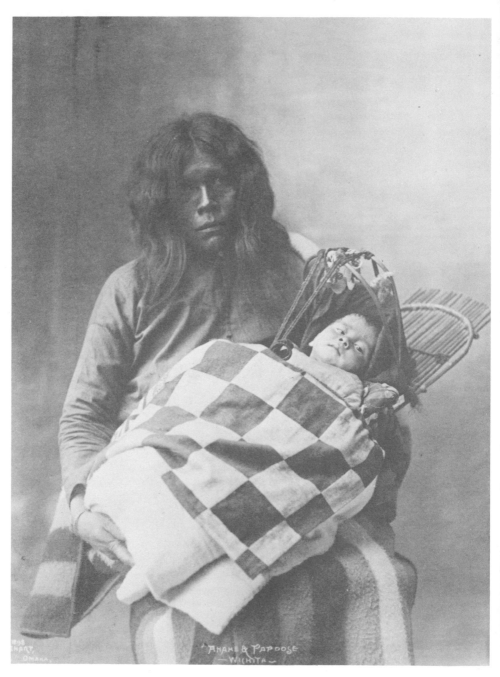

Ahahe, Wichita, and her infant.

Swift Dog, Sioux.

An interpreter and his entourage—a Cheyenne, a Comanche, and
Geronimo—photographed around the turn of the century.

front of a long counter, and out at another. They crowded and pushed a great deal, almost as much as their fairer sisters do in front of the box-office at a Patti matinée, and the babies blinked stoically at the sun, and seemed to wish they could get their arms out of the wrappings and rub away the tears. A man in a sombrero would look at the tag and call out, "One of flour, two of sugar, one soap, and one baking-powder," and his Indian assistants delved into the barrels behind the line of the counter, and emptied the rations into the squaw's open apron. She sorted them when she reached the outside. By ten o'clock the distribution was over, and the women followed the men to the cattle-pen on the prairie. There were not over three hundred Indians there, although they represented several thousand others, who remained in the different camps scattered over the reservation, wherever water and timber, and bluffs to shield them best from the wind, were to be found in common. Each steer is calculated to supply twenty-five Indians with beef for two weeks, or from one and a half to two pounds of beef a day; this is on the supposition that the steers average from one thousand to one thousand and two hundred pounds. The steers that I saw issued weighed about five hundred pounds, and when they tried to run, stumbled with the weakness of starvation. They were nothing but hide and ribs and two horns. They were driven four at a time through a long chute, and halted at the gate at the end of it until their owner's names were marked off the list. The Indians were gathered in front of the gate in long rows, or in groups of ten or twelve, sitting easily in their saddles, and riding off leisurely in bunches of four as their names were called out, and as their cattle were started off with a parting kick into the open prairie.

The Apaches, Comanches, Delawares, and Towacomics drove their share off towards their camps; the Caddoes and the Kiowas, who live near the agency, and who were served last, killed theirs, if they chose to do so, as soon as they left the pen. A man in charge of the issue held a long paper in his hand, and called out, "Eck-hoos-cho, Pe-an-voon-it, Hoos-cho, and Chonoo-chy," which meant that Red-Bird, Large-Looking-Glass, The Bird, and Deer-Head were to have the next four steers. His assistant, an Indian policeman, with "God helps them who help themselves" engraved on his brass buttons, with the figure of an Indian toiling at a plough in the centre,

repeated these names aloud, and designated which steer was to go
to which Indian.

A beef issue is not a pretty thing to watch. Why the Government does not serve its meat with the throats cut, as any reputable
butcher would do, it is not possible to determine. It seems to prefer,
on the contrary, that the Indian should exhibit his disregard for the
suffering of animals and his bad marksmanship at the same time.
When the representatives of the more distant tribes had ridden off,
chasing their beef before them, the Caddoes and Kiowas gathered
close around the gate of the pen, with the boys in front. They were
handsome, mischievous boys, with leather leggins, colored green
and blue and with silver buttons down the side, and beaded buckskin shirts. They sat two on each pony, and each held his bow and
arrows, and as the steers came stumbling blindly out into the open,
they let the arrows drive from a distance of ten feet into the animal's
flank and neck, where they stuck quivering. Then the Indian boys
would yell, and their fathers, who had hunted buffalos with arrows,
smiled approvingly. The arrows were not big enough to kill, they
merely hurt, and the steer would rush off into a clumsy gallop for
fifty yards, when its owner would raise his Winchester, and make the
dust spurt up around it, until one bullet would reach a leg, and the
steer would stop for an instant, with a desperate toss of its head, and
stagger forward again on three. The dogs to the number of twenty
or more were around it by this time in a snarling, leaping pack, and
the owner would try again, and wound it perhaps in the flank, and it
would lurch over heavily like a drunken man, shaking its head from
side to side and tossing its horns at the dogs, who bit at the place
where the blood ran, and snapped at its legs. Sometimes it would lie
there for an hour, until it bled to death, or, again, it would scramble
to its feet, and the dogs would start off in a panic of fear after a
more helpless victim.

The field grew thick with these miniature butcheries, the Winchesters cracking, and the spurts of smoke rising and drifting away,
the dogs yelping, and the Indians wheeling in quick circles around
the steer, shooting as they rode, and hitting the mark once in every
half-dozen shots. It was the most unsportsmanlike and wantonly
cruel exhibition I have ever seen. A bull in a ring has a fighting
chance and takes it, but these animals, who were too weak to stand,

and too frightened to run, staggered about until the Indians had finished torturing them, and then, with eyes rolling and blood spurting from their mouths, would pitch forward and die. And they had to be quick about it, before the squaws began cutting off the hide while the flanks were still heaving.

This is the view of a beef issue which the friend of the Indian does not like to take. He prefers calling your attention to the condition of the cattle served the Indian, and in showing how outrageously he is treated in this respect. The Government either purchases steers for the Indians a few weeks before an issue, or three or four months previous to it, feeding them meanwhile on the Government reservation. The latter practice is much more satisfactory to the contractor, as it saves him the cost and care of these cattle during the winter, and the inevitable loss which must ensue in that time through illness and starvation. Those I saw had been purchased in October, and had been weighed and branded at that time with the Government brand. They were then allowed to roam over the Government reservation until the spring, when they had fallen off in weight from one-half to one-third. They were then issued at their original weight. That is, a steer which in October was found to weigh eleven hundred pounds, and which would supply twenty or more people with meat, was supposed to have kept this weight throughout the entire winter, and was issued at eleven hundred although it had not three hundred pounds of flesh on its bones. The agent is not to blame for this. This is the fault of the Government, and it is quite fair to suppose that some one besides the contractor benefits by the arrangement. When the beef is issued two weeks after the contract has been made, it can and frequently is rejected by the army officer in charge of the issue if he thinks it is unfit. But the officers present at the issue that I saw were as helpless as they were indignant, for the beef had weighed the weight credited to it once when it was paid for, and the contractor had saved the expense of keeping it, and the Indian received just one-fourth of the meat due him, and for which he had paid in land.

Fort Sill, which is a day's journey in a stage from Anadarko, is an eight-company post situated on the table-land of a hill, with other hills around it, and is, though somewhat inaccessible, as interesting and beautiful a spot to visit as many others which we cross the ocean to see. I will be able to tell why this is so when I write something later about the army posts. There are any number of Indians here, and they add to the post a delightfully picturesque and foreign element. L Troop of the Seventh cavalry, which is an Indian troop, is the nucleus around which the other Indians gather. The troop is encamped at the foot of the hill on which the post stands. It shows the Indian civilized by uniform, and his Indian brother uncivilized in his blanket and war-paint; and although I should not like to hurt the feelings of the patient, enthusiastic officers who have enlisted the Indians for these different troops for which the Government calls, I think the blanket Indian is a much more warlike-looking and interesting individual. But you mustn't say so, as George the Third advised. The soldier Indians live in regulation tents staked out in rows, and with the ground around so cleanly kept that one could play tennis on it, and immediately back of these are the conical teepees of their wives, brothers, and grandmothers; and what Lieutenant Scott is going to do with all these pretty young squaws and beautiful children and withered old witches, and their two or three hundred wolf-dogs, when he marches forth to war with his Indian troop, is one of the questions his brother officers find much entertainment in asking.

The Indian children around this encampment were the brightest spot in my entire Western trip. They are the prettiest and most beautifully barbaric little children I have ever seen. They grow out of it very soon, but that is no reason why one should not make the most of it while it lasts. And they are as wild and fearful of the white visitor, unless he happens to be Lieutenant Scott or Second Lieutenant Quay, as the antelope in the prairie around him. It required a corporal's guard, two lieutenants, and three squaws to persuade one of them to stand still and be photographed, and whenever my camera and I appeared together there was a wild stampede of Indian children, which no number of looking-glasses or dimes or strings of beads could allay. Not that they would not take the bribes, but they would run as soon as they had snatched them. It was very distressing, for I did not mean to hurt them very much. The older people were kinder, and would let me sit inside the teepees, which were very warm on the coldest days, and watch them cook, and play their queer games, and work moccasins, and gamble at monte for brass rings if they were women, or for cartridges if they were men. And for ways that are dark and tricks that are vain, I think the Indian monte-dealer can instruct a Chinese poker-player in many things. What was so fine about them was their dignity, hospitality, and strict suppression of all curiosity. They always received a present as though they were doing you a favor, and you felt that you were paying tribute. This makes them difficult to deal with as soldiers. They cannot be treated as white men, and put in the guard-house for every slight offence. Lieutenant Scott has to explain things to them, and praise them, and excite a spirit of emulation among them by commending those publicly who have done well. For instance, they hate to lose their long hair, and Lieutenant Scott did not order them to have it cut, but told them it would please him if they did; and so one by one, and in bunches of three and four, they tramped up the hill to the post barber, and back again with their locks in their hands, to barter them for tobacco with the post trader. The Indians at Fort Sill were a temperate lot, and Lieutenant Harris, who has charge of the canteen, growled because they did not drink enough to pay for their share of the dividend which is returned to each troop at the end of the month.

Lieutenant Scott obtained his ascendency over his troop in several ways—first, by climbing a face of rock, and, with the assistance of Lieutenant Quay, taking an eagle from the nest it had built there. Every Indian in the reservation knew of that nest, and had long wanted the eagle's feathers for a war-bonnet, but none of them had ever dared to climb the mirrorlike surface of the cliff, with the rocks below. The fame of this exploit spread, by what means it is hard to understand among people who have no newspapers or letters, but at beef issues, perhaps, or Messiah dances, or casual meetings on the prairie, which help to build up reputations and make the prowess of one chief known to those of all the other tribes, or the beauty of an Indian girl familiar. Then, following this exploit, three little Indian children ran away from school because they had been flogged, and tried to reach their father's tent fifteen miles off on the reservation, and were found half-buried in the snow and frozen to death. One of them was without his heavier garments, which he had wrapped around his younger brother. The terrified school-teacher sent a message to the fort begging for two troops of cavalry to protect him from the wrath of the older Indians, and the post commander sent out Lieutenant Scott alone to treat with them. His words were much more effective than two troops of cavalry would have been, and the threatened outbreak was stopped. The schoolmaster fled to the woods, and never came back. What the Indians saw of Lieutenant Scott at this crisis made them trust him for the future, and this and the robbery of the eagle's nest explain partly, as do his gentleness and consideration, the remarkable hold he has over them. Some one was trying to tell one of the chiefs how the white man could bring lightning down from the sky, and make it talk for him from one end of the country to the other.

"Oh yes," the Indian said, simply, "that is quite true. Lieutenant Scott says so."

But what has chiefly contributed to make the lieutenant's work easy for him is his knowledge of the sign language, with which the different tribes, though speaking different languages, can communicate one with the other. He is said to speak this more correctly and fluently than any other officer in the army, and perhaps any other white man. It is a very curious language. It is not at all like the deaf-and-dumb alphabet, which *is* an alphabet, and is not pretty to watch. It is just what its name implies—a language of signs. The first time I saw the lieutenant speaking it, I confess I thought, having heard of his skill at Fort Reno, that he was only doing it because he could do it, as young men who speak French prefer to order their American dinners in that language when the waiter can understand English quite as well as themselves. I regarded it as a pleasing weakness, and was quite sure that the lieutenant was going to meet the Indian back of the canteen and say it over again in plain every-day words. In this I wronged him; but it was not until I had watched his Irish sergeant converse in this silent language for two long hours with half a dozen Indians of different tribes, and had seen them all laugh heartily at his witticisms delivered in semaphoric gestures, that I really believed in it. It seems that what the lieutenant said was, "Tell the first sergeant that I wish to see the soldiers drill at one o'clock, and, after that, go to the store and ask Madeira if there is to be a beef issue to-day." It is very difficult to describe in writing how he did this; and as it is a really pretty thing to watch, it seems a pity to spoil it. As well as I remember it, he did something like this. He first drew his hand over his sleeve to mark the sergeant's stripes; then he held his fingers upright in front of him, and moved them forward to signify soldiers; by holding them in still another position, he represented soldiers drilling; then he made a spyglass out of his thumb and first finger, and looked up through it at the sky—this represented the sun at one o'clock. "After that" was a quick cut in the air; the "store" was an interlacing of the fingers, to signify a place where one thing met or was exchanged for another; "Madeira" he named; beef was a turning up of the fingers, to represent horns; and how he represented issue I have no idea. It is a most curious thing to watch, for they change from one sign to the other with the greatest rapidity. I always regarded it with great interest as a sort of game, and tried to guess what the different gestures might mean. Some of the signs are very old, and their origin is as much in dispute as some of the lines in the first folios of Shakespeare, and have nearly as many commentators. All the Indians know these signs, but very few of them can tell how they came to mean what they do. "To go to war," for instance, is shown by sweeping the right arm out with the thumb and first finger at right angles; this comes from an early custom among the Indians of carrying a lighted pipe before them when going on the war-path. The thumb and finger in that position are supposed to represent the angle of the bowl of the pipe and the stem.

I visited a few of the Indian schools when I was in the Territory, and found the pupils quite learned. The teachers are not permitted to study the Indian languages, and their charges in consequence hear nothing but English, and so pick it up the more quickly. The young women who teach them seem to labor under certain disadvantages; one of them was reading the English lesson from a United States history intended for much older children—grown-up children, in fact— and explained that she had to order and select the school-books she used from a list furnished by the Government, and could form no opinion of its appropriateness until it arrived.

Some of the Indian parents are very proud of their children's progress, and on beef-issue days visit the schools, and listen with great satisfaction to their children speaking in the unknown tongue. There were several in one of the school-rooms while I was there, and the teacher turned them out of their chairs to make room for us, remarking pleasantly that the Indians were accustomed to sitting around on the ground. She afterwards added to this by telling us that there was no sentiment in *her*, and that she taught Indians for the fifty dollars there was in it. The mother of one of the little boys was already crouching on the floor as we came in, or squatting on her heels, as they seem to be able to do without fatigue for any length of time. During the half-hour we were there, she never changed her position or turned her head to look at us, but kept her eyes fixed only on her son sitting on the bench above her. He was a very plump, clean, and excited little Indian, with his hair cut short, and dressed in a very fine pair of trousers and jacket, and with shoes and stockings. He was very keen to show the white visitors how well he knew their talk, and read his book with a masterful shaking of the head, as though it had no terrors for him. His mother, kneeling at his side on the floor, wore a single garment, and over that a dirty blanket strapped around her waist with a beaded belt. Her feet were bare, and her coarse hair hung down over her face and down her back almost to her waist in an unkempt mass. She supported her chin on one hand, and with the other hand, black and wrinkled, and with nails broken by cutting wood and harnessing horses and ploughing in the fields, brushed her hair back from before her eyes, and then touched her son's arm wistfully, as a dog tries to draw his master's eyes, and as though he were something fragile and fine. But he paid no attention to her whatsoever; he was very much interested in the lesson. She was the only thing I saw in the school-room. I wondered if she was thinking of the days when she carried his weight on her back as she went about her cooking or foraging for wood, or swung him from a limb of a tree, and of the first leather leggings she made for him when he was able to walk, and of the necklace of elk teeth, and the arrows which he used to fire bravely at the prairie-dogs. He was a very different child now, and very far away from the doglike figure crouching by his side and gazing up patiently into his face, as if looking for something she had lost.

It is quite too presumptuous to suggest any opinion on the Indian question when one has only lived with them for three weeks, but the experience of others who have lived with them for thirty years is worth repeating. You will find that the individual point of view regarding the Indian is much biassed by the individual interests. A man told me that in his eyes no one under heaven was better than a white man, and if the white man had to work for his living, he could not see why the Indian should not work for his. I asked him if he thought of taking up Indian land in the Territory when it was open in the spring, and he said that was his intention, "and why?"

The officers are the only men who have absolutely nothing to gain, make, or lose by the Indians, and their point of view is accordingly the fairest, and they themselves say it would be a mistake to follow the plan now under consideration—of placing officers in charge of the agencies. This would at once strip them of their present neutral position, and, as well, open to them the temptation which the control of many thousands of dollars' worth of property entails where the recipients of this property are as helpless and ignorant as children. They rather favor raising the salary of the Indian agent from two thousand to ten thousand dollars, and by so doing bring men of intelligence and probity into the service, and destroy at the same time the temptation to "make something" out of the office. It may have been merely an accident, but I did not meet with one officer in any of the army posts who did not side with the Indian in his battle for his rights with the Government. As for the agents, as the people say in the West, "they are not here for their health." The Indian agents of the present day are, as every one knows, political appointments, and many of them—not all—are men who at home would keep their corner grocery or liquor store, and who would flatter and be civil to every woman in the neighboring tenement who came for a pound of sugar or a pitcher of beer. These men are suddenly placed in the control of hundreds of sensitive, dangerous, semi-civilized people, whom they are as capable of understanding as a Bowery boy would be of appreciating an Arab of the desert.

The agents are not the only people who make mistakes. Some friend mailed me a book the other day on Indian reservations, in order that I might avoid writing what has already been written. I read only one page of the book, in which the author described his manner of visiting the Indian encampments. He would drive to one of these in his ambulance, and upon being informed that the chiefs were waiting to receive him in their tents, would bid them meet him at the next camp, to which he would drive rapidly, and there make the same proposition. He would then stop his wagon three miles away on the prairie, and wait for the chiefs to follow him to that point. What his object was in this exhibition, with which he seemed very well satisfied, he only knows. Whether it was to teach the chiefs they were not masters in their own camps, or that he was a most superior person, I could not make out; but he might just as effectively have visited Washington, and sent the President word he could not visit him at the White House, but that he would grant him an interview at his hotel. I wonder just how near this superior young man got to the Indians, and just how wide they opened their hearts to him.

There was an Indian agent once—it was not long ago, but there is no need to give dates or names, for the man is dead—who when the Indians asked him to paint the wagons (with which the Government furnished them through him in return for their land) red instead of green, answered that he would not pander to their absurdly barbaric tastes. Only he did not say absurdly. He was a man who had his own ideas about things, and who was not to be fooled, and he was also a superior person, who preferred to trample on rather than to understand the peculiarities of his wards. So one morning this agent and his wife and children were found hacked to pieces by these wards with barbaric tastes, and the soldiers were called out, and shot many of the Indians; and many white women back of the barracks, and on the line itself, are now wearing mourning, and several officers got their first bar. It would seem from this very recent incident, as well as from many others of which one hears, that it would be cheaper in the end to place agents over the Indians with sufficient intelligence to know just when to be firm, and when to compromise in a matter; for instance, that of painting a wagon red.

Andy Adams

"He looked every inch a chief"

1903

Cowboys occasionally had dealings with Indians, especially with those whose land they crossed when driving trail herds to market. Here, Andy Adams, the foremost chronicler of cowboy life, describes negotiations between Indians and cowboys over the right to traverse Indian land. In Adams' view, the Indians were begging for beef, not bargaining for a toll, but even so, the parties met on equal terms, demonstrated a healthy mutual respect, and dealt courteously with each other throughout.

We were following the regular trail, which had been slightly used for a year or two, though none of our outfit had ever been over it, when late on the third afternoon, about forty miles out from Doan's, about a hundred mounted bucks and squaws sighted our herd and crossed the North Fork from their encampment. They did not ride direct to the herd, but came into the trail nearly a mile above the cattle, so it was some little time from our first sighting them before we met. We did not check the herd or turn out of the trail, but when the lead came within a few hundred yards of the Indians, one buck, evidently the chief of the band, rode forward a few rods and held up one hand, as if commanding a halt. At the sight of this gaudily bedecked apparition, the cattle turned out of the trail, and Flood and I rode up to the chief, extending our hands in friendly greeting. The chief could not speak a word of English, but made signs with his

From Andy Adams, *The Log of a Cowboy: A Narrative of the Old Trail Days* (Boston, Houghton Mifflin and Company, 1903), 136–43.

hands; when I turned loose on him in Spanish, however, he instantly turned his horse and signed back to his band. Two young bucks rode forward and greeted Flood and myself in good Spanish.

On thus opening up an intelligible conversation, I called Fox Quarternight, who spoke Spanish, and he rode up from his position of third man in the swing and joined in the council. The two young Indians through whom we carried on the conversation were Apaches, no doubt renegades of that tribe, and while we understood each other in Spanish, they spoke in a heavy guttural peculiar to the Indian. Flood opened the powwow by demanding to know the meaning of this visit. When the question had been properly interpreted to the chief, the latter dropped his blanket from his shoulders and dismounted from his horse. He was a fine specimen of the Plains Indian, fully six feet in height, perfectly proportioned, and in years well past middle life. He looked every inch a chief, and was a natural born orator. There was a certain easy grace to his gestures, only to be seen in people who use the sign language, and often when he was speaking to the Apache interpreters, I could anticipate his requests before they were translated to us, although I did not know a word of Comanche.

Before the powwow had progressed far it was evident that begging was its object. In his prelude, the chief laid claim to all the country in sight as the hunting grounds of the Comanche tribe,—an intimation that we were intruders. He spoke of the great slaughter of the buffalo by the white hide-hunters, and the consequent hunger and poverty amongst his people. He dwelt on the fact that he had ever counseled peace with the whites, until now his band numbered but a few squaws and papooses, the younger men having deserted him for other chiefs of the tribe who advocated war on the palefaces. When he had fully stated his position, he offered to allow us to pass through his country in consideration of ten beeves. On receiving this proposition, all of us dismounted, including the two Apaches, the latter seating themselves in their own fashion, while we whites lounged on the ground in truly American laziness, rolling cigarettes. In dealing with people who know not the value of time, the civilized man is taken at a disadvantage, and unless he can show an equal composure in wasting time, results will be against him. Flood had had years of experience in dealing with Mexicans in the land of *mañana*, where all maxims regarding the value of time are religiously discarded. So in dealing with this Indian chief he showed no desire to hasten matters, and carefully avoided all reference to the demand for beeves.

His first question, instead, was to know the distance to Fort Sill and Fort Elliott. The next was how many days it would take for cavalry to reach him. He then had us narrate the fact that when the first herd of cattle passed through the country less than a month before, some bad Indians had shown a very unfriendly spirit. They had taken many of the cattle and had killed and eaten them, and now the great white man's chief at Washington was very much displeased. If another single ox were taken and killed by bad Indians, he would send his soldiers from the forts to protect the cattle, even though their owners drove the herds through the reservation of the Indians—over the grass where their ponies grazed. He had us inform the chief that our entire herd was intended by the great white man's chief at Washington as a present to the Blackfeet Indians who lived in Montana, because they were good Indians, and welcomed priests and teachers amongst them to teach them the ways of the white man. At our foreman's request we then informed the chief that he was under no obligation to give him even a single beef for any privilege of passing through his country, but as the squaws and little papooses were hungry, he would give him two beeves.

The old chief seemed not the least disconcerted, but begged for five beeves, as many of the squaws were in the encampment across the North Fork, those present being not quite half of his village. It was now getting late in the day and the band seemed to be getting tired of the parleying, a number of squaws having already set out on their return to the village. After some further talk, Flood agreed to add another beef, on condition they be taken to the encampment before being killed. This was accepted, and at once the entire band set up a chattering in view of the coming feast. The cattle had in the mean time grazed off nearly a mile, the outfit, however, holding them under a close herd during the powwowing. All the bucks in the band, numbering about forty, now joined us, and we rode away to the herd. I noticed, by the way, that quite a number of the younger braves had arms, and no doubt they would have made a display of force had Flood's diplomacy been of a more warlike character. While drifting the herd back to the trail we cut out a big lame steer and two stray cows for the Indians, who now left us and followed the beeves which were being driven to their village.

Flood had instructed Quarternight and me to invite the two Apaches to our camp for the night, on the promise of sugar, coffee, and tobacco. They consulted with the old chief, and gaining his consent came with us. We extended the hospitality of our wagon to our guests, and when supper was over, promised them an extra beef if they would give us particulars of the trail until it crossed the North Fork, after that river turned west towards the Pan-handle. It was evident that they were familiar with the country, for one of them accepted our offer, and with his finger sketched a rude map on the ground where there had formerly been a camp-fire. He outlined the two rivers between which we were then encamped, and traced the trail until it crossed the North Fork or beyond the Indian reservation. We discussed the outline of the trail in detail for an hour, asking hundreds of unimportant questions, but occasionally getting in a leading one, always resulting in the information wanted. We learned that the big summer encampment of the Comanches and Kiowas was one day's ride for a pony or two days' with cattle up the trail, at the point where the divide between Salt and North Fork narrows to about ten miles in width. We leeched out of them very cautiously the information that the encampment was a large one, and that all herds this year had given up cattle, some as many as twenty-five head.

Having secured the information we wanted, Flood gave to each Apache a package of Arbuckle coffee, a small sack of sugar, and both smoking and chewing tobacco. Quarternight informed them that as the cattle were bedded for the night, they had better remain until morning, when he would pick them out a nice fat beef. On their consenting, Fox stripped the wagon sheet off the wagon and made them a good bed, in which, with their body blankets, they were as comfortable as any of us. Neither of them was armed, so we felt no fear of them, and after they had lain down on their couch, Flood called Quarternight and me, and we strolled out into the darkness and reviewed the information. We agreed that the topography of the country they had given was most likely correct, because we could verify much of it by maps in our possession. Another thing on which we agreed was, that there was some means of communication between this small and seemingly peaceable band and the main encampment of the tribe; and that more than likely our approach would be known in the large encampment before sunrise. In spite of the good opinion we entertained of our guests, we were also satisfied they had lied to us when they denied they had been in the large camp since the trail herds began to pass. This was the last question we had asked, and the artful manner in which they had parried it showed our guests to be no mean diplomats themselves.

Our camp was astir by daybreak, and after breakfast, as we were catching our mounts for the day, one of the Apaches offered to take a certain pinto horse in our *remuda* in lieu of the promised beef, but Flood declined the offer. On overtaking the herd after breakfast, Quarternight cut out a fat two year old stray heifer, and he and I assisted our guests to drive their beef several miles toward their village. Finally bidding them farewell, we returned to the herd, when the outfit informed us that Flood and The Rebel had ridden on ahead to look out a crossing on the Salt Fork. From this move it was evident that if a passable ford could be found, our foreman intended to abandon the established route and avoid the big Indian encampment.

The cover of a program for Pawnee Bill's Pioneer Days, a "representative exhibition" of "marvelous magnitude and unprecedented merit," featuring Indians and other exotics.

Indians with the 101 Ranch Wild West show entering the arena. Feathers, coup sticks, and war cries were the order of the day.

Another grand entrance by 101 Ranch Indians. Some of the horses wore bells to enhance the noise of the spectacle.

Behind the scenes a 101 Ranch Indian aims his pistol at the camera.

Amid the props and tent stakes 101 Ranch Indians rehearse the act they will later perform for white spectators.

101 Ranch Indians ride around the arena against a backdrop of painted canvas.

The cast of the 101 Ranch show, photographed on September 22, 1911—cowboys, cowgirls, Cossacks, and Indians.

A Wild West show Indian on a sawhorse demonstrates the use of bow and arrow for passersby.

157

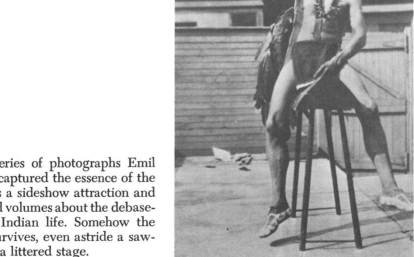

In this series of photographs Emil
Lenders captured the essence of the
Indian as a sideshow attraction and
suggested volumes about the debase-
ment of Indian life. Somehow the
Indian survives, even astride a sawhorse on a littered stage.

The back cover of a Pawnee Bill's Pioneer Days program, promising

C SCENES FROM
RONTIER DAYS
LY DEPICTED BY
BOYS AND INDIANS
JUNCTION WITH
S PIONEER DAYS

"realistic scenes . . . truthfully depicted by real cowboys and Indians."

The Plains Indian stereotype on a 101 Ranch poster.

Edward L. Wheeler

"The great warrior straightened up like an arrow"

1877

Edward L. Wheeler was twenty-two years old when he introduced his Deadwood Dick character to dime-novel readers. He had been only as far west as Titusville, Pennsylvania, but firsthand knowledge meant little to those who had enjoyed Wheeler's earlier novelette *Old Avalanche, the Great Injun Annihilator.* The young man knew all that he needed to know about Indians to please eastern readers and reach the pinnacle of dime-novel popularity: nothing. Here, from the first Deadwood Dick saga, is an exchange between Fearless Frank and Sitting Bull over the fate of a captive white girl.

Fearless Frank stepped back aghast, as he saw the inhuman chief of the Sioux—the cruel, grim-faced warrior, Sitting Bull; shrunk back, and laid his hand upon the butt of a revolver.

"Ha!" he articulated, "is that you, chief? You, and at such work as this?" There was stern reproach in the youth's tone, and certain it is that the Sioux warrior heard the words spoken.

"My friend, Scarlet Boy, is keen with the tongue," he said, frowning. "Let him put shackles upon it, before it leaps over the bounds of reason."

"I see no reason why I should not speak in behalf of yon suffering girl!" retorted the youth, fearlessly, "on whom you have been inflicting one of the most inhuman tortures Indian cunning could

From Edward L. Wheeler, "Deadwood Dick, the Prince of the Road; or, The Black Rider of the Black Hills," *Beadle's Half-Dime Library,* Vol. I, No. 1 ([October 15,] 1877), 5.

conceive. For shame, chief, that you should ever assent to such an act—lower yourself to the grade of a dog by such a dastard deed. For shame, I say!"

Instantly the form of the great warrior straightened up like an arrow, and his painted hand flew toward the pistols in his belt.

But the succeeding second he seemed to change his intention; his hand went out toward the youth in greeting:

"The Scarlet Boy is right," he said, with as much graveness as a red-skin can conceive. "Sitting Bull listens to his words as he would to those of a brother. Scarlet Boy is not stranger in the land of the Sioux; he is the friend of the great chief and his warriors. Once when the storm-gods were at war over the pine forests and picture rocks of the Hills; when the Great Spirit was sending fiery messengers down in vivid streaks from the skies, the Big Chief cast a thunder-bolt in playfulness at the feet of Sitting Bull. The shock of the hand of the Great Spirit did not escape me; for hours I lay like one slain in battle. My warriors were in consternation; they ran hither and thither in affright, calling on the Manitou to preserve their chief. You came, Scarlet Boy, in the midst of all the panic;—came, and though then but a stripling, you applied simple remedies that re-stored Sitting Bull to the arms of his warriors.

"From that hour Sitting Bull was your friend—is your friend, now, and will be as long as the red-men exist as a tribe."

"Thank you, chief," and Fearless Frank grasped the Indian's hand and wrung it warmly. "I believe you mean all you say. But I am surprised to find you engaged in such work as this. I have been told that Sitting Bull made war only on warriors—not on women."

An ugly frown darkened the savage's face—a frown wherein was depicted a number of slumbering passions.

"The pale-face girl is the last survivor of a train that the war-riors of Sitting Bull attacked in Red Canyon. Sitting Bull lost many warriors; yon pale squaw shot down a full half-score before she could be captured; she belongs to the warriors of Sitting Bull, and not to the great chief himself."

"Yet you have the power to free her—to yield her up to me. Con-sider, chief; are you not enough my friend that you can afford to give me the pale-face girl? Surely, she has been tortured sufficiently to satisfy your braves' thirst for vengence."

Sitting Bull was silent.

"What will the Scarlet Boy do with the fair maiden of his tribe?"

"Bear her to a place of safety, chief, and care for her until I can find her friends—probably she has friends in the East."

"It shall be as he says. Sitting Bull will withdraw his braves and Scarlet Boy can have the red-man's prize."

A friendly hand-shake between the youth and the Sioux chieftain, a word from the latter to the grim painted warriors, and the next instant the glade was cleared of the savages.

Prentiss Ingraham

" 'It's my Injun, boys,' he cried exultantly"

1881

Prentiss Ingraham, a soldier of fortune turned dime novelist, was in the business of making heroes where, in many cases, none had existed before. He was a friend and business associate of William F. Cody's, and it was perhaps inevitable that he would become Cody's biographer and, later, his ghost writer. In 1881, Ingraham prepared a dime-novel life of Cody for juvenile consumption, and in it he revealed to young readers the subtle fact that Cody was a hero principally because of his prowess at homicide. The eighth chapter of that opus, wherein the boy Cody kills his first Indian, follows. That it is largely fictional is irrelevant.

When the train and beef-herd, with which Billy Cody had gone, arrived in the vicinity of old Fort Kearney their first serious adventure occurred, and for a while the boy thought of his mother's prediction, that he "would be killed or captured by Indians."

Not expecting an attack from red-skins in that vicinity, the party had camped for dinner, and most of them were enjoying a *siesta* under the wagons, Billy being among the latter number, while but three men were on duty as herders.

But suddenly they were aroused by shots, wild yells, and rapid hoof-falls, and down upon them dashed a band of mounted warriors, while others had killed the three guards and the cattle were stam-

From Colonel Prentiss Ingraham, "Adventures of Buffalo Bill from Boyhood to Manhood," *Beadle's Boy's Library of Sport, Story and Adventure*, Vol. I, No. 1 (December 14, 1881), 5.

peding in every direction. But the train hands quickly sprung to their feet, rallied promptly for the fight, and met the advancing red-skins with a volley from their Mississippi yagers, which were loaded with ball and buck-shot, and checked their advance.

Knowing that they could not hold out there the train-master called out:

"Boys, make a run for the river, and the banks will protect us."

All started, when Billy called out:

"Don't let us leave these wounded boys."

They turned at his word, to find that two of their number had been wounded, one seriously in the side and the other in the leg.

Raising them in their arms they started at a run for the bank, ere the Indians had rallied from the fire that met them, and reached it in safety, though the man who had been shot in the side was dead ere they got there.

A short consultation was then held, and it was decided to make their way back to Fort Kearney, by wading in the river and keeping the bank as a breast work.

A raft of poles was constructed for the wounded man, and the party started down the stream, protected by the bank, and keeping the Indians at bay with their guns, for they followed them up closely.

As night came on, utterly worn out with wading and walking, Billy dropped behind the others; but trudged manfully along until he was suddenly startled by a dark object coming down over the bank.

It was moonlight, and he saw the plumed head and buckskin-clad form of an Indian, who, in peering over the bank to reconnoiter had lost his balance, or the earth had given way, and sent him down into the stream.

He caught sight of Billy as he was sliding down, and gave a wild war-whoop, which was answered by a shot from the boy's rifle, for though taken wholly by surprise he did not lose his presence of mind.

Hearing the war-whoop and the shot, and at the same time missing Billy, the men came running back and found him dragging the red-skin along in the stream after him.

"It's my Injun, boys," he cried exultantly.

"It are fer a fact, an' I'll show yer how ter take his scalp," replied

Frank McCarthy the train-master, and he skillfully cut off the scalp-lock and handed it to Billy, adding:

"Thar, thet is yer first scalp, boy, an' I'm willin' ter swear it won't be yer last, for Billy, you is ther boss boy I ever see."

Billy thanked McCarthy for the gory trophy, gave a slight shudder as he took it, and said significantly:

"I ain't so tired as I was, and I guess I'll keep up with you all now, for if the bank hadn't caved in that Injun would have had me."

At daylight they came in sight of Kearney, and after a volley or two at the Indians still dogging their steps, made for the fort and reached it in safety.

The commanding officer at once sent out a force in pursuit of the red-skins; but they neither found them or the cattle they had driven off.

After a short stay at Fort Kearney Billy returned with a train to Leavenworth, where the papers dubbed him the "Boy Indian-Killer," and made a hero of him for his exploit in the South Platte.

Helen Hunt Jackson

"Here is a picture of a helpless people!"

1881

Helen Hunt Jackson was born in Massachusetts, grew up with Emily Dickinson, and became the most prolific woman writer of her day. Her interest in federal treatment of Indians led her to publish *A Century of Dishonor* in 1881 and, three years later, her best-known work, *Ramona*, a novel. She sought to publicize the Indians' plight and hoped to do for Indians what Harriet Beecher Stowe had done for blacks. In the process she called Secretary of the Interior Carl Schurz a "blockhead" and was, in turn, labeled by Theodore Roosevelt a "foolish sentimentalist" who wrote "foul slanders." Unlike Roosevelt, Mrs. Jackson did not claim to be a historian. In this selection she discusses the Sioux.

The word Sioux is a contraction from the old French word "Nadouessioux," or "Enemies," the name given by the French traders to this most powerful and warlike of all the North-western tribes. They called themselves "Dakota," or "many in one," because so many bands under different names were joined together. At the time of Captain Carver's travels among the North American Indians there were twelve known bands of these "Nadouwessies." They entertained the captain most hospitably for seven months during the winter of 1766–'7: adopted him as one of their chiefs; and when the time came came for him to depart, three hundred of them ac-

From H. H. [Helen Hunt Jackson], *A Century of Dishonor: A Sketch of the United States Government's Dealings with Some of the Indian Tribes* (New York, Harper & Brothers, 1881), 136–43, 147–85.

companied him for a distance on his journey, and took leave with expressions of friendship for him, and good-will toward the Great Father, the English king, of whom he had told them. The chiefs wished him to say to the king "how much we desire that traders may be sent to abide among us with such things as we need, that the hearts of our young men, our wives, and children may be made glad. And may peace subsist between us so long as the sun, the moon, the earth, and the waters shall endure"; and "acquaint the Great King how much the Nadouwessies wish to be counted among his good children."

Nothing in all the history of the earliest intercourse between the friendly tribes of North American Indians and the Europeans coming among them is more pathetic than the accounts of their simple hospitality, their unstinted invitations, and their guileless expressions of desire for a greater knowledge of the white men's ways.

When that saintly old bigot, Father Hennepin, sailed up the Illinois River, in 1680, carrying his "portable chapel," chalice, and chasuble, and a few holy wafers "in a steel box, shut very close," going to teach the savages "the knowledge of the Captain of Heaven and Earth, and to use fire-arms, and several other things relating to their advantage," the Illinois were so terrified that, although they were several thousand strong, they took to flight "with horrid cries and howlings." On being reassured by signs and words of friendliness, they slowly returned—some, however, not until three or four days had passed. Then they listened to the good man's discourses with "great attention; afterward gave a great shout for joy," and "expressed a great gratitude"; and, the missionaries being footsore from long travel, the kindly creatures fell to rubbing their legs and feet "with oil of bears, and grease of wild oxen, which after much travel is an incomparable refreshment; and presented us some flesh to eat, putting the three first morsels into our mouths with great ceremonies."

It was a pity that Father Hennepin had no more tangible benefit than the doctrine of the "efficacy of the Sacraments" to communicate to the hospitable Illinois in return for their healing ointments. Naturally they did not appreciate this, and he proceeded on his way disheartened by their "brutish stupidity," but consoling himself, however, with the thought of the infants he had baptized. Hearing of the death of one of them, he says he is "glad it had pleased God to take this little Christian out of the world," and he attributed his own "preservation amidst the greatest dangers" afterward to "the care he took for its baptism." Those dangers were, indeed, by no means inconsiderable, as he and his party were taken prisoners by a roaming party of these Indians, called in the Father's quaint old book "Nadouwessians." He was forced to accompany them on their expeditions, and was in daily danger of being murdered by the more riotous and hostile members of the band. He found these savages on the whole "good-natured men, affable, civil, and obliging," and he was indebted for his life to the good-will of one of the chiefs, who protected him again and again at no inconsiderable danger to himself. The only evidence of religion among the Nadouwessies which he mentions is that they never began to smoke without first holding the pipe up to the sun, saying, "Smoke, sun!" They also offered to the sun the best part of every beast they killed, carrying it afterward to the cabin of their chief; from which Father Hennepin concluded that they had "a religious veneration for the sun."

The diplomatic relations between the United States Government and the Sioux began in the year 1815. In that year and the year following we made sixteen "treaties" of peace and friendship with different tribes of Indians—treaties demanding no cessions of land beyond the original grants which had been made by these tribes to the English, French, or Spanish governments, but confirming those to the United States; promising "perpetual peace," and declaring that "every injury or act of hostility committed by one or other of the contracting parties shall be mutually forgiven and forgot." Three of these treaties were made with bands of the Sioux—one of them with "the Sioux of the Leaf, the Sioux of the Broad Leaf, and the Sioux who shot in the Pine-tops."

In 1825 four more treaties were made with separate Sioux bands. By one of those treaties—that of Prairie du Chien—boundaries were defined between the Chippewas and the Sioux, and it was hoped that their incessant feuds might be brought to an end. This hostility had continued unabated from the time of the earliest travellers in the country, and the Sioux had been slowly but steadily driven south and west by the victorious Chippewas. A treaty could not avail very much toward keeping peace between such ancient enemies as these. Fighting went on as before; and white traders, being exposed to the attacks of all war-parties, suffered almost more than the Indians themselves. The Government consoled itself for this spectacle of bloody war, which it was powerless to prevent, by the thought that the Indians would "probably fight on until some one or other of the tribes shall become too reduced and feeble to carry on the war, when it will be lost as a separate power"—an equivocal bit of philosophizing which was unequivocally stated in these precise words in one of the annual reports of the War Department.

In the third Article of the next treaty, also at Prairie du Chien, in 1830, began the trouble which has been from that day to this a source of never ending misunderstanding and of many fierce outbreaks on the part of the Sioux. Four of the bands by this article ceded and relinquished to the United States "forever" a certain tract of country between the Mississippi and the Des Moines River. In this, and in a still further cession, two other bands of Sioux, who were not fully represented at the council, must join; also, some four or five other tribes. Landed and "undivided" estate, owned in common by dozens of families, would be a very difficult thing to parcel out and transfer among white men to-day, with the best that fair intentions and legal skill combined could do; how much more so in those days of unsurveyed forests, unexplored rivers, owned and occupied in common by dozens of bands of wild and ignorant Indians, to be communicated with only by interpreters. Misconstructions and disputes about boundaries would have been inevitable, even if there had been all possible fairmindedness and good-will on both sides; but in this case there was only unfairmindedness on one side, and unwillingness on the other. All the early makers of treaties with the Indians congratulated themselves and the United States on the getting of acres of valuable land by the million for next to nothing, and, as years went on, openly lamented that "the Indians were beginning to find out what lands were worth"; while the Indians, anxious, alarmed, hostile at heart, seeing themselves harder and harder pressed on all sides, driven "to provide other sources for supplying their wants besides those of hunting, which must soon entirely fail them," yielded mile after mile with increasing sense of loss, which they were powerless to prevent, and of resentment which it would have been worse than impolitic for them to show.

The first annuities promised to the Sioux were promised by this treaty—$3000 annually for ten years to the Yankton and Santee bands; to the other four, $2000. The Yankton and Santee bands were to pay out of their annuity $100 yearly to the Otoes, because part of some land which was reserved for the half-breeds of the tribe had originally belonged to the Otoes. "A blacksmith, at the expense of the United States; also, instruments for agricultural purposes; and iron and steel to the amount of $700 annually for ten years to some of the bands, and to the amount of $400 to the others; also, $3000 a year for educational purposes, and $3000 in presents distributed at the time," were promised them.

It was soon after these treaties that the artist Catlin made his famous journeys among the North American Indians, and gave to the world an invaluable contribution to their history, perpetuating in his pictures the distinctive traits of their faces and their dress, and leaving on record many pages of unassailable testimony as to their characteristics in their native state. He spent several weeks among the Sioux, and says of them: "There is no tribe on the continent of finer looking men, and few tribes who are better and more comfortably clad and supplied with the necessaries of life. * * * I have travelled several years already among these people, and I have not had my scalp taken, nor a blow struck me, nor had occasion to raise my hand against an Indian; nor has my property been stolen as yet to my knowledge to the value of a shilling, and that in a country where no man is punishable by law for the crime of stealing. * * * That the Indians in their native state are drunken, is false, for they are the only temperance people, literally speaking, that ever I saw in my travels, or expect to see. If the civilized world are startled at this, it is the fact that they must battle with, not with me. These people manufacture no spirituous liquor themselves, and know nothing of it until it is brought into their country, and tendered to them by Christians.

"That these people are naked, is equally untrue, and as easily disproved with the paintings I have made, and with their beautiful costumes which I shall bring home. I shall be able to establish the fact that many of these people dress not only with clothes comfortable for any latitude, but that they dress also with some considerable taste and elegance. * * * Nor am I quite sure that they are entitled to the name of 'poor' who live in a country of boundless green fields, with good horses to ride; where they are all joint tenants of the soil together; where the Great Spirit has supplied them with an abundance of food to eat."

Catlin found six hundred families of the Sioux camped at one time around Fort Pierre, at the mouth of the Teton River, on the west bank of the Missouri. There were some twenty bands, each with their chief, over whom was one superior chief, called Ha-won-je-tah (the One Horn), whose portrait is one of the finest in Catlin's book. This chief took his name, "One Horn," from a little shell which he wore always on his neck. This shell had descended to him from his father, and he said "he valued it more than anything which he possessed: affording a striking instance of the living affection which these people often cherish for the dead, inasmuch as he chose to carry this name through life in preference to many others and more honorable ones he had a right to have taken from different battles and exploits of his extraordinary life." He was the fleetest man in the tribe; "could run down a buffalo, which he had often done on his own legs, and drive his arrow to the heart."

This chief came to his death, several years later, in a tragic way. He had been in some way the accidental cause of the death of his only son—a very fine youth—and so great was the anguish of his mind at times that he became insane. In one of these moods he mounted his favorite war-horse, with his bow and arrows in his hand, and dashed off at full speed upon the prairies, repeating the most solemn oath that he would slay the first living thing that fell in his way, be it man or beast, friend or foe. No one dared follow him, and after he had been absent an hour or two his horse came back to the village with two arrows in its body covered with blood. Fears of the most serious kind were now entertained for the fate of the chief, and a party of warriors immediately mounted their horses and retraced the animal's tracks to the place of the tragedy, where they found the body of their chief horribly mangled and gored by a buffalo-bull, whose carcass was stretched by the side of him.

A close examination of the ground was then made by the Indians, who ascertained by the tracks that their unfortunate chief, under his unlucky resolve, had met a buffalo-bull in the season when they are very stubborn, and unwilling to run from any one, and had incensed the animal by shooting a number of arrows into him, which had brought him into furious combat. The chief had then dismounted and turned his horse loose, having given it a couple of arrows from his bow, which sent it home at full speed, and then had thrown away his bow and quiver, encountering the infuriated animal with his knife alone, and the desperate battle had resulted in the death of both. Many of the bones of the chief were broken, and his huge antagonist lay dead by his side, weltering in blood from a hundred wounds made by the chief's long and two-edged knife.

Had the provisions of these first treaties been fairly and promptly carried out, there would have been living to-day among the citizens of Minnesota thousands of Sioux families, good and prosperous farmers and mechanics, whose civilization would have dated back to the treaty of Prairie du Chien. . . .

In 1849 the "needs" of the white settlers on the east side of the Mississippi made it imperative that the Sioux should be again removed from their lands. "The desirable portions of Minnesota east of the Mississippi were already so occupied by a white population as to seem to render it absolutely necessary to obtain without delay a cession from the Indians on the west side of the river, for the accommodation of our citizens emigrating to that quarter, a large portion of whom would probably be compelled to precipitate themselves on that side of the Mississippi."

Commissioners were accordingly sent to treat with the Indians owning these desired lands. In the instructions given to these commissioners there are some notable sentences: "Though the proposed purchase is estimated to contain some twenty millions of acres, and some of it no doubt of excellent quality," there are "sound reasons why it is comparatively valueless to the Indians, and a large price should not be paid for it." Alive to the apparent absurdity of the statement that lands which are "absolutely necessary" for white farmers are "comparatively valueless" to Indians whom the Government is theoretically making every effort to train into farmers, and who have for the last ten years made appreciable progress in that direction, the commissioner adds, "With respect to its being valuable to the United States, it is more so for the purpose of making room for our emigrating citizens than for any other; and only a small part of it is now actually necessary for that object.*** The extent of the proposed cession should be no criterion of the amount that should be paid for it. On a full consideration of the whole matter, it is the opinion of this office that from two to two and a half cents an acre would be an ample equivalent for it." Some discretion is left to the commissioners as to giving more than this if the Indians are "not satisfied;" but any such increase of price must be "based on such evidence and information as shall fully satisfy the President and Senate."

Reading farther on in these instructions, we come at last to the real secret of this apparent niggardliness on the part of the Government. It is not selfishness at all; it is the purest of philanthropy. The Government has all along been suffering in mind from two conflicting desires—"the desire to give these Indians an equivalent for their possessions," and, on the other hand, "the well-ascertained fact that no greater curse can be inflicted on a tribe so little civilized as the Sioux than to have large sums of money coming to them as annuities."*** On the whole, the commissioner says that we are called on, "as a matter of humanity and duty toward this helpless race, to make every exertion in our power not to place much money at their discretion." The Government is beginning very well in this direction, it must be admitted, when it proposes to pay for Mississippi Valley lands in Minnesota only two and a half cents per acre. "Humanity and duty" allied could hardly do more at one stroke than that.

We cannot ascribe to the same philanthropy, however, the withholding from 1837 to 1850 the $3000 a year which the treaty of 1837 provided should be expended "annually" as the President might direct, and which was not expended at all, because President after President directed that it should be applied to educational purposes; and there being no evident and easy way of expending it in that manner, it was allowed to accumulate, until in 1850 it amounted, according to the report of Governor Ramsey, of Minnesota, to $50,000. The governor also thinks better than the United States Government does of the country to be relinquished this year by the Sioux. He says that it will be "settled with great rapidity, possessing as it does from its situation considerable prospective commercial as well as agricultural advantages." It was evidently very cheap at two and a half cents an acre.

In this same code of instructions by the Indian Bureau there is a record of another instance of the Government's disregard of treaty stipulations. At the time of the treaty of Prairie du Chien, in 1850, the Sioux chiefs had requested that a certain tract be set apart and bestowed upon the half-breeds of their nation. This was provided for in the ninth Article of that treaty; but the Government refused to give to the half-breeds any title to this land, except "in the same manner as other Indian titles are held." It was agreed, however, that the President might "assign to any of said half-breeds, to be held by him or them in fee-simple, any portion of said tract not exceeding a section of six hundred and forty acres to an individual." This tract of land was known as the "Half-breed Reservation on Lake Tepin."

The half-breeds had made almost unintermitting efforts to have these assignments made, but the Government had as constantly refused to do it. The Indian Bureau now assigns two reasons why this treaty stipulation was never fulfilled: 1st, that "the half-breeds, or most of them, would be speculated upon by designing persons, and cheated out of their reservations;" 2d, that, "on account of the quality of the lands, some would necessarily have much better reservations than others, which would engender dissatisfaction and heart-burning among themselves as well as against the United States." The Bureau felicitates itself that "the only title they now have to this land, therefore, is that by which other Indians hold their lands, viz., the occupant or usufruct right, and this they enjoy by the permission of the United States." Such being the case, and as the Government would properly never find it expedient and advisable to make the assignment referred to, this tract, whatever may be the character of the land, must be and would continue comparatively worthless to them.

Nevertheless, it appears that in 1841 one of the three treaties made with the Sioux, but not ratified, was with these very half-breeds for this same "valueless" tract of 384,000 acres of land; that they were to be paid $200,000 for it, and also to be paid for all the improvements they had made on it; and that the treaty commissioners are still instructed "to allow them for it now whatever sum the commissioners deem it to be" fairly worth; "under no circum-

stances," however, "to exceed the sum stipulated in 1841." Putting
this all into plain English, it simply means that in 1830 the Government promised to let a band of men take out tracts of land in fee-
simple, and settle down like other men on their homesteads; that for
ten years the men begged to do so, and were refused; that at the end
of ten years, thinking there was no hope of anything better, they
agreed to sell the whole tract back to the Government for $200,000;
that this bargain, also, the Government did not fulfil (the treaties
never being ratified), and nine years later was found congratulating
itself on the fact that, by reason of all these unfulfilled agreements,
the land was still "held only in the same manner as other Indian titles
are held"—*i.e.*, not "held" at all—only used on sufferance of the Government, and could be taken possession of at any time at the Government's pleasure. (This matter was supposed to be finally settled in
1854 by a law of Congress; but in 1856 the thing appears to have
been still unsettled. A commission had been sent out to investigate it,
and the report was that "the subject has been one of some difficulty
and intricacy; but the final report of the commissioners has just been
received, and steps will be taken at once to cause the scrip to issue to
the parties entitled thereto.")

A little farther on in this same notable document is a mention
of another tract, of which it is now "desirable to extinguish the title."
This was set apart by the tenth Article of the same old treaty for the
half-breeds of the Omahas, Otoes, Iowas, and Yankton and Santee
Sioux. This contains about 143,000 acres, but is "supposed to be of
much less value than that on Lake Tepin:" much less value than
"valueless;" but the "amount to be paid for it is left to the discretion"
of the commissioners.

At this time the bands of the Medewakanton Sioux were occupying a tract of over two hundred miles along the west shore of the
Mississippi, reaching also some twenty-five miles up the St. Peter's.
The Yanktons, Santees, and the other bands lived high up the St.
Peter's, reaching over into the lands west of the Missouri, out of
reach of ordinary facilities of intercourse. These bands were often
in great distress for food, owing to the failure of the buffalo. They
never lost an occasion to send imploring messages to the Great
Father, urging him to help him. They particularly ask for hoes, that
they may plant corn. In his report for 1850 the superintendent of the

territory embracing these Indians says: "The views of most of those who have lived the longest among the Indians agree in one respect—that is, that no great or beneficial change can take place in their condition until the General Government has made them amenable to local laws—laws which will punish the evil-disposed, and secure the industrious in their property and individual rights."

Superintendents, agents, commissioners, secretaries, all reiteratedly recommending this one simple and necessary step toward civilization—the Indians themselves by hundreds imploring for titles to their farms, or at least "hoes"—why did the United States Government keep on and on in its obstinate way, feeding the Indian in gross and reckless improvidence with one hand, plundering him with the other, and holding him steadily down at the level of his own barbarism? Nay, forcing him below it by the newly added vices of gambling and drunkenness, and yet all the while boasting of its desire to enlighten, instruct, and civilize him. It is as inexplicable as it is infamous: a phenomenal thing in the history of the world.

In the summer of 1851 the desired treaties were made, the upper and lower bands of Sioux being treated with separately at Traverse de Sioux and at Mendota. The upper bands were soon disposed of, though "some few of them, having been taught to read," had become impressed with the idea that their country was of immense value, and at first demanded six million dollars for the lands to be ceded. The treaty with the lower bands—the Medawakantons and Wahpacootas—was "exceedingly difficult of attainment" on account of, firstly, "their proximity to the flourishing settlements on the east side of the Mississippi producing necessarily frequent contact with the whites, whose ideas of the great value of the country had been imparted to these Indians; secondly, their great experience in Indian diplomacy, being in the enjoyment already of liberal annuities under former stipulations"—all these things rendered them as "indifferent to the making of another treaty at present as the whites on their borders were anxious that their lands should he acquired." In consequence of this indomitable common-sense on the part of the Indians the sessions of the commissioners were tedious and long; not until a month had passed did they prevail on these Indians to sign away the coveted lands, "the garden-spot of the Mississippi Valley," and they were obliged to more than treble the number of cents per acre which they had been instructed to pay. For thirty-five millions of acres of land they agreed to pay nominally $3,075,000, which would be between eight and nine cents an acre. But as $2,500,000 was to be held in trust, and only the interest at five per cent to be paid to the Indians, and this only for the term of fifty years, at which time the principal was to revert to the Government, it will be easily reckoned that the Indians would receive, all told, only about six and one-quarter cents an acre. And taking into account the great value of the relinquished lands, and the price the Government would undoubtedly obtain for them, it will be readily conceded that Governor Ramsey was not too sanguine when he stated, in his report to the Interior Department, that the "actual cost to the Government of this magnificent purchase is only the sum paid in hand" ($575,000).

The governor says that it was "by no means the purpose" of the commission "to act other than justly and generously toward the Indians;" that "a continuation of the payment of large sums of interest annually would do them no further good" after fifty years had expired, and would be "inconsistent with sound governmental policy." He says that the Dakota nation, although warlike, is "friendly to the whites," and that it may be reasonably expected that, "by a judicious expenditure of the civilization and improvement funds provided for in these treaties," they will soon take the lead "in agriculture and other industrial pursuits."

One of the provisions of this treaty forbade the introduction of ardent spirits into the new reservation. This was put in in accordance with the "earnest desire" of the chiefs, who requested that "some stringent measures should be taken by the Government to exclude all kinds of liquors from their new home."

By this treaty the four great bands of Minnesota Sioux were all to be "consolidated together on one reservation in the upper part of the Mississippi Valley." This region was thought to be "sufficiently remote to guarantee" them against any pressure from the white population for many years to come. Farms were to be opened for them, mills and schools to be established, and dwelling-houses erected. They were to have now a chance to own "that domestic country called home, with all the living sympathies and all the future hopes and projects which people it." From this time "a new era was to be dated in the history of the Dakotas: an era full of brilliant promise." The tract of territory relinquished by them was "larger than the State of New York, fertile and beautiful beyond description," far the best part of Minnesota. It is "so far diversified in natural advantages that its productive powers may be considered almost inexhaustible.***Probably no tract on the surface of the globe is equally well watered.***A large part is rich arable land; portions are of unsurpassed fertility, and eminently adapted to the production in incalculable quantities of the cereal grains. The boundless plains present inexhaustible fields of patronage, and the river bottoms are richer than the banks of the Nile. In the bowels of the earth there is every indication of extensive mineral fields."

It would seem that the assertion made only a few lines before this glowing paragraph—"to the Indians themselves the broad regions which have been ceded are of inconsiderable value"—could not be true. It would seem that for eight thousand people, who, according to this same writer, "have outlived in a great degree the means of subsistence of the hunter state," and must very soon "resort to the pursuits of agriculture," nothing could have been more fortunate than to have owned and occupied thirty-five millions of acres of just such land as this.

They appear to be giving already some evidence of a disposition to turn this land to account. The reports from the different farms and schools show progress in farming industry and also in study. The farming is carried on with difficulty, because there are only a few carts and ploughs, which must be used in turn by the different farmers, and therefore must come to some quite too late to be of use, and there is much quarrelling among them owing to this trouble. Nevertheless, these bands have raised over four thousand bushels of corn in the year. There is also a great opposition to the schools, because the Indians have been told that the accumulated fifty thousand dollars which is due to them would be paid to them in cash if it were not for the schools. Nevertheless, education is slowly progressing; in this year fifty copies of a little missionary paper called *The Dakota Friend* were subscribed for in the one mission station of Lac qui Parle, and sixty scholars were enrolled at the school. The blacksmith at St. Peter's reports that he has made during the year 2506 pieces of one sort and another for the Indians, and repaired 1430 more. Evidently a community keeping blacksmiths so busy as this are by no means wholly idle themselves.

It is worth while to dwell upon these seemingly trivial details at this point in the history of the Minnesota Sioux, because they are all significant to mark the point in civilization they had already reached, and the disposition they had already shown toward industry before they were obliged to submit to their first great removal. Their condition at the end of two years from the ratification of these treaties is curtly told in the official reports of the Indian Bureau:

"The present situation of that portion of the Sioux Indians parties to the treaties of July 23d and August 5th, 1851, is peculiar, unfortunate, and to them must prove extremely injurious. By these treaties they reluctantly parted with a very large extent of valuable country, which it was of the greatest importance to the Government to acquire. An insignificant portion of it near its western boundary, not deemed necessary or desirable for a white population for many years, if at all, was agreed to be reserved and assigned to them for their future residence. The Senate amended the treaties, striking out this provision, allowing ten cents an acre in lieu of the reservations, and requiring the President, with the assent of the Indians, if they agreed to the amendments, to assign them such tracts of country, beyond the limits of that ceded, as might be satisfactory for their future home. To the amendments was appended a proviso 'that the President may, by the consent of the Indians, vary the conditions aforesaid, if deemed expedient.' The Indians were induced to agree to the amendments; 'confiding in the justice, liberality, and humanity of the President and the Congress of the United States, that such tracts of country will be set apart for their future occupancy and home as will be to them acceptable and satisfactory.' Thus, not only was the assent of the Indians made necessary to a country being assigned to them without the limits of that ceded, but, by the authority given to the President to vary the conditions of the amendments to the treaties, he was empowered, with the consent of the Indians, to place them upon the designated reservations, or upon any other portion of the ceded territory, 'if deemed expedient.'

"To avoid collisions and difficulties between the Indians and the white population which rapidly commenced pouring into the ceded country, it became necessary that the former should vacate at least a large portion of it without delay, while there was neither the time nor the means to make the requisite explorations to find a suitable location for them beyond the limits of the cession.

"Under these pressing and embarrassing circumstances the late President determined to permit them to remain five years on the designated reservations, if they were willing to accept this alternative. They assented, and many of them have been already removed. However unavoidable this arrangement, it is a most unfortunate one. The Indians are fully aware of its temporary character, and of the uncertainty as to their future position, and will consequently be disinclined and deterred from any efforts to make themselves comfortable and improve their condition. The inevitable result must be that, at the end of the time limited, they will be in a far worse condition than now, and the efforts and expenditures of years to infuse into them a spirit of improvement will all have been in vain.

"The large investments in mills, farms, mechanic shops, and other improvements required by the treaties to be made for their benefit, will be entirely wasted if the Indians are to remain on their reservations only during the prescribed five years. At the very period when they would begin to reap the full advantage of these beneficial provisions they would have to remove. Another unfortunate feature of this arrangement, if temporary, is that the Indians will have expended the considerable sums set apart in the treaties for the expenses of their removal to a permanent home, and for subsistence until they could otherwise provide it, leaving nothing for these important and necessary purposes in the event of another emigration. In view of these facts and considerations, no time should be lost in determining upon some final and permanent arrangement in regard to them."

The Governor of Minnesota also writes at this time: "The doubtful tenure by which this tribe hold their supposed reservation is well understood by their chiefs and headmen, and is beginning to give deep dissatisfaction, and throwing daily more and more obstacles in the way of their removal. This reservation will not be wanted for white men for many years.

"There is not wood, or timber, or coal sufficient for the purposes of civilization, except immediately on the St. Peter's and its tributaries. From near the vicinity of the new agency there commences a vast prairie of more than one hundred miles in extent, entirely destitute of timber, and I feel confident that we never shall be able to keep any very large number of them at their new agency, or near there.

"Already the fund set apart for the removal and subsistence the first year of the Sissetons and Wah-pa-tons has been expended, and all their provisions eaten up. Seventeen thousand dollars and upward have been expended by Governor Ramsey, and one year in advance of the time fixed by the treaty for their removal. This expenditure was made while he was getting them to sign the Senate amendments to the treaty of 1851, which they were very reluctant to do, and which not more than half the chiefs have signed. These Indians want the Government to confirm this reservation to them. I would recommend that this be done as the only means to satisfy them, and humanity demands it."

Here is a picture of a helpless people! Forced to give up the "garden-spot of the State," and accept in its stead an "insignificant tract, on the greater part of which there is not wood, or timber, or coal sufficient for civilization;" and then, before the ink of this treaty is dry, told that even from this insignificant tract they must promise to move at the end of five years. What words could characterize such a transaction between man and man? There is not a country, a people, a community in which it would be even attempted! Was it less base, or more, being between a strong government and a feeble race?

From the infamy of accomplishing this purpose the United States was saved. Remonstrances, and still more the resistance of the Indians, prevailed, and in 1854 we find the poor creatures expressing "much satisfaction" that the President has decreed that they are to remain permanently on their "insignificant tract."

The Upper Missouri Sioux are still suffering and destitute; a few of them cultivating little patches of ground, depending chiefly on the chase, and on roots and wild berries; when these resources fail there is nothing left for them but to starve, or to commit depredations on white settlers. Some of the bands, nevertheless, have scrupulously observed the stipulations of the Fort Laramie treaty in 1851, show a "strong desire for improvement," and are on the most friendly terms with the whites. These peaceable and friendly bands are much distressed, as well they may be, at the reckless course pursued by others of their tribe. They welcome the presence of the soldiers sent to chastise the offenders, and gladly render all the service to them they can, even against their relatives and friends.

In 1855 it is stated that "various causes have combined to prevent the Minnesota Sioux from deriving, heretofore, much substantial benefit from the very liberal provisions of the treaties of 1851. Until after the reservations were permanently assured to the Indians (1854) it would have been highly improper to have made the expenditures for permanent improvements, and since then the affairs of the agency have not been free from confusion."

"Large sums of money have been expended for these Sioux, but they have been indolent, extravagant, intemperate, and have wasted their means without improving, or seeming to desire to improve their condition."

Both these statements are made in grave good faith; certainly without any consciousness of their bearing on each other. It is not stated, however, what specific means the Sioux could have employed "to improve their condition," had they "desired" to do so.

The summer of 1857 was one which will long be remembered by the citizens of Minnesota. It was opened by terrible massacres, which were all the work of a strolling outcast band of Sioux, not more than fifteen in number. They had been driven out of their tribe some sixteen years previous, and had been ever since then leading a wandering and marauding life. The beginning of the trouble was a trivial difficulty between one of the white settlers on Rock River and an Indian. The settler's dog bit the Indian, and the Indian shot the dog. For this the white settlers beat the Indian severely, and then went to the camp and by force took away all the guns of the band. This was at a season of the year when to be without guns meant simply to be without food, and the Indians were reduced at once to a condition of great suffering. By some means they either repossessed themselves of their guns or procured others, and, attacking the settlement, killed all the inhabitants except four women, whom they carried away with them, and treated with the utmost barbarity. The inevitable results of such horrors followed. The thousands of peaceable Indians in Minnesota, who did not even know of this outrage, were all held in one common terror and hatred by the general public; only the very great firmness and discretion of the military officers sent to deal with the outbreak saved Minnesota from a general uprising and attack from all the Sioux bands, who were already in a state of smouldering discontent by reason of the non-payment of their annuities. However, they obeyed the demands of the Government that they themselves should pursue this offending band, and either capture or exterminate it. They killed four, and took three prisoners, and then returned "much jaded and worn," and said they could do no more without the help of United States soldiers; and that they thought they had now done enough to show their loyalty, and to deserve the payment of their annuities. One of the chiefs said: "The man who killed white people did not belong to us, and we did not expect to be called to account for the people of another band. We have always tried to do as our Great Father tells us." Another said: "I am going to speak of the treaty. For fifty years we were to be paid $50,000 per annum. We were also promised $300,000 that we have not seen. I wish to say to my Great Father we were promised these things, but have not seen them yet. Why does not the Great Father do as he promised?"

These hostilities were speedily brought to an end, yet the situation was by no means reassuring for the Indians. But one sentiment seemed to inspire the whole white population, and this was the desire to exterminate the entire Indian race.

"For the present," writes the superintendent, "it is equally important to protect the Indians from the whites as the whites from the Indians;" and this in spite of the fact that all the leading bands of the treaty Sioux had contributed warriors to go in pursuit of the murderers, had killed or captured all they could find, and stood ready to go again after the remaining eight, if the United States troops would go also and assist them. Spite of the exertions of one of the chiefs of the Lower Sioux, "Little Crow," who, the superintendent says, labored with him "night and day in organizing the party, riding continually between the lower and upper agencies," so that they "scarcely slept" till the war-party had set out on the track of the murderers; spite of the fact that the whole body of the Sioux, without exception, "received the intelligence with as much indignation and disapprobation as the whites themselves, and did their best to stand clear of any suspicion of or connection with the affair—spite of all this, they were in continual danger of being shot at sight by the terrified and unreasoning settlers. One band, under the chief Sleepy Eyes, were returning to their homes from a hunt; and while they were "wondering what the panic among the whites meant" (they having heard nothing of the massacre), were fired into by some of the militia volunteers.

The next day a white settler was found killed near that spot—presumably by some member of Sleepy Eyes' band. This excitement slowly abated, and for the next four years a steady improvement was visible in the Minnesota Sioux. Hundreds of them threw aside the blanket—the distinctive badge of their wild state; schools were well attended, and farms were well tilled. That there was great hostility to this civilization, on the part of the majority of the tribe, cannot be denied; but that was only natural—the inevitable protest of a high-spirited and proud race against abandoning all its race distinctions. When we see the men of Lorraine, or of Montenegro, ready to die for the sake merely of being called by the name of one power rather than by that of another, we find it heroic, and give them our sympathies; but when the North American Indian is ready to die rather than wear the clothes and follow the ways of the white man, we feel for him only unqualified contempt, and see in his instinct nothing more than a barbarian's incapacity to appreciate civilization. Is this just?

In 1861 the Commissioner of Indian Affairs, visiting these Sioux, reports: "I was much surprised to find so many of the Sioux Indians wearing the garb of civilization, many of them living in frame or brick houses, some of them with stables or out-houses, and their fields indicating considerable knowledge of agriculture." Their condition, he says, afford "abundant evidence of what may be accomplished among the Sioux Indians by steadily adhering to a uniform, undeviating policy.

"The number that live by agricultural pursuits is yet small compared with the whole; but their condition is so much better than that of the wild Indian, that they, too, are becoming convinced that it is the better way to live; and many are coming in, asking to have their hair cut, and for a suit of clothes, and to be located on a piece of land where they can build a house and fence in their fields."

Many more of them would have entered on the agricultural life had the Government provided ways and means for them to do so. In this same report is a mention of one settlement of two thousand Indians at Big Stone Lake, who "have been hitherto almost entirely neglected. These people complain that they have lived upon promises for the last ten years, and are really of opinion that white men never perform what they promise. Many of them would go to work if they had any reasonable encouragement."

The annuities are still in arrears. Every branch of the industries and improvements attempted suffers for want of the promised funds, and from delays in payments expected. The worst result, however, of these delays in the fulfilment of treaty stipulations was the effect on the Indians. A sense of wrong in the past and distrust for the future was ever deepening in their minds, and preparing them to be suddenly thrown by any small provocation into an antagonism and hostility grossly disproportionate to the apparent cause. This was the condition of the Minnesota Sioux in the summer of 1862.

The record of the massacres of that summer is scarcely equalled in the history of Indian wars. Early in August some bands of the Upper Sioux, who had been waiting at their agency nearly two months for their annuity payments, and had been suffering greatly for food during that time—so much so that "they dug up roots to appease their hunger, and when corn was turned out to them they devoured it uncooked, like wild animals"—became desperate, broke into the Government warehouse, and took some of the provisions stored there. This was the real beginning of the outbreak, although the first massacre was not till the 18th. When that began, the friendly Indians were powerless to resist—in fact, they were threatened with their lives if they did not join. Nevertheless, some of them rescued whole families, and carried them to places of safety; others sheltered and fed women and children in their own lodges; many fled, leaving all their provisions behind—as much victims of the outbreak as the Minnesota people themselves. For three days the hostile bands, continually re-enforced, went from settlement to settlement, killing and plundering. A belt of country nearly two hundred miles in length and about fifty in width was entirely abandoned by the population, who flocked in panic to the towns and forts. Nearly a thousand were killed—men, women and children—and nameless outrages were committed on many. Millions of dollars' worth of property were destroyed. The outbreak was quickly quelled by military force, and a large number of Indians captured. Many voluntarily surrendered, bringing with them over two hundred whites that they had taken prisoners. A military commission tried these Indians, and sentenced over three hundred to be hung. All but thirty-nine were reprieved and put into prison. The remainder were moved to Dakota, to a barren desert, where for three years they endured sufferings far worse than death. The remainder escaped to the Upper Missouri region or to Canada.

Minnesota, at a terrible cost to herself and to the United States Government, was at last free from the presence of Indians within her borders—Indians who were her enemies only because they had been treated with injustice and bad faith.

During this time the bands of Sioux in the Upper Missouri region had been more or less hostile, and military force in continual requisition to subdue them. Re-enforced by the Minnesota refugees, they became more hostile still, and in the summer of 1863 were in almost incessant conflict. In 1864 the Governor of Dakota Territory writes to the Department that the war is spreading into Nebraska and Kansas, and that if provision is not made for the loyal treaty Indians in that region before long, they also will join the hostiles. One band of the Sioux—the Yanktons—has been persistently loyal, and rendered great service through all the troubles. Fifty of these Yankton Sioux had been organized by General Sibley into a company of scouts ,and had proved "more effective than twice the number of white soldiers." The only cost to the Government "of this service on the part of the Yanktons had been fifty suits of condemned artillery uniforms, arms, and rations in part to the scouts themselves."

In 1865 the Government, having spent about $40,000,000 on these campaigns, began to cast about for cheaper, if not more humane methods, and, partly at the instance of the Governor of Dakota, who knew very well that the Indians desired peace, sent out a commission to treat with them. There were now, all told, some 14,000 Sioux in this region, nearly 2000 being the refugees from Minnesota.

The report of this commission is full of significant statements. There seems to be no doubt that the great majority of the Indians are anxious for peace; but they are afraid to meet the agents of the Government, lest they be in some way betrayed. Such bands as are represented, however, gladly assent to a treaty of peace and good-will. The commissioners speak with great feeling of the condition of the loyal Yanktons. "No improvements have been made on their lands, and the commissioners were obliged to issue provisions to them to keep them from starving.* * *No crops met the eye, nor is there the semblance of a school-house."

Yet by Article four of the treaty with the Yankton Sioux the United States Government had agreed to expend $10,000 in erecting a suitable building or buildings, and to establish and maintain one or more normal labor schools; and it is to be read in the United States Statutes at Large that in each of the years 1860, 1861, 1862, and 1863, Congress appropriated $65,000, as per treaty, for the bene-fit of the Yankton Sioux.

"With the exception of a few miserable huts, a saw-mill, and a small amount of land enclosed, there are few vestiges of improve-ment.* * *They are reduced to the necessity of hunting for a living, and, unless soon reassured and encouraged, they will be driven to despair, and the great discontent existing among them will culmi-nate in another formidable Indian war."

Nine treaties were concluded by this commission with as many different bands of Sioux, the Indians pledging themselves to abstain from all hostilities with each other and with the whites, and the Government agreeing to pay to the Indians fifteen dollars a head per annum, and to all who will settle down to farming twenty-five dollars a head.

In the winter following these treaties all these Indians faithfully kept their promises, in spite of terrible sufferings from cold and from lack of food. Some of them were at the old Crow Creek Reservation in Dakota, where they were "kept from absolute starvation only by the issue to them of such scanty supplies as could be spared from the stores at Fort Sully, and from the agency." It is much to the credit of these Indians that, in spite of their manifold sufferings, scarcely a case of stealing occurred among them, they being determined to keep their faith to the Government.

"They will run like chickens to gather the offal from the slop buckets that are carried from the garrison kitchens; while they pass a pile of corn and hundreds of loose cattle without touching a thing, except when told they may gather up the grains of corn from the ground where the rats in their depredations have let it fall from the sacks," says the report of one of the commissioners.

In the summer of 1865 still further treaties were concluded with the Indians of the plains, and all the Sioux, with the exception of those in the British possessions, were now pledged to peace. This summer also saw the first recognition on the part of the Government of its flagrant injustice toward the friendly Minnesota Sioux who were moved to Crow Creek, Dakota, at the time of the massacre. There were nearly one thousand of these—mostly old men, women, and children—many of them the widows and children of those who had been hung or were in prison at Davenport. For three years they had been "quiet and patient in their sufferings."

The two hundred prisoners in Davenport had also shown "an excellent disposition and entire submission," although many of them were known and proved to have been "absolutely guiltless of any acts of hostility; and not only this, but deserving of reward for the rescue of white captives." Certificates, petitions, and letters showing these facts were forwarded from Iowa to the Department, but the commissioner says, in his report for 1866, that "they have been mislaid in their passage through the various departments, and cannot be found!"

There was still another class of these Indians deserving of help from the Government—some two hundred and fifty friendly farmer Indians, who were living in 1862 quietly on their farms, "who have acted as scouts for the Government; who never committed any acts of hostility, nor fled with those who did commit them," and have still remained friendly through these four years," while compelled to a vagabond life by the indiscriminate confiscation of all their land and property."

"The crops belonging to these farmer Indians were valued at $125,000, and they had large herds of stock of all kinds, fine farms, and improvements. The United States troops engaged in suppressing the massacre, also the prisoners taken by them—in all, some 3500 men—lived for fifty days on this property."

Strong efforts were made by Bishop Whipple and others to obtain from the Government some aid for these friendly Indians, and the sum of $7500 was appropriated by Congress for that purpose. The letter of Bishop Whipple, who was requested to report on the division of this sum, is so eloquent a summing up of the case of these Indians, that it ought to be placed on permanent record in the history of our country. He writes:

"There is positive injustice in the appropriation of so miserable a pittance.* * *A much larger sum would not pay the amount which we honestly owe these men. The Government was the trustee of the Upper and Lower Sioux. It held several millions of dollars for their benefit— the joint property of the tribes. These friendly Sioux had abandoned their wild life, and adopted the dress, habits, and customs of civilization; and in doing this, which placed them in open opposition to the traditions of their tribes, they were pledged the protection of the Government. By a mistaken policy, by positive neglect to provide a government, by the perversion of funds due them for the sale of one-half their reservations, by withholding their annuities until two months after they were due (which was caused by the use of a part of these funds for claims), by permitting other causes of dissatisfaction to go on unheeded, we provoked the hostility of the wild Indians, and it went on until it ripened in massacre. These farmer Indians had been pledged a patent for their farms: unless we violated our solemn pledge, these lands were theirs by a title as valid as any title could be. They had large crops, sufficient to support General Sibley's army for a number of weeks. They lost all they had—crops, stock, clothing, furniture. In addition to this, they were deprived of their share in these annuities, and for four years have lived in very great suffering. You can judge whether $5000 shall be deemed a just reward for the bravery and fidelity of men who, at the risk of their own lives, were instrumental in saving white captives, and maintained their friendship to the whites.

"I submit to you, sir, and through you hope to reach all who fear God and love justice, whether the very least we can do for all the friendly Sioux is not to fulfil the pledges we made years ago, and give to each of them a patent of eighty acres of land, build them a house, and provide them cattle, seeds, and implements of husbandry?"

In 1866 all these Sioux were removed, and, in spite of the protestations of the Nebraska citizens, settled on reservations on the

Niobrara River, in Northern Nebraska. It soon became evident that this place was undesirable for a reservation, both on account of its previous occupancy by the whites and scarcity of timber.

In the fall they removed again to the month of Bazile Creek. Temporary buildings were again erected, and here they spent the winters of 1866 and 1867. In February they were cheered by the invitation sent their chiefs and headmen to visit Washington. They went, feeling sure that they should get a home for themselves and people. "All they got was a promise that a commission should be sent out to visit them the next year." They were told, however, to move to Breckenridge, on the west bank of the Missouri, plant crops there, and were promised that, if they liked the place, they should have it "secured to them as a permanent home." Accordingly, the "agency buildings" were once more removed, and two hundred acres of land were planted. Before the crops were harvested the commission arrived, and urged the Indians to move farther up the Missouri. The Indians being averse to this, however, they were allowed to remain, and told that if they would cultivate the soil like white men—take lands in severalty—the Government would assist them. The Indians gladly consented to this, and signed a treaty to that effect. But in 1868 their agent writes: "That treaty is not yet ratified, and, instead of assistance to open farms, their appropriation has been cut down one half. After paying for supplies purchased on credit last year, it is entirely insufficient for clothing and subsistence, and leaves nothing for opening farms, procuring cattle," etc. These Indians, only five years previous, had been living on good farms, and had $125,000 worth of stock, implements, etc. No wonder their agent writes: "Leave them without a home a few years longer, and you offer strong inducements for them to become idle and worthless."

It is an intricate and perplexing task to attempt now to follow the history of the different bands of the Sioux tribe through all their changes of location and affiliation—some in Dakota, some in Nebraska, and some on the Upper Arkansas with the hostile Cheyennes and Arapahoes—signing treaties one summer, and on the war-path the next—promised a home in spring, and ordered off it before harvest—all the time more and more hemmed in by white settlers, and more and more driven out of their buffalo ranges by emigrations—

liable at any time to have bodies of United States soldiers swoop down on them and punish whole bands for depredations committed by a handful of men, perhaps of a totally distinct band—the wonder is not that some of them were hostile and vindictive, but that any of them remained peaceable and friendly. Bandied about from civil authorities to military—the War Department recommending "that all Indians not on fixed reservations be considered at war," and proceeded against accordingly, and the Interior Department neglecting to provide them with "fixed reservations," or to define or enforce the boundaries of even their temporary reservations—tricked, cheated on all sides—starving half the time—there is not a tribe of all the persecuted tribes of Indians that has a more piteous record than the Sioux. Neverthless, we find many of the bands, in 1870, advancing in civilization. In the Yankton band nearly one hundred children are in school, and eight hundred acres of land are under cultivation. The Lower Yanktons are peaceful and quiet, although they are near the Brulés, who are always roving and hostile. The Sissetons and Wahpetons, who were by a treaty of 1867 placed on reservations in Dakota, are "industrious, and fast advancing in agricultural pursuits." Four schools are in operation among them. The Yanktons are "anxious to farm, and state that the Government has promised to assist and teach them to farm; that they are and have been ready for some time, but as yet the agent has not received any instructions or funds to permit of their accomplishing their desire."

Two events, important in the history of the Sioux tribe, happened in 1869 and 1870. One was the visit of a delegation of chiefs and headmen from several of the bands, under the leadership of the chief Red Cloud, to Washington, Philadelphia, and New York. They had thus an opportunity of relating all their grievances, and of receiving the Government's declarations of good intentions toward them. Red Cloud, after his return home, became an ardent and determined advocate of peace and loyalty. The other was the withdrawal of a portion of the Santee Sioux from their band, for the purpose of taking up farms under the Homestead Act, and becoming independent citizens. The story of this experiment, and the manner in which it was met by the United States Government, is best told in the words of Dr. Williamson, a missionary, who had lived thirty-five years among them, and who pleaded thus warmly for them in a letter addressed to the Department in the summer of 1870: "Several considerations have influenced the Dakotas in going to the Big Sioux River: 1st. The soil and climate are more similar to that to which they have been accustomed in Minnesota, their former home, than is that of their reservation on the Missouri; 2d. Feeling that they were men capable of sustaining themselves if a fair opportunity is afforded them, they felt that it was degrading to live as sinecures and pensioners dependent on Government for food and clothing; 3d. And chiefly a desire to make homes for their families where they could be subjected to, and protected by, the laws of the United States, the same as all other men are. This they thought could not be the case on their reservation.

"These Sioux were parties to the treaties made in 1851, by which they and other bands ceded to the United States all the best settled parts of Minnesota west of the Mississippi for less than one-hundredth part of its present value, and much less than the lands were worth to them as hunting-grounds. And while as hunters they needed no protection of the law, they knew that as agriculturists they could not live without it; and they positively refused to sell their hunting-grounds till the Commissioner of the United States promised that they should be protected in their persons and property the same as white men. Government never accorded to them this protection, which, in the view of the Indians, was a very important consideration in selling the lands. This neglect on the part of the Government led to yearly complaints, and the massacres of 1862.*** These Sioux were most of them previous to the war living in comfortable homes, with well-cultivated farms and teams," and were receiving by annuity provisions, either in money or the equivalent, about $50 a head annually, from interest on their money invested in the bonds of the Government. These Indians, in taking up their new homesteads, were required by the Department to renounce, on oath, all claims on the United States for annuities. Without doubt, citizenship of the United States, the protection of our laws, is worth a great sum; but is it wise or right in our Government to require these natives of the country to purchase, at a price of several thousands of dollars, that which is given without money or price to every immigrant from Asia, Europe, or Africa that asks for it?

"Besides their annuities, there is due them from the Government the proceeds of the sale of their old reservation on the Minnesota River, which is more than forty miles long and ten wide; which, after paying expenses of survey and sale, are, according to a law of the United States, to be expended in assisting them to make homes elsewhere; and as these lands were valued at $1.25 an acre and upward, and are rapidly selling, the portion which will be due each of the Indians cannot be less than $200 or $300—or $1000 for each family. The oath required of them is supposed to bar them from any claim to this also. Now, I cannot see how this decision of the Indian Department is consistent either with justice or good policy, and it is certainly inconsistent with both the spirit and letter of Articles six and ten of a treaty between the United States of America and different bands of Sioux Indians, concluded in 1868, and ratified and proclaimed February, 1869.***What I ask for them is that our Government restore to them a part of what we took from them, and give them the same chance to live and thrive which we give to all the other inhabitants of our country, whether white or black.***That some aid is very necessary must be obvious to you, who know how difficult it is for even white men, trained to work, and with several hundred dollars in property, to open a new farm in this Western wilderness. Their number is probably greater than you are aware of. When I administered the Lord's Supper there on the first Sabbath of this month, there were present seventy-seven communicants of our church, besides quite a number of other persons.***It is owing to the Santee Sioux—partly to those on the Big Sioux River, chiefly to those near Fort Wadsworth—that in the last five years not a single white inhabitant of Minnesota or Iowa has been murdered by the wild Indians, while many have been cut off in every frontier State and Territory south-west of the Missouri. So long as the Christian Sioux can be kept on the frontier, the white settlements are safe.*** In conclusion, I wish again to call your attention to the fact that these Indians on the Big Sioux purchase citizenship at a very great sum, and to entreat you to do all in your power to secure for them that protection of person or property for which they bargain, and without which nothing our Government can do will make them prosperous or happy."

No attention was paid to this appeal; and the next year the indefatigable missionary sent a still stronger one, setting forth that this colony now numbered fifty families; had been under the instruction of the American Board of Commissioners for Foreign Missions for many years; had a church of one hundred members; a native preacher, partly supported by them; had built log-cabins on their claims, and planted farms, "many of them digging up the ground with hoes and spades."

Dr. Williamson reiterates the treaty provisions under which he claims that these Indians are entitled to aid. The sixth Article of the treaty of 1868 closes as follows: "Any Indian or Indians receiving a patent for land under the foregoing provisions, shall thereby and henceforth become and be a citizen of the United States, and be entitled to all the privileges and immunities of such citizenship, and shall at the same time retain all his rights and benefits accruing to Indians under this treaty."

This treaty goes on to provide most liberally for all Indians adopting the civilized mode of life. Article eighth specially provides for supplying them with seed and agricultural implements, and this is what they most of all need.

The encouragement held forth in this treaty was one great motive in leading these people to break tribal influences, so deleterious to improvement, and adopt our democratic civilization. Is it not base tyranny to disappoint them? They are the first Sioux, if not the first Indians in the United States to adopt the spirit and life of our American civilization. They have of their own accord done just what the Government has been for generations trying to get the Indians to do. And now will the Government refuse this helping hand? To our shame, it has for two years refused. And why? Because the Indians said, "If we become civilized, it is necessary for us to break up tribal relations, and settle down like white men."

In 1873 the Government at last yielded to this request, and sent out oxen, wagons, ploughs, etc., enough to stock thirty farms. In 1874, Dr. Williamson, having been appointed a special agent for them, reports their progress: "They all live in log-houses and wear citizens' dress.***One hundred and nineteen can read their own language fluently. They all go to church regularly. They have broken one hundred and seventy-seven acres of new prairie. Twenty new houses have been built.***They have cut and hauled two hundred cords of wood, hauling some of it forty miles to market.***They

have done considerable freighting with their teams, going sometimes a hundred miles away. They have earned thirty-five hundred
dollars, catching small furs.***One Indian has the contract for
carrying the mail through Flandreau, for which he receives one
thousand dollars a year.***It is but a few miles from Flandreau to
the far-famed pipe-stone quarry, and these Indians make many little
sums by selling pipes, rings, ink-glasses, etc., made of this beautiful
red stone.***They are anxious to be taught how to make baskets,
mats, cloth; and the young men ask to be taught the blacksmith and
carpenter trades."

This is a community that only five years before had pushed out
into an unbroken wilderness without a dollar of money, without a
plough, to open farms. "Without ploughs, they had to dig the sod
with their hoes, and at the same time make their living by hunting.
They suffered severe hardships, and a number of their best men
perished in snow-storms. Believing they were carrying out the
wishes of the Great Father, as expressed in the treaty of 1868, to
which they were parties, they were disappointed when for three
years no notice was taken of them." There is something pathetic in
the gratitude they are said now to feel for the niggardly gift of a few
oxen, wagons, and ploughs. They have apparently given over all
hope of ever obtaining any of the money due them on account of
their lands sold in Minnesota. No further allusion is made to it by
Dr. Williamson.

From the Yankton Sioux this year comes a remarkable report:
"We have no jail, no law except the treaty and the agent's word, yet
we have no quarrels, no fighting, and, with one or two exceptions,
not a single case of drunkenness during the year. This I consider remarkable, when we take into consideration the fact that the reservation is surrounded by ranches where liquors of all kinds can be
obtained." Is there another village of two thousand inhabitants in the
United States of which this can be said?

In this year a commission was sent to treat with some of the
wilder bands of Sioux for the relinquishment of their right to hunt
and roam over a large part of their unneeded territory in Kansas and
Nebraska. Some of the chiefs consented. Red Cloud's band refused
at first; "but on being told that the right would soon be taken from
them," after a delay of two days they "agreed to accept," merely

stipulating that their share of the twenty-five thousand dollars promised should be paid in horses and guns. They insisted, however, on this proviso: "That we do not surrender any right of occupation of the country situated in Nebraska north of the divide, which is south of and near to the Niobrara River and west of the one hundredth meridian."

It was a significant fact that, when these Sioux gave up this hunting privilege, "they requested that nearly all the $25,000 they received in compensation for this relinquishment should be expended in cows, horses, harness, and wagons," says the Commissioner of Indian Affairs in 1875.

There are still some thousand or more of hostile Sioux roaming about under the famous chief Sitting Bull—living by the chase when they can, and by depredations when they must; occasionally, also, appearing at agencies, and drawing rations among the other Indians unsuspected. The remainder of the bands are steadily working their way on toward civilization. The Santees are a Christian community; they have their industrial-schools, Sabbath-schools, and night-schools; they publish a monthly paper in the Dakota tongue, which prints twelve hundred copies. The Yanktons have learned to weave, and have made cloth enough to give every Indian woman in the tribe one good dress. The Flandreau citizen Sioux have a Presbyterian church of one hundred and thirty-five members, and pay half the salary of the native preacher. On the occasion of an anniversary meeting of the Dakota missionaries there, these people raised one hundred dollars to pay for their entertainment. These three bands are far the most advanced, but all the others are making steady progress.

In 1876 the news from the Sioux on the agencies is that, owing to the failure of appropriations, the Indian Bureau had been unable to send the regular supplies, and the Indians, being in "almost a starving condition," had been induced, by the "apparent purpose of the Government to abandon them to starvation," to go north in large numbers, and join the hostile camps of Sitting Bull. This was in the spring; again in mid-summer the same thing happened, and many of the Indians, growing still more anxious and suspicious, left their agencies to join in the war.

Congress would probably have paid little attention at this time to the reading of this extract from "Kent's Commentaries:" "Treaties of peace, when made by the competent power, are obligatory on the whole nation. If the treaty requires the payment of money to carry it into effect, and the money cannot be raised but by an act of the legislature, the treaty is morally obligatory upon the legislature to pass the law; and to repeal it would be a breach of the public faith."

A disturbed and unsettled condition of things prevailed at all the Sioux agencies, consequent on this state of things. Companies of troops were stationed at all of them to guard against outbreaks. Owing to lack of funds, the Yanktons were obliged to give up their weaving and basket-making. At the Standing Rock Agency, after the Indians had planted eight hundred and seventy-two dollars' worth of seeds—of corn, potatoes, and other vegetables—the grasshoppers came and devoured them. "Many of these Indians, with their whole families, stood all day in their fields fighting these enemies, and in several places succeeded so far as to save a considerable part of their crops." The Santees were made very anxious and unhappy by fresh rumors of their probable removal. Public sentiment at the East, knowing no difference between different tribes of Sioux, regarded it as maudlin sentimentalism to claim for the Santees any more rights than for the hostiles that had murdered General Custer. One of the agents in Dakota writes:

"The recent troubles in the Indian country, and the existing uncertainty as to the future intentions of the Government toward the Indians, occasion considerable uneasiness among them. * * *Reports are circulated that no further assistance will be rendered by the Government, as the Great Council in Washington refuses to furnish money unless the Indians are turned over to the War Department. Every inducement is held out to encourage secession from the agencies, and strengthen the forces of the hostile camp. It is not surprising that, in view of the non-arrival of supplies, and the recent order of the War Department to arrest parties leaving and arriving, that people less credulous than Indians would feel undecided and uneasy. * * * It must be remembered that the whole Sioux nation is related, and that there is hardly a man, woman, or child in the hostile camp who has not blood relations at one or the other of the agencies."

Contrast the condition into which all these friendly Indians are

suddenly plunged now, with their condition only two years previous: martial law now in force on all their reservations; themselves
in danger of starvation, and constantly exposed to the influence of
emissaries from their friends and relations, urging them to join in
fighting this treacherous government that had kept faith with nobody—neither with friend nor with foe; that made no discrimination
in its warfare between friends and foes; burning villages occupied
only by women and children; butchering bands of Indians living
peacefully under protection of its flag, as at Sand Creek, in Colorado
—no wonder that one of the military commander's official reports
says, "The hostile body was largely re-enforced by accessions from
the various agencies, where the malcontents were, doubtless, in
many cases, driven to desperation by starvation and the heartless
frauds perpetrated on them;" and that the Interior Department is
obliged to confess that, "Such desertions were largely due to the
uneasiness which the Indians had long felt on account of the infrac-
tion of treaty stipulations by the white invasion of the Black Hills,
seriously aggravated at the most critical period by irregular and insufficient issues of rations, necessitated by inadequate and delayed
appropriations."

It was at this time that Sitting Bull made his famous reply: "Tell
them at Washington if they have one man who speaks the truth to
send him to me, and I will listen to what he has to say."

The story of the military campaign against these hostile Sioux
in 1876 and 1877 is to be read in the official records of the War Department, so far as statistics can tell it. Another history, which can
never be read, is written in the hearts of widowed women in the
Sioux nation and in the nation of the United States.

Before midsummer the Sioux war was over. The indomitable
Sitting Bull had escaped to Canada—that sanctuary of refuge for the
Indian as well as for the slave. Here he was visited in the autumn by
a commission from the United States, empowered by the President
to invite him with his people to return, and be "assigned to agencies,"
and treated "in as friendly a spirit as other Indians had been who had
surrendered." It was explained to him that every one of the Indians
who had surrendered had "been treated in the same manner as those
of your nation who, during all the past troubles, remained peaceably
at their agencies." As a great part of those who had fled from these

same agencies to join Sitting Bull had done so because they were starving, and the Government knew this (had printed the record of the fact in the reports of two of its Departments), this was certainly a strange phraseology of invitation for it to address to Sitting Bull. His replies and those of his chiefs were full of scathing sarcasm. Secure on British soil, they had for once safe freedom of speech as well as of action, and they gave the United States Commissioners very conclusive reasons why they chose to remain in Canada, where they could "trade with the traders and make a living," and where their women had "time to raise their children."

The commissioners returned from their bootless errand, and the Interior Department simply entered on its records the statement that "Sitting Bull and his adherents are no longer considered wards of the Government." It also enters on the same record the statement that "in the months of September and October, 1876, the various Sioux agencies were visited by a commission appointed under the Act of Congress, August 15th of that year, to negotiate with the Sioux for an agreement to surrender that portion of the Sioux Reservation which included the Black Hills, and certain hunting privileges outside that reserve, guaranteed by the treaty of 1868; to grant a right of way across their reserve; and to provide for the removal of the Red Cloud and Spotted Tail bands to new agencies on the Missouri River. The commission were also authorized to take steps to gain the consent of the Sioux to their removal to the Indian Territory.***The commission were successful in all the negotiations with which they were charged, and the Indians made every concession that was desired by the Government, although we were engaged at that very time in fighting their relatives and friends." The only comment needed on this last paragraph is to suggest that a proper list of errata for that page should contain: "For 'although' read 'because!'" "On behalf of the United States the agreement thus entered into provided for subsisting the Sioux on a stated ration until they should become self-supporting; for furnishing schools, and all necessary aid and instruction in agriculture and the mechanical arts, and for the allotment of lands in severalty."

In accordance with this act, a commission was sent to select a location on the Missouri River for the two new Sioux agencies (the Red Cloud and Spotted Tail).

"For the former the site chosen is the junction of Yellow Medicine and Missouri rivers, and at that point agency buildings have just been erected," says the Report of the Indian Bureau for 1877. "For the latter the old Ponca Reserve was decided on, where the agency buildings, storehouses, one hundred and fifty Indian homes, and five hundred acres of cultivated fields, left vacant by the Poncas, offer special advantages for present quarters."

The commissioner says: "The removal of fourteen thousand Sioux Indians at this season of the year, a distance of three hundred miles from their old agencies in Nebraska to their new quarters near the Missouri River, is not a pleasant matter to contemplate. Neither the present Secretary of the Interior nor the present Commissioner of Indian Affairs is responsible for the movement, but they have carried out the law faithfully though reluctantly. The removal is being made in accordance with the Act of August 15th, 1876. It is proper to say here that I cannot but look on the necessity thus imposed by law on the executive branch of the Government as an unfortunate one, and the consequences ought to be remedied as speedily as possible.

"Let us for a moment consider that the Spotted Tail Agency was in 1871 on the west bank of the Missouri River, where the whites became exceedingly troublesome, and the river afforded abundant facilities for the introduction of intoxicating liquors. In 1874 the Red Cloud and Spotted Tail agencies were removed to what a subsequent survey proved to be the State of Nebraska—the former agency one hundred and sixty-five miles from Cheyenne, and the latter one hundred and eight miles from Sidney, the nearest points on the Union Pacific Railroad. Here the usual ill-fortune attending the removal of these Indians was again exemplified in placing the agencies on absolutely barren land, where there was no possibility of cultivating the soil, no hope of their being enabled to become self-supporting, and where they have of necessity been kept in the hopeless condition of paupers."

In the hope of placing these Indians upon arable land, where they might become civilized and self-supporting, the determination was hastily taken to remove them back to the Missouri River. This step was taken without a proper examination of other points on their reservation, where it is stated that "a sufficient quantity of excellent wheat lands can be found on either bank of the White River, and where there is also timber sufficient in quantity and quality for all practical purposes.***The Indian chiefs, in their interview with the President in September last, begged that they might not be sent to the Missouri River, as whiskey-drinking and other demoralization would be the consequence. This was the judgment of the best men of the tribe; but the necessity was one that the President could not control. The provisions and supplies for the ensuing winter had been placed, according to law, on the Missouri, and, owing to the lateness of the season, it was impossible to remove them to the old agencies. Accordingly, the necessities of the case compelled the removal of these Indians in the midst of the snows and storms of early winter, which have already set in."

If there were absolutely no other record written of the management of Indian affairs by the Interior Department than this one page of the history of these two bands of the Sioux tribe, this alone would be enough to show the urgent need of an entirely new system. So many and such hasty, ill-considered, uninformed, capricious, and cruel decisions of arbitrary power could hardly be found in a seven years' record of any known tyrant; and there is no tyrant whose throne would not have been rocked, if not upset, by the revolutions which would have followed on such oppressions.

There is a sequel to this story of the removal of the Red Cloud and Spotted Tail bands—a sequel not recorded in the official reports of the Department, but familiar to many men in the Western country. Accounts of it—some humorous, some severe—were for some time floating about in Western newspapers.

The Red Cloud and Spotted Tail bands of Sioux consented to go to the old Ponca Reserve only after being told that all their supplies had been sent to a certain point on the Missouri River with a view to this move; and it being too late to take all this freight northward again, they would starve if they stayed where they were. Being assured that they would be allowed to go back in the spring, and having a written pledge from General Crook (in whose word they had implicit faith) that the Government would fulfil this promise, they at last very reluctantly consented to go to the Ponca Reserve for the winter. In the spring no orders came for the removal. March passed, April passed—no orders. The chiefs sent word to their friend,

General Crook, who replied to them with messages sent by a swift runner, begging them not to break away, but to wait a little longer. Finally, in May, the Commissioner of Indian Affairs went himself to hold a council with them. When he rose to speak, the chief Spotted Tail sprung up, walked toward him, waving in his hand the paper containing the promise of the Government to return them to White Clay Creek, and exclaimed, "All the men who come from Washington are liars, and the bald-headed ones are the worst of all! I don't want to hear one word from you—you are a bald-headed old liar! You have but one thing to do here, and that is to give an order for us to return to White Clay Creek. Here are your written words; and if you don't give this order, and everything here is not on wheels inside of ten days, I'll order my young men to tear down and burn everything in this part of the country! I don't want to hear anything more from you, and I've got nothing more to say to you:" and he turned his back on the commissioner and walked away. Such language as this would not have been borne from unarmed and helpless Indians; but when it came from a chief with four thousand armed warriors at his back, it was another affair altogether. The order was written. In less than ten days everything was "on wheels," and the whole body of these Sioux on the move to the country they had indicated; and the Secretary of the Interior says, naïvely, in his Report for 1868, "The Indians were found to be quite determined to move westward, and the promise of the Government in that respect was faithfully kept."

The reports from all the bands of Sioux for the past two years have been full of indications of their rapid and encouraging improvement. "The most decided advance in civilization has been made by the Ogallalla and Brulé Sioux," says the Report of the Indian Bureau for 1879. "Their progress during the last year and a half has been simply marvellous."

And yet this one band of Ogallalla Sioux has been moved, since 1863, eight times. Is it not a wonder that they have any heart to work, any hope of anything in the future?

"It is no longer a question," says this same report, "whether Indians will work. They are steadily asking for opportunities to do so, and the Indians who to-day are willing and anxious to engage in civilized labor are largely in the majority; * * *there is an almost universal call for lands in severalty; * * *there is a growing desire to live in houses; the demand for agricultural implements and appliances, and for wagons and harness for farming and freighting purposes, is constantly increasing."

That all this should be true of these wild, warlike Sioux, after so many years of hardships and forced wanderings and removals, is incontrovertible proof that there is in them a native strength of character, power of endurance, and indomitable courage, which will make of them ultimately a noble and superior race of people, if civilization will only give them time to become civilized, and Christians will leave them time and peace to learn Christianity.

James Willard Schultz

"The squawman fought their battles"

1907

James Willard Schultz was a white man who for many years lived with the Blackfoot Indians in Montana. He married a Blackfoot woman and therefore was, in the vernacular of whites, a squawman. Here he describes the role that such men played in Blackfoot society in the late nineteenth century and the reaction that some whites had to them. His is a different perspective on Indian life.

The very last of the buffalo herds disappeared in 1883. In the spring of 1884 a large flotilla of steamboats was tied up at the Fort Benton levee; among them the "Black Hills" and "Dacotah," boats of great size and carrying capacity. The latter came up but once in a season—when the Missouri was bank full from the melting snow in the mountains—and this was their last trip for all time to come. Not only was it the last trip for them, but for all the smaller boats. The railroad was coming. It had already crossed Dakota, and was creeping rapidly across the Montana plains. Tying up at night, using enormous quantities of wood fuel in order to overcome the swift current of the Missouri, the steamboats could not compete with the freight carrier of the rails.

When the railroad did finally enter the Rocky Mountain country, a branch running to Fort Benton, Great Falls, Helena, and Butte, the main line crossing the divide through the Two Medicine Pass, it

From J. W. Schultz, *My Life as an Indian: The Story of a Red Woman and a White Man in the Lodges of the Blackfeet* (New York, Doubleday, Page & Company, 1907), 411–26.

brought in its coaches many immigrants from the "States," at whom the old-timers laughed. "What are they coming here for?" they asked. "What are they going to do—these hard-hatted men and delicate looking women?"

They soon found out. The new-comers settled here and there in the valleys, and took up the available water rights; they opened stores in the towns and crossroads places and reduced prices to a five-cent basis; they even gave exact change in pennies. Heretofore a spool of thread, even a lamp-wick, had been sold for two bits. The old storekeepers and traders, with their easy, liberal ways, could not hold their own in this new order of things; they could not change their life-long habits, and one by one they went to the wall.

The men married to Indian women—squawmen, as they were contemptuously called—suffered most, and, strange to say, the wives of the new-comers, not the men, were the bitterest enemies. They forbade their children to associate with the half-breed children, and at school the position of the latter was unbearable. The white ones beat them and called them opprobrious names. This hatred of the squawman was even carried into politics. One of them, as clean-minded, genial, fearless, and honest a man as I ever knew, was nominated for sheriff of the county upon the party ticket which always carried the day; but at that election he and he alone of all the candidates of his party was not elected. He was actually snowed under. The white women had so badgered their husbands and brothers, had so vehemently protested against the election of a squawman to any office, that they succeeded in accomplishing his defeat. And so, one by one, these men moved to the only place where they could live in peace, where there was not an enemy within a hundred and more miles of them, the Reservation; and there they settled to pass their remaining days. There were forty-two of them at one time; few are left.

Let me correct the general impression of the squawmen, at least as to those I have known, the men who married Blackfeet women. In the days of the Indians' dire extremity, they gave them all they could, and were content so long as there remained a little bacon and flour for their families; and some days there was not even that in the houses of some of them for they had given their all. With the Indian they starved for a time, perchance. Scattered here and there upon the Reservation, they built for themselves neat homes and corrals, and fenced their hay lands, all of which was an object lesson to the Indian. But they did more than that. They helped to build their red neighbours' cabins and stables; surveyed their irrigating ditches; taught them how to plough, and to manage a mowing machine. All this without thought of pay or profit. If you enter the home of a Blackfoot, you nearly always find the floor clean, the windows spotless, everything about in perfect order, the sewing machine and table covered with pretty cloths; the bed with clean, bright-hued blankets; the cooking utensils and tableware spotless and bright. No Government field-matrons have taught them to do this, for they have had none. This they learned by observing the ways of the squawmen's wives. I have seen hundreds of white homes —there are numbers of them in any city—so exceedingly dirty, their inmates so slovenly, that one turns from them in absolute disgust; but I have seen nothing like that among the Blackfeet.

In their opulent days, under a good agent, and when they had numbers of steers to sell, they bought much furniture, even good carpets. There came to me one day at that time a friend, and we smoked together. "You have a book with pictures of furniture," he said, "show me the best bedstead it tells about."

I complied. "There it is," pointing to the cut. "All brass, best of springs; price $80."

"Send for it," he said, "I want it. It costs only two steers, and what is that?"

"There are others," I went on, "just as good looking, part iron, part brass, which cost much less."

"Huh!" he exclaimed. "Old Tail-feathers-coming-over-the-hill has one that cost fifty dollars. I'm going to have the best."

Without the squawman, I do not know what the Blackfeet would have done in the making of their treaties with the Government; in getting rid of agents, of whom the less said the better—for the squawman fought their battles and bore the brunt of all the trouble. I have known an agent to order his police to kill a certain squawman on sight, because the man had reported to Washington his thievery; and others to order squawmen to leave the Reservation, separating them from their families, because they had spoken too openly regarding certain underhand doings. But at intervals there were good, honest, capable men in charge, under whom the Indians regained in a measure the prosperity they had lost. But such men did not last; with a change of administration they were always dismissed by the powers that be.

One thing the squawmen never succeeded in doing—they were never able to rid the Reservation of the great cattle kings' stock. The big men had an "understanding" with some agents, and at other times with certain politicians of great influence. So their stock remained and increased and fed down the rich grasses. Most of the Indians and most of the squawmen carefully tended their little herds in some favourable locality as near as possible to their homes; but always, once in the spring, once in the fall, the great round-up of the cattle kings swept like wild fire across the Reservation. Thirty or forty swift riders would swoop down on one of these little herds. Some of their cattle would be mixed in with them; but they did not stop to cut them out; there wasn't time; and they drove them all to some distant point or branding corral, and the owner of the little herd lost forever more or less of them. At last, so I am told, the Indians prevailed upon the Department to fence the south and east sides of the Reservation in order to keep the foreign stock out, and their own inside. There was no need of fencing the west and north sides, for the Rocky Mountains form the western boundary, and the Canadian line the northern. It cost $30,000 to build that fence, and then the cattle kings obtained permission to pasture 30,000 head of cattle within it. But perhaps it is as well. It is only hastening the end a bit, for the Blackfeet, as I have said before, are to have their lands allotted. Then will come the sheepmen, desolation in their wake, and then the end. It has been nearly the end for them this past winter. The Department decreed that no able-bodied person should receive rations. In that bleak country there is no chance of obtaining work, for the white men's ranches are few and far between. Even if a man obtained three months' work in summer time—something almost impossible—his wages could not by any means support his family for a year. A friend wrote me in January: "I was over on the Reservation to-day and visited many old friends. In most of the homes there was little, generally no food, and the people were sitting sadly around the stove, drinking wild tea."

In the hegira of the old-timers to the Reservation, Berry and I took part. Fort Conrad had been sold. Berry bought out the Reservation trader, goodwill and goods, for three hundred dollars.

I got an insane idea in my head that I wanted to be a sheepman, and locating some fine springs and hay ground about twelve miles above Fort Conrad, I built some good sheds, and a house, and put up great stacks of hay. The cattlemen burned me out. I guess they did right, for I had located the only water for miles around. I left the blackened ruins and followed Berry. I am glad that they did burn me out, for I thus can truthfully say that I had no part in the devastation of Montana's once lovely plains.

We built us a home, Nät-ah'-ki and I, in a lovely valley where the grass grew green and tall. We were a long time building it. Up in the mountains where I cut the logs, our camp under the towering pines was so pleasant that we could hardly leave it for a couple of days to haul home a wagon-load of material. And there were so many pleasant diversions that the axe leaned up against a stump during long dreamy days, while we went trout fishing, or trailed a deer or bear, or just remained in camp listening to the wind in the pine tops, watching the squirrels steal the remains of our breakfast, or an occasional grouse strutting by.

"How peaceful it all is here," Nät-ah'-ki once said, "How beautiful the pines, how lovely and fragile the things that grow in the damp and shadowy places. And yet, there is something fearsome about these great forests. My people seldom venture into them alone. The hunters always go in couples or three or four together, the women in large numbers when they come to cut lodge poles, and their men always with them."

"But why are they afraid?" I asked. "I don't see why they should be."

"There are many reasons," she replied. "Here an enemy can easily lie in wait for one and kill without risk to himself. And then— and then they say that ghosts live in these long, wide, dark woods; that they follow a hunter, or steal along by his side or in front of him; that one knows they are about, for they sometimes step on a stick which snaps, or rustle some loose leaves with their feet. Some men, it is said, have even seen these ghosts peering at them from behind a distant tree. They had terrible, big, wide faces, and big, wicked eyes. Sometimes I even have thought that I was being followed by them. But, though I was terribly afraid, I have just kept on going, away down there to the spring for water. It is when you are away off there chopping and the blows of your axe cease, that I am most afraid. I stop and listen; if you begin to chop again soon, then all is well, and I go on with my work. But if there is a long silence then I begin to fear, I know not what; everything; the dim shadowy places away out around; the wind in the tree-tops which seems to be saying something I cannot understand. Oh, I become afraid, and I steal out to see if you are still there—if anything has happened to you——"

"Why—how is that?" I interposed, "I never saw you."

"No, you didn't see me. I went very quietly, very cautiously, just like one of those ghosts they talk about; but I always saw you. You would be sitting on a log, or lying on the ground, smoking, always smoking, and then I would be satisfied, and go back as quietly as I came."

"But when you came out that way, why didn't you come further and sit down and talk with me?" I asked.

"Had I done so," she replied, "you would have sat still longer idle, smoked more, and talked of those things you are ever dreaming and thinking about. Don't you know that the summer is nearly gone? And I do so much want to see that house built. I want to have a home of my own."

Thereupon I would for a time wield the axe with more vigour, and then again there would be a reaction—more days of idleness, or of wandering by the stream, or on the grim mountain slopes. But before snow came we had our modest home built and furnished, and were content.

It was the following spring that Nät-ah'-ki's mother died, after a very short illness. After the body had been wrapped with many a blanket and robe and securely bound with rawhide thongs, I was told to prepare a coffin for it. There was no lumber for sale within a hundred and fifty miles, but the good Jesuits, who had built a mission nearby, generously gave me the necessary boards and I made a long, wide box more than three feet in height. Then I asked where the grave should be dug. Nät-ah'-ki and the mourning relatives were horrified. "What," the former cried "bury mother in a hole in the dark, heavy, cold ground?

"No!! our Agent has forbidden burials in trees, but he has said nothing about putting our dead in coffins on the top of the ground. Take the box up on the side of the hill where lie the remains of Red Eagle, of other relatives, and we will follow with all the rest in the other wagon."

I did as I was told, driving up the valley a half-mile or so, then turning up on the slope where lay half a dozen rude coffins side by side on a small level place. Removing the box from the wagon, I placed it at some little distance from the others and with pick and spade made an absolutely level place for it. Then came the others, a number of friends and relatives, even three men, also relatives of the good woman. Never before nor since have I known men to attend a funeral. They always remained in their lodges and mourned; so this was even greater proof of the love and esteem in which Nät-ah'-ki's mother had been held.

Nät-ah'-ki, from the moment her mother had died, had neither slept nor partaken of food, crying, crying all the time. And now she insisted that none but she and I should perform the last ceremonies. We carried the tightly wrapped body and laid it in the big box, very carefully and tenderly you may be sure, and then placed at the sides and feet of it various little buckskin sacks, small parfleche pouches, containing needles, awls, thread and all the various implements and trinkets which she had kept and guarded so carefully. I raised and placed in position the two boards forming the cover. Everyone was now crying, even the men. I held a nail in position, and drove it partly down. How dreadfully they sounded, the hammer blows hollowly, loudly reverberating from the big, half-empty box. I had kept up thus far pretty well, but the cold, harsh, desecrating hammering unnerved me. I tossed the implement away, sat down, and in spite of all my efforts to control myself, I cried with the rest. "I cannot do it," I said, over and over, "I cannot drive those nails."

Nät-ah'-ki came and sat down, leaned on my shoulder and reached out her trembling hands for mine.

"Our mother!" she said, "Our mother! just think; we shall never, never see her again. Oh, why must she have died while she had not even begun to grow old?"

One of the men stepped forward, "Go you two home," he said, "I will nail the boards."

So, in the gathering dusk, Nät-ah'-ki and I drove home, unhitched the horses and turned them loose; and then entering the silent house we went to bed. The Crow Woman, always faithful and kind, came later, and I heard her build a fire in the kitchen stove. Presently she brought in a lamp, then some tea and a few slices of bread and meat. Nät-ah'-ki was asleep; bending over me she whispered; "Be more than ever kind to her now, my son. Such a good mother as she had! There was not one quite so good in all the earth; she will miss her so much. You must now be to her both her man and mother."

"I will," I replied, taking her hand. "You know that I will," whereupon she passed as silently out of the room and out of the house as she had come. It was a long, long time though before Nät-ah'-ki recovered her naturally high spirits, and even years afterward she would awake me in the night, crying, to talk about her mother. . . .

Since the rails of the great road had crossed the land which Big Lake had said should never be desecrated by fire-wagons, I thought that we might as well ride upon them, but it was some time before I could persuade Nät-ah'-ki to do so. But at last she fell grievously ill, and I prevailed on her to see a famous physician who lived in a not far distant city, a man who had done much for me, and of whose wonderful surgical work I never tired telling. So, one morning we took the seats in the rear Pullman of a train and started, Nät-ah'-ki sitting by the open window. Presently we came to a bridge spanning an exceedingly deep cañon, and looking down she gave a little cry of surprise, and terror, dropped to the floor and covered her face with her hands. I got her back on the seat, but it was some time before she recovered her composure. "It looked so awfully far down there," she said, "and supposing the bridge had broken, we would all have been killed."

I assured her that the bridges could not break, that the men who built them knew just how much they could hold up, and that was more than could be loaded on a train. Thenceforth she had no fear and loved the swift glide of a train, her favourite place in suitable weather being a seat on the rear platform of the last Pullman.

We hadn't been on the train fifteen minutes when I suddenly realised something that I had never thought of before. Glancing at the women seated here and there, all of them dressed in neat and rich fabrics, some of them wearing gorgeous hats, I saw that Nät-ah'-ki was not in their class so far as wearing apparel was concerned. She wore a plain gingham dress, and carried a shawl and a sun-bonnet, all of which were considered very "swell" up on the Reserva-tion, and had been so regarded in the days of the buffalo traders at Fort Benton. To my surprise, some of these ladies in the car came to talk with Nät-ah'-ki, and said many kind things to her. And the little woman was highly pleased, even excited by their visits. "Why," she said to me in surprise, "I did not think that white women would speak to me. I thought they all hated an Indian woman."

"Many do," I answered, "but they are not women of this class. There are women, and women. My mother is like these you have spoken to. Did you notice their dresses?" I added. "Well, so you must dress. I am glad that we arrive in the city at night. You shall be dressed like them before we go to the hospital."

Our train pulled into the city on time, and I hurried Nät-ah'-ki into a cab, and thence to the side entrance of a hotel, thence upstairs to a room which I had telegraphed for. It was a Saturday night and the stores were still open. I found a saleswoman in a department store to accompany me to the hotel and take Nät-ah'-ki's measure. In a little while we had her fitted out with waists and skirts, and a neat travelling coat. How pleased she was with them, and how proud I was of her. There was nothing, I thought, good enough to clothe that true and tried little body, whose candour, and gentleness, and innate refinement of mind were mirrored in her eyes.

We had dinner in our room. I suddenly remembered that I had not thought of one article of costume, a hat, and out I went to get it. In the lobby of the hotel I met an artist friend, and besought his aid in selecting the important gear. We looked at about five hundred, I thought, and at last decided upon a brown velvet thing with a black feather. We took it up to the room and Nät-ah'-ki tried it on. " 'Twas too small," we all declared, so back we went after another one. There didn't seem to be any larger ones, and we were discouraged. "They don't fit down," I told the woman, "can't be made to fit like this," raising my hat and jamming it down in place. The woman looked at me in astonishment. ""Why, my dear sir!" she exclaimed, "Women do not wear their hats that way. They place them lightly on the top of the head, and secure them there with large pins, hat pins, running through the hair."

"Oh, I see," I said. "That's the way, is it? Well, give us back the hat and some pins, and we'll be fixed this time, sure."

But we weren't. Nät-ah'-ki wore her hair in two long braids, tied together and hanging down her back. There was no way of skewering that hat on, unless she wore her hair pompadour, or whatever you call it, bunched up on top of the head, you know, and of course she wouldn't do that. Nor did I wish her to; I liked to see those great heavy braids falling down, away down below the waist.

"I have it," said my friend, who had ridden some himself—in fact, had been a noted cowpuncher—"we'll just get a piece of rubber elastic sewed on, like the string on a sombrero. That will go under the braids, close to the skin, and there you are."

The store was just closing when I finally got the elastic, some thread and needles, and Nät-ah'-ki sewed it on. The hat stayed. One could hardly knock it off. Tired and thirsty, the artist and I withdrew in search of a long, fizzing drink, and Nät-ah'-ki went to bed. I found her wide awake when I returned. "Isn't this splendid!" she exclaimed, "everything as one could wish it. You merely push a little black thing and someone comes up to wait on you, to bring you your dinner, or water, or whatever you want. You turn faucets, and there is your water. With one turn you make the lightning-lamps burn, or go out. It is wonderful, wonderful. I could live here very happily."

"Is it better than the neat lodge we had, when we travelled about, when we camped right here where this city stands and hunted buffalo?"

"Oh, no, no," she cried, "it is not like those dear, dead, past times. But they are gone. Since we must travel the white man's road, as the chiefs say, let us take the best we can find along the way, and this is very nice."

In the morning we drove to the hospital, and took the elevator to the floor and room assigned to us. Nät-ah'-ki was put to bed by the Sisters, with whom she immediately became infatuated. Then came the doctor. "It is he," I told her, "the one who saved me."

She rose up in bed and grasped one of his hands in both her own. "Tell him," she said, "that I will be good and patient. That no matter how bad his medicines taste, I will take them, that no matter how much he hurts me, I will not cry out. Tell him I wish to get well quickly, so I can walk around, and do my work, and be happy and healthy once more."

"It is nothing organic," said the doctor. "It does not even need the knife. A week in bed, some medicine, and she can go home as well as ever."

This was pleasing news to Nät-ah'-ki, when she came to her senses. The chloroform did not even make her ill, and she was as cheerful as a lark from morning until night. The Sisters and nurses were always coming in to talk and joke with her, and when I was not on hand to interpret, they still seemed to understand one another, Nät-ah'-ki in some way making her thoughts known. One could hear her cheery laughter ringing out of the room and down the hall at almost any hour of day.

"Never in my life," said the Sister Superior, "have I known such another cheerful, innocent, happy woman. You are a lucky man, sir, to have such a wife."

Then came the happy day when we could set out for home again. We went, and for a long time Nät-ah'-ki talked of the wonderful things she had seen. Her faith in the Blackfoot men and women doctors was shattered, and she did not hesitate to say so. She told of the wonderful way in which her doctor had cut patients in the hospital and made them well; of his wonderful lightning-lamp (X-ray), with which one's bones, the whole skeleton, could be seen through the flesh. The whole tribe became interested and came from far and near to listen. After that, many a suffering one went to the great hospital and to her doctor, no matter what their ailment, in full faith that they would be cured.

On our homeward way, I remember, we saw a man and two women loading a hay wagon, the man on top of the load, the women sturdily pitching up great forkfuls of hay to him, regardless of the extreme heat of the day. The little woman was astonished, shocked. "I did not think," she said, "that white men would so abuse their women. A Blackfoot would not be so cruel. I begin to think that white women have a much harder time than we do."

"You are right," I told her," most poor white women are slaves; they have to get up at three or four o'clock in the morning, cook three meals a day, make, mend, and wash their children's clothes, scrub floors, work in the garden, and when night comes they have hardly strength left to crawl to bed. Do you think you could do all that?"

"No," she replied, "I could not. I wonder if that is not why some white women so dislike us, because they have to work so dreadfully hard, while we have so much time to rest, or go visiting, or ride around here and there on the beautiful plains. Surely our life is happier than theirs, and you, oh, lucky was the day when you chose me to be your little woman." . . .

The years passed happily for Nät-ah'-ki and me. We had a growing bunch of cattle which were rounded-up with the other Reservation stock twice a year. I built two small irrigating ditches and raised some hay. There was little work to do, and we made a trip somewhere every autumn, up into the Rockies with friends, or took a jaunt by rail to some distant point. Sometimes we would take a skiff and idly drift and camp along the Missouri for three or four hundred miles below Fort Benton, returning home by rail. I think that we enjoyed the water trips the best. The shifting, boiling flood, the weird cliffs, the beautifully timbered, silent valley had a peculiar fascination for us such as no place in the great mountains possessed. It was during one of these river trips that Nät-ah'-ki began to complain of sharp pain in the tips of her right hand fingers. "It is nothing but rheumatism," I said, "and will soon pass away."

But I was wrong. The pain grew worse, and abandoning our boat at the mouth of Milk River, we took the first train for the city where our doctor lived, and once more found ourselves in the hospital, in the very same room; the same good Sisters and nurses surrounding Nät-ah'-ki and trying to relieve her of the pain, which was now excruciating. The doctor came, felt her pulse, got out his stethoscope and moved it from place to place until, at last, it stopped at a point at the right side of the neck, close to the collar bone. There he listened long, and I began to feel alarmed. "It is not rheumatism," I said to myself. "Something is wrong with her heart."

The doctor gave some directions to the nurse; then turning to Nät-ah'-ki he said, "Take courage, little friend, we'll pull you through all right."

Nät-ah'-ki smiled. Then she grew drowsy under the influence of an opiate; and we left the room.

"Well, old man," said the doctor, "this time I can do little. She may live a year, but I doubt it."

For eleven months we all did what we could, and then one day, my faithful, loving, tender-hearted little woman passed away, and left me. By day I think about her, at night I dream of her. I wish that I had that faith which teaches us that we will meet again on the other shore. But all looks very dark to me.

A Sioux Sun Dance. In this demonstration, the thongs appear to be tied around the dancer's body rather than through his skin. The ordeal was popularized for white audiences in the motion picture *A Man Called Horse*.

Chiefs.

Cheyenne and Kiowa Indians and a Buick, in a pose that must have sug-

gested to the photographer a meeting between past and present.

Between two worlds. A father and his daughter at the Darlington Agency, in western Oklahoma, in the 1890's.

The Indian as a white man. Comanche Jack (1853–1926), or Per-man-su, was one of Quanah Parker's subchiefs. Shorn of his braids and dressed in a suit, he posed for this portrait at Fort Sill in the late 1870's.

A Ghost Dance in a Cheyenne-Arapaho camp two miles northwest of Fort Reno in August, 1889. The photographer was as near as he dared to be. Messianic movements among conquered peoples generally evoke paranoid reactions from their conquerors, and so it was with the American Indian.

Burying the dead after the Battle
of Wounded Knee, S.D. -1890.

The dead await burial in a common grave at Wounded Knee, South
Dakota, in 1890. The slaughter of approximately 150 Indian men, women,
and children by Indian police and United States troops marked the end
of the Indian wars and active resistance to federal Indian policies, as well
as the old ways of Indian life.

W. Fletcher Johnson

*"He was lazy and vicious, and never told the truth
when a lie would serve better"*

1891

Sitting Bull, the Hunkpapa Sioux leader, was shot to death at
Wounded Knee in 1890. A few years earlier he had been a popular
attraction in Buffalo Bill's Wild West show, and patrons had remarked on the fact that he gave away his salary, a bit at a time, to
undernourished bootblacks and newsboys. He was hardly the "inhuman chief" of Edward L. Wheeler's fiction, but within a year after
his death W. Fletcher Johnson gave the public yet another account
of this brutal Indian. Johnson, a popular writer who, in earlier works,
had treated such diverse subjects as the Johnstown flood and Henry
M. Stanley's African exploits, seemed to suggest that the United
States government would not have had a hand in the killing of a
humane man. This selection gives an interesting summary of the
various notions about Sitting Bull's origins.

Among the countless relics and records in the Army Medical Museum at Washington, most of them ghastly and tragic in their nature,
is conspicuous the Autobiography of Ta-tan-kah-yo-tan-kah, the
Sioux chieftain best known to fame as Sitting Bull. The work is
unique, and it has itself a curious history. In the fall of 1870, a
Yankton Sioux brought to the army officers at Fort Buford an old
roll-book of the Thirty-first Regiment of Infantry, U.S.A., which
bore, on the backs of the leaves, originally blank, a remarkable series

From W. Fletcher Johnson, *Life of Sitting Bull and History of the Indian War
of 1890–'91* (N.p., Edgewood Publishing Company, 1891), 17–48.

of portraitures, representing the doings of a mighty Indian warrior. The pictures were outlined in ink, and shaded with colored chalks and pencils, brown, blue, and red. In the corner of each picture was a "totem," or Indian signature, just like the "remarque" on an etching. This totem was a buffalo bull on its haunches, and it revealed at once the authorship of the work. The Yankton Indian wanted to sell it, and finally did so, for one dollar and a half, confessing, frankly, that he had stolen it from Sitting Bull himself, whose autobiography it was, down to date.

This literary and artistic work, which is now likely to be famous, fell into the hands of Assistant Surgeon James C. Kimball, of the army, who was then stationed at Fort Buford, Dakota. He had the pictures translated and sent them, with the translation and an index, to the curator of the Army Medical Museum, Washington, Surgeon George A. Otis, United States Army, who filed them, in book shape, among the archives of the museum. The introduction, written by Dr. Kimball, says that the autobiography contains a description of the principal adventures in the life of Sitting Bull, an Unk-pa pa chief. It was sketched by himself in the picture language in common use with the Indians.

The index, explanatory of the drawings, was prepared through the assistance of Indians and interpreters. The word "coup," which occurs frequently in the index, has been appropriated by the Sioux from the French. "Counting coup" signifies the striking of an enemy, either dead or alive, with a stick, bow, lance, or other weapon. The number of "coups" counted are enumerated along with the number of horses stolen and scalps taken in summing up the brave deeds of a warrior. Sitting Bull was not at all modest in recounting his deeds for the edification of posterity. The scalping of a soldier and the theft of a mule are pictured with equal pride and with an equally artistic display of pigments. The plates are enumerated and described in the index as follows:

No. 1. Sitting Bull, a young man without reputation and therefore wearing no feather, engages in his first battle and charges his enemy, a Crow Indian, who is in the act of drawing his bow, rides him down and strikes him with a "coup" stick.

Sitting Bull's autograph, a buffalo bull sitting on his haunches, is inscribed over him. His shield suspended in front has on it the figure of an eagle, which he considers his medicine, in the Indian sense of the term.

No. 2. Sitting Bull, wearing a war bonnet, is leader of a war party who take a party of Crows, consisting of three women and a man, so completely by surprise that the man has not time to draw his arrows from the quiver. Sitting Bull kills one woman with his lance and captures another, the man meanwhile endeavoring to drag him from the horse, from which it is supposed he is forced to destroy others of the war party.

The fate of Sitting Bull and his victims is given in this history.

No. 3. Sitting Bull pursuing his enemy, a Crow Indian, whom he strikes with his lance.

No. 4. Lances a Crow woman.

No. 5. Lances a Crow Indian.

No. 6. Sitting Bull twice wounded and unhorsed; his enemy, a Crow, at length killed by a shot in the abdomen and his scalp taken and hung to Sitting Bull's saddle.

No. 7. In an engagement with the Crows, Sitting Bull mortally wounds one of the enemy, and, dropping his lance, rides up and strikes him with his whip. The lines and dashes in the picture represent the arrows and bullets that were flying in the air during the combat.

No. 8. Counts "coup" on a Gros Ventre de Prairie by striking him with his lance. Gros Ventre distinguished from Crow by manner of wearing his hair.

No. 9. Lances a Crow Indian.

No. 10. A Crow Indian attempts to seize Sitting Bull's horse by the bridle; Sitting Bull knocks him down with a "coup" stick, takes his scalp and hangs it to his bridle.

No. 11. Sitting Bull, with his brother mounted behind him, kills a white man, a soldier.

No. 12. Counts "coup" on a white man by hitting him with a "coup" stick.

No. 13. In a warm engagement with the whites, as shown by the bullets flying about, Sitting Bull shoots an arrow through the body of a soldier, who turns and fires, wounding Sitting Bull in the hip.

No. 14. Sitting Bull counts "coup" on a white man by striking him with his bow. Sitting Bull wears a red jacket and bandanna handkerchief taken from some of his victims.

Nos. 15 to 22 are repetitions of No. 14, Sitting Bull in each counting "coup" on a white man.

No. 23. Sitting Bull shoots a frontiersman wearing a buckskin shirt, takes his scalp, which he hangs to his own bridle, and captures his horse. Sitting Bull wears a blanket.

No. 24. Sitting Bull strikes a white soldier with his "coup" stick, takes his scalp and mule.

No. 25. counts "coup" on a soldier mounted, with overcoat on, gun slung across his back, by riding up and striking him with his riding-whip.

No. 26. Kills a white man and takes his scalp.

No. 27. Captures a mule and a scalp.

No. 28. In a warm engagement captures a horse and a scalp.

No. 29. Steals a mule.

No. 30. Captures two horses in action.

No. 31. Steals a horse.

No. 32. Steals and runs off a drove of horses from the Crows.

No. 33. In an engagement captures a government horse and mule and a scalp.

No. 34. Steals a horse.

No. 35. Captures three horses and a scalp.

No. 36. Steals a drove of horses from the Crows.

No. 37. Steals a government horse.

No. 38. Steals a drove of horses from the Crows.

No. 39. In an engagement captures a mule. Sitting Bull first appears here as chief of the band of Strong Hearts, to which dignity his prowess had raised him. The insignia of his rank, a bow having on end a lance head, he carries in his hand.

No. 40. Sitting Bull, chief of the band of Strong Hearts, captures two horses in an engagement, in which his horse is wounded in the shoulder.

No. 41. Captures a horse in a fight.

No. 42. Steals a mule.

No. 43. Captures two horses in a fight, in which his horse is wounded in the leg.

No. 44. Mounted on a government horse captures a white man.

No. 45. Steals two horses.

No. 46. Captures four mules in a fight, in which his horse is wounded in the hip.

Nos. 47 and 48. Counts "coup" on white men.

No. 49. Steals a government horse.

No. 50. Fastens his horse to his lance, driven into the earth, and in a hand-to-hand fight kills a white man with his own gun. The black marks show the ground fought and trampled over.

No. 51. A fort into which his enemies, the Crows, have retreated, and from which they maintain a hot fire, through which Sitting Bull charges the fort.

No. 52. In a fight with Crows, Sitting Bull kills and scalps one Indian and counts "coup" on another, and fires at him, barely missing him.

No. 53. Steals a drove of mules.

No. 54. Sitting Bull, at the head of his band, charges into a camp of Crows and kills thirty of them. This happened in the winter of 1869–70.

No. 55. Kills one Crow and counts "coup" on two others, who run from him disgracefully.

Such was the self-told story of this red desperado's career down to the summer of 1870, and in it he doubtless did himself no injustice. Rather was his life more venturesome and lawless than even that criminal calendar would indicate. Since the establishment of Fort Buford, in 1866, Sitting Bull, at the head of from sixty to seventy warriors, had been the terror of mail-carriers, wood-choppers and small parties in the vicinity of the post, and from 100 to 200 miles from it either way, up and down the Missouri River. During the time from 1866 to 1870, when the biography was written, this band had several times captured and destroyed the mail, and had stolen and run off over 200 head of cattle and killed near a score of white men in the immediate vicinity of the fort.

Despite this autobiography, however, the origin and early life of Sitting Bull are involved in much of mystery. Many different stories have been told concerning him, and he has himself told the story of his early years on various occasions in various versions. Once he said:

"I was born near old Fort George, on Willow Creek, below the mouth of the Cheyenne River. Cannot tell exactly how old I am. We count our years from the moons between great events. The event from which I date my birth is the year in which Thunder Hawk was born. I have always been running around. Indians that remain on the same hunting grounds all the time can remember years better. I have nine children and two living wives and one wife that has gone to the Great Spirit. I have two pairs of twins. I think as much of one as the other. If I did not I would not keep them. I believe if I had a white wife I would think more of her than the other two. My father's name was The Jumping Bull, and he was a chief. At the age of fourteen I killed an enemy and I began to make myself great in battle and became a chief."

Again, in 1877, after the Custer massacre, and while he was in the British territory for safety, a correspondent wrote as follows concerning the famous chief:

"The mystery that has hitherto shrouded the person of the great Sioux warrior has been removed. In conversation after dinner with one of the police officers, the other day he said that he was a native of Fort Garry, and an alumnus of St. John's College there—statements which he himself afterward confirmed. Several old traders who have had a look at him declare that they remember him well as Charlie Jacobs, a half-breed, who attended the college in its infancy thirty years ago. This young Jacobs was of Ojibway birth, and was a remarkably intelligent lad, with ambition to become a 'big Injun.' He disappeared from Fort Garry about 1853.

"When asked by the police officer if he recollected anything about Fort Garry, Sitting Bull laughed heartily and said he knew the principal people there, among others Donald A. Smith, the Hudson Bay factor; James Sutherland, and Father Vary, now a missionary at the Sault. He was also well acquainted with the late James Ross, Chief Justice of the Riel-Lepine Government in 1869–70; indeed, he says, they were boys together. Ross was a half-breed, who, after graduating at St. John's College, went to Toronto University, where he was a gold medalist. Sitting Bull says his father, Henry Jacobs, was at one time employed as interpreter by Father Proulx on Manitoulin Island, but whether the old gentleman is dead or not he does not know. Sitting Bull is thoroughly familiar with French and English and several Indian languages. He is about forty-two or forty-three years of age, a medium-sized athletic-built man, of no distinguishing traits beyond those always found in the half-breed. He is an excellent conversationalist, and will talk on every subject but his plans for the future."

Captain McGarry, of an Upper Missouri steamboat, knew Sitting Bull well for many years, and in August, 1876, gave this account of him:

"Sitting Bull is a Teton-Sioux, and is thirty-five years old. He is a Roman Catholic convert, and said to be a firm believer in all the tenets of that church. He was converted by Father de Smet. By this priest he was taught French, and he is able to read and speak that tongue with fluency. He has always doggedly refused to learn English. He is well versed in the Delaware language also, and is pronounced by the native tribes a greater orator than Little Pheasant, chief of the Yanktonnais. Sitting Bull has read French history carefully, and he is especially enamored of the career of Napoleon, and endeavors to model his campaigns after those of the "Man of Destiny." In 1868 Sitting Bull became a chief. Previously he had been repudiated by the other chiefs, and had been for several years a malcontent and at variance with the other chiefs of the Sioux nation, often coming into open conflict with them. After he contemplated his present war with the whites his ranks were filled by hundreds of young braves, who were seduced into revolt by his persuasive eloquence. At length the other chiefs deemed it policy to recognize him, and from that moment his supremacy was insured. Every summer, for years, he has been North into the country of the Assiniboins and Crees, and the acquaintance and friendship which he cultivated there are ripening into a harvest."

About the same time a well-known resident of Manitoba, made another contribution to the history of Sitting Bull. He described him as a Sac or Fox, and not a Sioux at all. He attended, says this historian, the school at Fort Garry, when a young man, having moved thither from Prairie du Chien. He acquired a good education, especially in French, and was noted as a superb marksman with pistol or rifle. While in Manitoba, his great object in life seemed to be the establishment of a great Indian commonwealth, governed exclusively by aborigines or half-breeds. In the summer of 1869, he made a proposition to Louis Riel, looking to the establishment of an inde-

pendent province either on British or Canadian soil, stating at the
same time that he could obtain money from London and through
the Hudson Bay company, in support of such a governmental enter-
prise. He told Reil that he would stand at his back with 5,000 Sioux
warriors, if he would only enter into an agreement providing that
none but Indian and half breed officers should be chosen to govern
his proposed independent province. This proposition was declined
by Reil on the ground that the church authorities of Manitoba would
refuse any sanction to the programme, being opposed to an independent principality in Northern America. Nor does this conclude
the catalogue of conflicting records. An army officer, in the summer
of 1876, propounded the startling inquiry, "Is Sitting Bull a West
Point graduate?" "This question," he continued, "is asked in sober
earnest, with the view of eliciting information, there being reasons
for believing that this formidable warrior and so-called savage, now
occupying so much of public attention, from the unquestioned skill
and extraordinary courage with which he has met our soldiers, is
really a graduate of the Military Academy. There may be some
foundation for the reports as to his reading French and being
familiar with the campaigns of the great Napoleon. Graduates of
West Point, between 1846 and 1850, will remember the new cadet
of both singular and remarkable appearance, hailing from the western borders of Missouri, who reported for duty in 1845, 1846 or
1847. Above medium height, apparently between eighteen and
twenty years old, heavy set frame, long, bushy hair, growing close to
his brow and overhanging his neck and shoulders, his face covered
with thin patches of fuzzy beard, the general get-up of this plebe
was such as to cause the old cadets to hesitate in the heretical jokes
usually played off on new cadets. Nicknames are often applied to
cadets that they carry with them among their friends into the army,
and even to their graves. The thick neck, broad shoulders, and long,
bushy hair, caused the name of "Bison" to be applied to this new
comer, and it adhered to him ever afterward. The West Point course
he learned with ease, graduating in the upper third of his class. He
had no disposition to be social, kept to himself, talked but little and
was never known to either smile or laugh. During hours of recreation
he did not mingle with his classmates, but was often seen in solitary
walks around the plain or scaling the neighboring mountains, even

to their very summits. He was often out of his quarters after night, eluding successfully the vigilance of sentinels and officers, visiting the neighboring villages in quest of strong drink, but never seen under its influence until he had graduated.

"This remarkable character passed his graduating examination creditably, received his diploma, but before doffing the cadet gray, visited the village of Buttermilk Falls, below West Point a short distance, got intoxicated and became involved in a broil, in which stones and sticks were used freely. Several of the participants were badly hurt, and the Bison himself much bruised. This conduct was regarded as so unbecoming and discreditable that on the recommendation of the academic board he was refused a commission in the army. He was heard of three times after leaving the academy, once at Galveston, Texas. There he had a terrible fight with some desperadoes, and was forced to leave. He was next seen on one of the California steamers, and going upon the western coast he got into an altercation with the officers of the steamer, and was placed under guard down in the hold, and made to work. The third and last time, as far as we know, he was seen and recognized under the following circumstances; In 1858, about ten years after the Bison had graduated, Lieutenant Ives, of the Topographical Engineer Corps, was engaged in making an exploration and survey of the Colorado River, emptying into the Gulf of California. While engaged in this work he would quite often leave his boat in the afternoon and go on shore and bivouac till morning. On one of these occasions a party of Mohave Indians came into his camp, and after talking some time in Spanish, the chief says, in English, "Ives, do you know me?" The Lieutenant was startled at hearing his name called so distinctly in English by this naked and painted-face chief; he replied that he did not, and asked the chief where he had learned to speak English so well. The chief replied: "Never mind that, but do you know me, Ives?" The Lieutenant scanned closely the huge painted chief, with feathers in head, rings through his nose and ears, and again answered he did not, and again asked the chief where he had learned English, and how did it happen that he knew him. The chief replied that he did not wonder at his not knowing him, as his change of nationality had brought with it a great change in habits, dress and appearance, and then added: "I am the Bison; we were together at

West Point. I have with this little party been watching you for several days. My band wanted to kill you and your little party, but I told them we had better wait and see, and try and talk; that we might do better than kill you. I have made them understand that after you have left and gone back trade will spring up, and we can then do better by trading or robbing the boats loaded with goods and supplies of all kinds." The Indians retired and were seen no more, nor did I bivouac on land any more. A year or two before this, Captain Lyon (killed in the late war) of the army, had a desperate fight with the Indians on an island in the Colorado River, the Indians supposed to have been commanded by the Bison. He was successful for years in raiding on the settlements and extending as far off as Arizona. It may be, and we think it probable, with the settlements extending from the West to the East, and from East to West, and the Indian area diminishing constantly, that this Indian chief may have gone as far North as the Black Hills, and may be even the veritable Sitting Bull, for to the close observer, Sitting Bull has shown as much skill and judgment as any educated civilized soldier could have done. It would not be strange if Sitting Bull proves to have been educated at West Point, and it seems to us probable that such is the case."

To this remarkable story the following was added by another West Pointer:

"Bison" McLean was a cadet at West Point from Missouri from 1844 to 1848, and stood *well intellectually* in a large and bright class. His diploma was refused him when his class graduated in 1848, he, having been convicted before a court-martial of dishonorable conduct. During the Summer of 1852 I met him in New Mexico. He had joined the Gila Apache Indians, had been adopted into the tribe, and had with him a wife or two from among the squaws. At this meeting he declared to me that he would never forget nor forgive the injustice and injuries he conceived he had received from his classmates and the academic authorities at West Point. If "Bison" McLean is living he is forty-nine or fifty years old. In character he is strong and rugged. His nature is untamed and licentious, his courage superb, and his physical qualities almost herculean, except in size. He is fair-complexioned, light colored hair, very full-bearded and hairy-bodied man, with a large head, and bold, irregular, full face.

His height is five feet ten or eleven inches, and twenty-four years ago he would have weighed about 175 or 180 pounds.

"When a cadet there was no disguise he would not assume and no hazard he would not venture for the gratification of his appetites. He never used strong drink when I knew him, and notwithstanding the great circumspection and vigilance of West Point authority, he thwarted it until the very end of his career at that institution, and was then brought to grief by the testimony of his own classmates, against whose watchfulness he had perhaps taken no precaution. Such a man, after near thirty years of experience among the savages, might well fill the position of Sitting Bull. While he was a cadet, under the cloak of a false marriage, he ruined a pretty girl, Effie Conklin, who lived at Buttermilk Falls, a mile or two below West Point."

This startling theory, however, was generally discredited. A correspondent writing from Huntsville, Mo., to *The St. Louis Republican*, thus inveighed against it:

"Bison, as he was known at West Point, was born and raised in this (Randolph) county. He was of highly respectable parentage. A nephew of John McLean, once a U.S. senator from Illinois, and brother of Finis M. McLean, a prominent citizen of this county. He entered West Point about the year 1846, and, I think, graduated in the class of which Stonewall Jackson was a member. He (Bison) was killed by Indians near Tubac, Arizona, about the year 1870. A gentleman then living in Tucson, Arizona, who had formerly lived here, and who knew Bison here and there, informed his relatives of his death, and sent them what money he left. Lieut. Hall of the Fifth cavalry, who was with Crook in Arizona, and now with him, and who is well acquainted with Bison's relatives here, confirms the statements received by his relatives of his death and the manner of his death. Of Bison I suppose it may be said that his greatest fault was that of having an ungovernable temper, which he knew, and which no doubt led him to pass his life beyond the confines of civilization. It was through the influence of Senator Benton that he received the appointment as a cadet to West Point, though his father, Charles McLean, was a zealous Whig. As to who Sitting Bull is, the writer of this does not know. But certain it is that he is not Bison." ...

The general concensus of opinion now is that Sitting Bull was born at a camp on Willow Creek, near the mouth of the Cheyenne River, and near old Fort George, about 1830. He was the son of Jumping Bull, a Sioux chief, and a nephew of Four Horns and Hunting His Lodge, who were also chiefs. His father was, for an Indian, a wealthy man, and was "the owner of a great many ponies in four colors." Although not destined to be a warrior, Sitting Bull, who was at first called Sacred Standshot, soon became a famous hunter. At ten years old he was famous all through the tribe as a killer of buffalo calves. As his father was rich and did not need the meat, the boy gave away all the game he killed to the poorer members of the tribe, and thus gained great popularity. When he was thirteen years old his father died, and he thereupon "killed buffaloes and fed his people." The next year he fought with and killed a young Indian a few years older than himself, and his name was then changed to Lame Bull or Sitting Bull, on account of a wound which he then received, which made him permanently lame.

Before he reached his fifteenth year Sitting Bull began to develop those traits which afterward made him a terror to the white settlers of the frontier. He is described by an old Western scout as a boy of rather stocky appearance, not "straight as an arrow" like the traditional Indian, and not given to any of those boyish sports which Fennimore Cooper has set up as standard. He was lazy and vicious, and never told the truth when a lie would serve better. But with all these traits he was fearless under all circumstances, a magnificent rider, an accurate shot, and capable of enduring an extraordinary amount of fatigue. As he approached 21 the cruelty of his nature became more marked, but he did nothing to indicate that he had in him the making of one of the representative men of his race.

He was three times married, one of his wives dying soon after the wedding. The other two wives were named She That Was Seen by the Nation, and She That Had Four Robes. They bore in all nine children, including a pair of twins—a most unusual thing among Indians. When, after the Custer massacre, Sitting Bull at last surrendered at Fort Buford, one of his sons, a young man of 18, was at school in Chicago. Another, a boy of six years, was with the chief, and at the formal pow-wow the chief put his heavy rifle in the little fellow's hands and ordered him to give it to Major Brotherton, saying: "I surrender this rifle to you through my young son, whom I now desire to teach in this way that he has become a friend of the whites. I wish him to live as the whites do and be taught in their schools. I wish to be remembered as the last man of my tribe who gave up his rifle. This boy has now given it to you, and he wants to know how he is going to make a living."

Sitting Bull is commonly thought of as a warrior. In point of fact he was not. He was a "medicine man;" which means that he included within himself the three professions of the priesthood, medicine and law. He inherited from his father the chieftanship of a part of the Sioux tribe. But his remarkable ascendancy over the whole tribe or nation was due to his miracle-working and to his talents as a politician. He played upon the credulity of the Sioux with his "medicine" or pretended miracles, until they believed him to possess supernatural powers, and were ready to follow his lead in everything. Some other chiefs inherited wider authority, such as Red Cloud and Crazy Horse, and some minor chiefs were inclined now and then to dispute his sway, such as Gall, Rain-in-the-face, and Broad Trail. But when Sitting Bull made an appeal to the religious fanaticism of the people, there was no withstanding him. To the day of his death he was the principal chief of all the Sioux and leader of 6,000 braves, who at all times were ready at his command to commit any crime from murder up or down. As a medicine man he had the squaws of his tribe abjectly subservient, and through them was assisted in maintaining control of the bucks.

Just what sort of a man a "medicine man" is, not many people are prepared to say. Even those who have traveled in the Indian country have not the most definite ideas. As explained by a well-versed writer in *The New York Sun*, every tribe has many of these personages, some of them chiefs, and all important men. They may be either young or old; and they are the leaders in all religious and social functions. No one can visit any Indians at any festival time, or time of general excitement from any cause, without seeing the medicine men figuring very conspicuously in whatever is going on. Sometimes they are merely beating drums, or perhaps they are only crooning, while a dance or feast is in progress. At other times they appear in the most grotesque costumes, painted all over, hung with feathers and tails and claws, and carrying some wand or staff, gorgeous with color, and smothered with Indian finery.

The term medicine is a white man's expression which the Indians have adopted. It was applied to the priests of the tribes—for that is what they really are—because the first white men often found them making their incantations at the side of the sick, the wounded, or the dying. In reality they were exorcising the evil spirits of disease or death, but the white travelers, seeing them in the presence of the sick, put two and two together and called them medicine men. The term is two centuries old, and the Indians have so fully adopted it that when one of these officials is at his offices they say he is "making medicine."

The medicine-man is a conjurer ,a magician, a dealer in magic, and an intermediary between the men of this world and the spirits of the other. He may know something of the rude pharmacopoeia of his fellows, and may prescribe certain leaves or roots to allay fever, to arrest a cold, or to heal a wound. That is not his business, however, and such prescriptions are more apt to be offered by the squaws or by any member of the patient's family. The medicine-man's work comes in when medicine fails, and it is pursued until death is seen to be certain, when—among most of the tribes—the sick or wounded man is abandoned to meet his fate. Far from thinking the only good Indian is a dead one, the Indians themselves have little regard for one who is half dead or seems certain to die.

In the Spring of 1890 as many medicine men as could crowd into a tepee of the largest size, beat their tomtoms and rattled their gourds all day and night for nearly a week to save the life of a dying plain chieftain, and then, as he seemed to get worse, deliberately withdrew from the tepee and turned the chief over to the ministrations of a Roman Catholic priest, whom they had excluded while they thought the man might live. They secured the best horse the old man had, and, leading it to the side of the tent, shot it through the head, that its carcass might be buried with him. Then they engaged in the politics of the situation and made themselves warmly friendly in the eyes of the heir apparent to the leadership. The old chief lived two or three days and was dosed with the physics of both the whites and red men. He begged for more "medicine," but the conjurors had diagnosed his case and decided it to be a waste of time to bother the spirits any longer in his behalf.

No more weird sight is to be seen on the face of this continent than a view of such a group of medicine men at work to save a life. Seen at night the effect is awesome. They sit in a circle, broken only by the body of the invalid stretched on a blanket, at the head of the tent opposite the door or tent opening. The wavering light is from a candle stuck ingeniously in a loop of birch bark, fastened tight in a slit in the end of a stick that has been thrust in the earth. The medicine men are painted in their own colors, green and yellow predominating. They are in full regalia, but their hair falls over their hideous faces as they bend forward to swing to and fro or to beat their drums. All are singing. Often they sing only the tunes of ancient songs, the words being forgotten or having grown tiresome. Now and then one leaps to his feet, waving his befeathered rattle and yelling louder than the others. He sings the words that occur to him as suiting the case. He has on no clothing but moccasins and a breech-clout, or "gee-string," as they call that garment on the plains.

His thin, bony, bare red legs have the effect of their nakedness increased by the jumping, dangling tail of feathers that flutters down from his head and mixed its colors with the paint stripes on his flesh. His dancing is rather more like pounding something beneath him than like what we call dancing. He lifts his feet by bending his knees; lifts them and thumps them down monotonously, though he turns his body first to one side and then to the other. When the dancer tired and fell back in his place in the circle the spirit moved another to take his place.

The queer resemblances between the Indians and those Hebrew bands of whose history the Old Testament is a record have often been pointed out, but the writer has never seen attention called to the similarity of certain of the Hebrew incidents to the common practices of Indian medicine men. In their early history the Hebrew leaders were continually holding converse with the Almighty. They went apart from their followers, up in mountains or in secret places and talked with Jehovah. That is precisely what the medicine men do to-day, or pretend to do. Every man who knows the Indians knows that during all this Messiah craze the medicine men of the various tribes have with great formality prepared to talk with

Gitchie-Manitou or whatever they happen to call the Good Spirit. In some tribes they have built little wickiups of saplings and leaves and have gone into them and held conversations that were audible, though not intelligible, to the red men listening outside. The savages have heard the medicine man's voice and then have heard the voice of some other person replying to him in a jargon they could not unravel. In other tribes the medicine men have merely reported having held such conversations precisely as the Israelitish leaders did. It is not for us to say that the grounds for such reports of the words of the Almighty were as slight in one case as the other, but it is true that the Indians have believed that their priests have really believed such conversations took place.

Those that have followed Sitting Bull's history know that his tribe has long been divided as to his power. One contingent has held that his "medicine" is no good, by which they mean that if he ever had genuine power to converse with spirits that power has left him. This often happens. Medicine men have their day and their decline, and he is a very sagacious Indian who can keep up faith in his ministrations for many years at a time or until he dies.

The following authentic story illustrates how much Sitting Bull was feared in his tribe. In January, 1876, when Major Alderson was Indian agent at Fort Peck, he received from the government a letter which he was ordered to convey to Sitting Bull, commanding that worthy to come into the reservation or consider himself an outlaw. Alderson was in a quandary. His instructions were clear and peremptory. He sent for Sitting Bull, but Sitting Bull was just then too busy to visit Fort Peck; so the letter had, if possible, to be sent to him. A gentleman of unquestioned bravery, who could speak the Indian language fluently, was sent for and offered $500. and an escort if he would take the letter to the Indian camp. After consideration, however, the offer was declined. "For," said he, "if I could see Sitting Bull myself, I believe my life would be safe, but he would cut my ears off, sure." Finally, a party of Indians were dispatched with the missive after it had been very carefully explained and interpreted. After an absence of five days they returned and confessed that their hearts "were not big enough" to carry such a message to Sitting Bull. Consequently the benevolent intentions of the government were never conveyed to the contumacious chief.

And yet he was often magnanimous, from an Indian's point of view. For example, it is told that in 1873 he was coming with a small band to Fort Peck, and he found a short distance from the fort, three white men lying asleep under a tree. His followers wanted to kill and scalp them on the spot, and secure their arms and horses. This the chief would not allow, and stood over them till all his band had passed. Next day in the fort, Sitting Bull walked up to the leader, Mr. Campbell, and shook hands. Campbell said he did not know him. "I am Sitting Bull," was the reply, "and I gave you your life yesterday." "How was that?" said Campbell. The chief proceeded to explain in a manner that satisfied Campbell that what he said was true, and, in gratitude, offered rewards, but Sitting Bull declined all such proffers, and after another handshaking, strode away.

Commissioner of Indian Affairs

"A shot was fired and carnage ensued"

1891

Bureaucrats charged with the management of Indian affairs conveyed their own images of Indians. The diligent ones strived for objectivity in their literary treatments, but they were hardly more qualified than journalists or novelists to discuss the varieties of Indian life. In the following extract concerning the Sioux, the Ghost Dance, and Wounded Knee, agency and Washington officials alike describe events with a vocabulary that suggests the contours of the bureaucratic image. A religious movement is a "craze," and Indians who participate in it are "wild and crazy," while those who do not are "friendly, progressive Indians," and so forth.

During the summer and fall of 1890 reports reaching this office from various sources showed that a growing excitement existed among the Indian tribes over the announcement of the advent of a so-called Indian Messiah or Christ, or Great Medicine Man of the North. The delusion finally became so widespread and well-defined as to be generally known as the "Messiah Craze." Its origin is somewhat obscure and its manifestations have varied slightly among different tribes. A few instances may be cited as representative.

In June, 1890, through the War Department, came the account of a "Cheyenne medicine man, Porcupine," who claimed to have left his reservation in November, 1889, and to have traveled by command and under divine guidance in search of the Messiah to the

From *Sixtieth Annual Report of the Commissioner of Indian Affairs to the Secretary of the Interior, 1891* (Washington, D.C., Government Printing Office, 1891), 123–35.

Shoshone Agency, Salt Lake City, and the Fort Hall Agency, and thence—with others who joined him at Fort Hall—to Walker River Reservation. Nev. There "the Christ," who was scarred on wrist and face, told them of his crucifixion, taught them a certain dance, counseled love and kindness for each other, and foretold that the Indian dead were to be resurrected, the youth of good people to be renewed, the earth enlarged, etc.

From the Tongue River Agency, in Montana, came a report, made by the special agent in charge, dated August 20, 1890, that Porcupine, an Indian of that agency, had declared himself to be the new Messiah, and had found a large following ready to believe in his doctrine. Those who doubted were fearful lest their unbelief should call down upon them the curse of the "Mighty Porcupine." The order went forth that in order to please the Great Spirit a six days and nights' dance must be held every new moon, with the understanding that at the expiration of a certain period the Great Spirit would restore the buffalo, elk, and other game, resurrect all dead Indians, endow his believers with perpetual youth, and perform many other wonders well calculated to inflame Indian superstition. Dances, afterward known as "ghost dances," were enthusiastically attended, and the accompanying feasts were so associated by stockmen with the disappearance of their cattle that very strained relations resulted between the rancher and Indian, which at one time threatened serious trouble.

About the same time the Cheyenne and Arapaho agent in Oklahoma reported that during the autumn of 1889 and the ensuing winter rumors had reached that agency from the Shoshones of Wyoming that an Indian Messiah was located in the mountains about 200 miles north of the Shoshones; that prominent medicine men had seen and held conversation with him, and had been told by him that the whites were to be removed from the country, the buffalo to come back, and the Indians to be restored to their original status. This report excited considerable interest among the Cheyennes and Arapahoes, particularly the Arapahoes, and they raised money to defray the expenses of sending two of their number to Wyoming to investigate the matter. After an absence of about two months these delegates returned, reporting that they had been prevented by snow from making the journey to the mountains to see the "Christ," but that the rumors concerning him were verified by the Indians at Shoshone. Great excitement soon prevailed; all industrial work came to a standstill; meetings were held in which hundreds of Indians would rise from the ground, circle around, and sing and cry until apparently exhausted. At one time they even contemplated leaving their reservation in a body to go and seek the "Christ."

During my absence from the office last fall on a tour of observation among the Indian agencies and schools, which lasted from September 5 to early in December, I had occasion to notice the effect of this craze among several tribes, and it was brought up prominently in a council with the Kiowas, Comanches, etc., of Oklahoma. As I stated in the supplement to my annual report of December 8 last, I found that among the tribes which I visited the excitement was comparatively harmless, and although it had seriously retarded progress in civilization for the time being, it had been readily controlled and had furnished no occasion for alarm; and I added:

> The only danger to be apprehended is that influences from without, emanating from those who in some manner might be benefited by the Indians uprising or the movement of troops, or by the excitement growing out of "wars and rumors of wars," may precipitate a needless conflict and bring on a disastrous and costly war. Of course this is said in regard to the Indians whom I have visited. I have not been among the Sioux of the Dakotas.

Among some of the Sioux the matter became more serious.

In August, 1890, Agent Gallagher stated that many at the Pine Ridge Agency were crediting the report made to them in the preceding spring that a great medicine man had appeared in Wyoming whose mission was to resurrect and rehabilitate all the departed heroes of the tribe, restore to the Indians herds of buffalo which would make them entirely independent of aid from the whites, and bring such confusion upon their enemies, the whites, that they would flee the country, leaving the Indians in possession of the entire Northwest for all time to come. Indians fainted during the performances which attended the recital of the wondrous things soon to come to pass, and one man died from the excitement. The effect of such meetings or dances was so demoralizing that on August 22, 1890, when about 2,000 Indians were gathered on White Clay Creek, about 18 miles from the agency, to hold what they called a religious dance connected with the appearance of this supernatural being, the agent instructed his Indian police to disperse them. This they were unable to do. Accompanied by about 20 police the agent himself visited the place, and on hearing of his approach most of the Indians dispersed. Several men, however, with Winchester rifles in their hands, and a good storing of cartridges belted around their waists, stood stripped for fight, prepared to die in defense of the new faith. They were finally quieted.

But the dances continued, and October 12, 1890, Agent Royer, who had just taken charge of the agency, reported that more than half the Indians had already joined the dancing, and when requested to stop would strip themselves ready for fight; that the police had lost control, and if his endeavors to induce the chiefs to suppress the craze should be unavailing, he hoped for hearty coöperation in invoking military aid to maintain order.

About the same time the Cheyenne River agent reported that Big Foot's band were much excited about the coming of a "Messiah," were holding "ghost dances" and, armed with Winchester rifles and of very threatening temper, were beyond police control.

A similar condition of affairs existed among the Rosebud Sioux.

Agent McLaughlin also reported from Standing Rock October 17, as follows:

> I feel it my duty to report the present craze and nature of the excitement existing among the Sitting Bull faction of Indians over the expected Indian millenium, the annihilation of the white man and supremacy of the Indian, which is looked for in the near future and promised by the Indian medicine men as not later than next spring, when the new grass begins to appear, and is known among the Sioux as the "return of the Ghosts."
>
> They are promised by some members of the Sioux tribe, who have lately developed into medicine men, that the Great Spirit has promised them that their punishment by the dominant race has been sufficient, and that their numbers having now become so decimated will be reinforced by all Indians who are dead; that the dead are all returning to reinhabit this earth, which belongs to the Indians; that they are driving back with them, as they return, immense herds of buffalo, and elegant wild horses to have for the catching; that the Great Spirit promises them that the white man will be unable to make gunpowder in future, and all attempts at such will be a failure, and that the gunpowder now on hand will be useless as against

Indians, as it will not throw a bullet with sufficient force to pass through the skin of an Indian; that the Great Spirit had deserted the Indians for a long period, but is now with them and against the whites, and will cover the earth over with thirty feet of additional soil, well sodded and timbered, under which the whites will all be smothered, and any whites who may escape these great phenomena will become small fishes in the rivers of the country, but in order to bring about this happy result the Indians must do their part and become believers and thoroughly organize.

It would seem impossible that any person, no matter how ignorant, could be brought to believe such absurd nonsense, but as a matter of fact a great many of the Indians of this agency actually believe it, and since this new doctrine has been engrafted here from the more southern Sioux agencies, the infection has been wonderful, and so pernicious that it now includes some of the Indians who were formerly numbered with the progressive and more intelligent, and many of the very best Indians appear dazed and undecided when talking of it, their inherent superstition having been thoroughly aroused.

Sitting Bull is high priest and leading apostle of this latest Indian absurdity; in a word he is the chief mischief-maker at this agency, and if he were not here, this Sitting Bull is a man of low cunning, devoid of a single manly principle in his nature, or an honorable trait of character, but on the contrary is capable of instigating and inciting others (those who believe in his promise) to do any amount of mischief. He is a coward and lacks moral courage; he will never lead where there is danger, but is an adept in influencing his ignorant henchmen and followers, and there is no knowing what he may direct them to attempt. He is bitterly opposed to having any surveys made on the reservation, and is continually agitating and fostering opposition to such surveys among his followers, who are the more worthless, ignorant, obstinate, and non-progressive of the Sioux.

On Thursday, the 9th instant, upon an invitation from Sitting Bull, an Indian named Kicking Bear, belonging to the Cheyenne River Agency, the chief medicine man of the ghost dance among the Sioux, arrived at Sitting Bull's camp on Grand River, 40 miles south of this agency, to inaugurate a ghost dance and initiate the members. Upon learning of his arrival there I sent a detachment of 13 policemen, including the captain and second lieutenant, to arrest and escort him from the reservation, but they returned without executing the order, both officers being in a dazed condition and fearing the powers of Kicking Bear's medicine. Several members of the force tried to induce the officers to permit them to make the arrest but the latter would not allow it, but simply told Sitting Bull that it was the agent's orders that Kicking Bear and his six companies should leave the reservation and return to their agency. Sitting Bull was very insolent to the officers and made some threats against some members of the force, but said that the visitors would leave the following day. Upon return of the detachment to the agency on Tuesday, the 14th, I immediately sent the lieutenant and one man back to see whether the party had left or not, and to notify Sitting Bull that this insolence and bad behavior would not be tolerated longer, and that the ghost dance must not be continued. The lieutenant returned yesterday and reported that the party had not started back to Cheyenne before his arrival there on the morning of the 15th, but left immediately upon his ordering them to do so, and that Sitting Bull told him that he was determined to continue the ghost dance, as the Great Spirit had sent a direct message by Kicking Bear that to live they must do so, but that he would not have any more dancing until after he had come to the agency and talked the matter over with me; but the news comes in this morning that they are dancing again and it is participated in by a great many Indians who become silly and like men intoxicated over the excitement. The dance is demoralizing, indecent, and disgusting.

Desiring to exhaust all reasonable means before resorting to extremes, I have sent a message to Sitting Bull, by his nephew One Bull, that I want to see him at the agency and I feel quite confident that I shall succeed in allaying the present excitement and put a stop to this absurd "craze" for the present at least, but I would respectfully recommend the removal from the reservation and confinement in some military prison, some distance from the Sioux country, of Sitting Bull and the parties named in my letter of June 18 last, hereinbefore referred to, some time during the coming winter before next spring opens.

At other Sioux agencies the Messiah craze seems to have made little or no impression. At Lower Brulé it was easily checked by the arrest by Indian police of twenty-two dancers, of whom seventeen were imprisoned for eight weeks at Fort Snelling. The Crow Creek, Santee, Yankton, and Sisseton Sioux, through schools, missions, and industrial pursuits, had been brought to give too valuable hostages to civilization to be affected by such a delusion.

This illegal appearance of a Messiah was not an entirely new thing. Some 6 or 8 years ago one of the Puyallup Indians claimed that in a trance he had been to the other world. As a result of his visions a kind of society was formed, churches were built, one of the Indians claimed to be the "Christ," and the band became so infatuated and unmanageable that the agent was obliged to imprison the alleged "Christ," punish his followers, and discharge a number of Indian judges and policemen in order to regain control.

During the past six months ghost dances have almost entirely disappeared, and although the Messiah craze prevailed to an unusual extent among a large number of widely separated tribes, and aroused a general feeling of discontent and unrest, yet it is doubtful if it would have had any history as more than one of many such ephemeral superstition of an ignorant and excitable people, if it had not been complicated with other disorders among the Sioux in the Dakotas so that it became one of the causes which led to the so-called Sioux war.

As early as June, 1890, a rumor that the Sioux were secretly planning an outbreak and needed close watching led this office to call upon the agents for the Sioux for reports as to the status and temper of the Indians in their charge. The replies indicated that no good grounds for apprehending trouble existed. The Rosebud agent, however, referred to the fact that secret communications had been passing between dissatisfied nonprogressive Indians at the various agencies who had refused to sign the agreement under which a large portion of the Sioux reserve had been opened to settlement by the President's proclamation of February 10, 1890. The Standing Rock agent reported as follows:

> So far as the Indians of this agency are concerned there is nothing in either their words or actions that would justify the rumor, and I do not believe that such an imprudent step is seriously meditated by any of the Sioux.
> There are, however, a few malcontents here, as at all of the Sioux agencies, who cling tenaciously to the old Indian ways and are slow to accept the better order of things, whose influence is exerted in the wrong direction, and this class of Indians are ever ready to circulate idle rumors and sow dissensions, to discourage the more progressive; but only a few of the Sioux could now possibly be united in attempting any overt act against the Government, and the removal from among them of a few individuals (the leaders of disaffection) such as Sitting Bull, Circling Bear, Black Bird, and Circling Hawk of this agency, Spotted Elk (Big Foot) and his lieutenants of Cheyenne River, Crow Dog and Low Dog of Rosebud, and any of like ilk of Pine Ridge, would end all trouble and uneasiness in the future.

The agent at Cheyenne River reported some little excitement

regarding the coming of an Indian "Messiah," as did the agent at Pine Ridge Agency, who also expressed his belief that it would soon die out without causing trouble.

After receiving later reports, already mentioned, which showed that ghost dancing was becoming a serious element of disturbance, the office instructed the agents at Standing Rock, Crow Creek and Lower Brûlé, Rosebud, and Pine Ridge Agencies, to exercise great caution in the management of the Indians, with a view to avoiding an outbreak, and, if deemed necessary, to call upon this office to secure military aid to prevent disturbances.

Agent Royer, of the Pine Ridge Agency, was especially advised, October 18, that Major-General Miles, commander of the military division in which the agency was situated, also chairman of the Commission recently appointed to negotiate with the Northern Cheyennes, would shortly visit the agency, and that he would have opportunity to explain the situation to him and ask his advice as to the wisdom of calling for troops.

October 24, 1890, this office recommended that the War Department be requested to cause Sitting Bull, Circling Hawk, Black Bird, and Circling Bear to be confined in some military prison, and to instruct the proper military authorities to be on the alert to discover any suspicious movements of the Indians of the Sioux agencies.

Early in November reports received from the agents at Pine Ridge, Rosebud, and Cheyenne River showed that the Indians of those agencies, especially Pine Ridge, were arming themselves and taking a defiant attitude towards the Government and its representatives, committing depredations, and likely to go to other excesses, and November 13 this office recommended that the matter be submitted to the War Department, with request that such prompt action be taken to avert an outbreak as the emergency might be found by them to demand.

On that day the President of the United States addressed the following communication to the Secretary of the Interior:

Replying to your several communications in regard to the condition of the Indians at the Sioux and Cheyenne agencies, I beg to say that some days ago I directed the War Department to send an officer of high rank to investigate the situation and to report upon it from a military standpoint. General Ruger, I understand, has been assigned to that duty, and is now probably at, or on his way to, these agencies. I have to-day directed the Secretary of War to assume a military responsibility for the suppression of any threatened outbreak, and to take such steps as may be necessary to that end. In the meantime, I suggest that you advise your agents to separate the well-disposed from the ill-disposed Indians, and while maintaining their control and discipline so far as may be possible, to avoid forcing any issue that will result in an outbreak, until suitable military preparations can be made.

November 15 Agent Royer sent to this office the following telegram frmo Pine Ridge:

> Indians are dancing in the snow and are wild and crazy. I have fully informed you that employés and Government property at this agency have no protection and are at the mercy of these dancers. Why delay by further investigation? We need protection, and we need it now. The leaders should be arrested and confined in some military post until the matter is quieted, and this should be done at once.

A military force under Gen. John R. Brooke, consisting of five companies of infantry, three troops of cavalry, and one Hotchkiss and one Gatling gun, arrived at Pine Ridge November 20, 1890. Two troops of cavalry and six companies of infantry were stationed at Rosebud. Troops were ordered to other agencies until finally nearly half the infantry and cavalry of the U.S. Army were concentrated upon the Sioux reservations. When the troops reached Rosebud about 1,800 Indians—men, women, and children—stampeded toward Pine Ridge and the bad lands, destroying their own property before leaving and that of others en route.

On December 1, 1890, in accordance with Department instructions, the following order was sent to the Sioux agents:

> During the present Indian troubles you are instructed that while you shall continue all the business and carry into effect the educational and other purposes of your agency, you will, as to all operations intended to suppress any outbreak by force, coöperate with and obey the orders of the military officer commanding on the reservation in your charge.

In the latter part of November the military authorized the arrest of Sitting Bull by W. F. Cody ("Buffalo Bill"), but at the request of Agent McLaughlin, who deemed it prudent to postpone the arrest until colder weather, the order was canceled by direction of the President.

Sitting Bull's camp where the dancing had been going on was on Grand River 40 miles from the agency. The number of Indian policemen in that vicinity was increased and he was kept under close surveillance. December 12 the commanding officer at Fort Yates was instructed by General Ruger, commanding the Department of Dakota, to make it his special duty to secure the person of Sitting Bull, and to call on Agent McLaughlin "for such coöperation and assistance as would best promote the object in view." December 14 the police notified the agent that Sitting Bull was preparing to leave the reservation. Accordingly, after consultation with the post commander it was decided that the arrest should be made the following morning by the police under command of Lieutenant Bullhead, with United States troops within supporting distance.

At daybreak, December 15, 39 Indian police and 4 volunteers went to Sitting Bull's cabin and arrested him. He agreed to accompany them to the agency, but while dressing caused considerable delay, and during this time his followers began to congregate to the number of 150, so that when he was brought out of the house they had the police entirely surrounded. Sitting Bull then refused to go and called on his friends, the ghost dancers, to rescue him. At this juncture one of them shot Lieutenant Bullhead. The lieutenant then shot Sitting Bull, who also received another shot and was killed outright. Another shot struck Sergeant Shavehead and then the firing became general. In about two hours the police had secured possession of Sitting Bull's house and driven their assailants into the woods. Shortly after, when 100 United States troops, under command of Capt. Fechet reached the spot the police drew up in line and saluted. Their bravery and discipline received highest praise from Capt. Fechet. The ghost dancers fled from their hiding places to the Cheyenne River Reservation, leaving their families and dead behind them. Their women who had taken part in the fight had been disarmed by the police and placed under guard and were turned over to the troops when they arrived. The losses were six policemen killed (including Bullhead and Shavehead who soon died at the agency hospital) and one wounded. The attacking party lost eight killed and three wounded.

Groups of Indians from the different reservations had commenced concentrating in the "bad lands," upon or in the vicinity of the Pine Ridge Reservation. Killing of cattle and destruction of other property by these Indians almost entirely within the liimts of Pine Ridge and Rosebud reservations occurred, but no signal fires were built, no warlike demonstrations were made, no violence was done to any white settler, nor was there cohesion or organization among the Indians themselves. Many of them were friendly Indians who had never participated in the ghost dance but had fled thither from fear of soldiers, in consequence of the Sitting Bull affair, or through the over persuasion of friends. The military gradually began to close in around them, and they offered no resistance, and a speedy and quiet capitulation of all was confidently expected.

Among them was Big Foot's band belonging to the Cheyenne River Agency, numbering with others who had joined him, about 120 men and 230 women and children. They had escaped to the bad lands, after arrest by the military at Cheyenne River, but soon started from the bad lands for the Pine Ridge Agency, and with a flag of truce advanced into the open country and proposed a parley with the troops whom they met. This being refused they surrendered unconditionally, remained in camp at Wounded Knee Creek over night, expecting to proceed next morning under escort of the troops to Pine Ridge, whither most of the quondam bad-land Indians were moving. The next day, December 29, when ordered to turn in their arms, they surrendered very few. By a search in the teepees 60 guns were obtained. When the military—a detachment of the Seventh Cavalry (Custer's old command), with other troops—began to take the arms from their persons a shot was fired and carnage ensued. According to reports of military officers, the Indians attacked the troops as soon as the disarmament commenced. The Indians claim that the first shot was fired by a half crazy, irresponsible Indian. At any rate, a short, sharp, indiscriminate fight immediately followed, and, during the fighting and the subsequent flight and pursuit of the Indians, the troops lost 25 killed and 35 wounded, and of the Indians, 84 men and boys, 44 women, and 18 children were killed and at least 33 were wounded, many of them fatally. Most of the men, including Big Foot, were killed around his tent where he lay sick. The bodies of women and children were scattered along a distance of two miles from the scene of the encounter.

Frightened and exasperated, again the Indians made for the bad lands. Indians en route thence to the agency turned back and others rushed away from Pine Ridge.

On January 6, 1891, military officers were assigned to the five Sioux agencies, under the following telegraphic instructions of that date to General Miles from Major-General Schofield:

> You are hereby authorized under existing orders of the President to assign Capt. E. P. Ewers, Capt. J. M. Lee, Capt. C. A. Earnest, and Capt. F. E. Pierce to the charge of the Indians of the several Sioux and Cheyenne agencies, to exercise over those Indians such military supervision and control as in your judgment is necessary, without interfering unnecessarily with the administration of the agents of the Indian Bureau under the regulations and instructions received by them from the Interior Department. It is not deemed advisable to detail two captains from the First Infantry. You will, therefore, please recommend another officer in the place of Captain Dougherty. Also, if you need other officers in addition to those, named recommend such as you think best qualified for that service.

A few skirmishes with the Indians followed the Wounded Knee affair, but by the end of January the Indians had come into the agencies and all serious troubles were practically ended.

Soon afterward a delegation of Sioux representing the different agencies and factions visited this city, had full conference with the Secretary of the Interior and the Commissioner of Indian Affairs relative to their rights and grievances, and were given an audience by the President.

It is worthy of note that the Christian Indians among the Sioux, those who had accepted the teaching of missionaries, were almost universally loyal, and in fact that the large body of the Sioux had no participation in the disturbances except to suffer from the consequences. Undoubtedly the large number among them in the bad lands who had abandoned their homes against their own desire, and were unwilling followers of their leaders, contributed in no small degree to bringing all hostilities to an end. While the damage done to the property of white settlers is slight, many friendly, progressive

Indians suffered severely in the destruction of houses, stock, and other property, a loss from which it will take them longer to recover.

On several occasions the office has been informed that the Sioux contemplated a renewal of hostilities, and very recently information was received, from a source deemed reliable, that they were endeavoring to induce other tribes to join them in a contemplated outbreak; but these reports prove, upon investigation, to have but little foundation in fact. Although some factions among the Indians are, undoubtedly, sullen and dissatisfied, and idle and vicious Indians have indulged in incendiary utterances, yet good feeling and satisfaction prevail almost universally on the Sioux reservations, and I do not consider that there are reasonable grounds for belief that any portion of the Sioux Nation of sufficient strength to be dangerous contemplates any overt act against the Government or the settlers.

It should also be recorded that no attempt was made by the Indians to reach and ravage any white settlements, no white person was killed off the reservation, and except in battle, only two were killed on the reserve.

A government herder, an old man named Miller, was wantonly murdered by a son of No Water. Lieut. E. W. Casey, of the Twenty-second Infantry, was killed by Plenty Horses. The death of this gallant young officer was much lamented. He was deeply interested in the welfare of the Indians, and was zealous in enlisting and drilling them as soldiers. All the facts in the case clearly show that the killing was without provocation, premeditated, and deliberate. Plenty Horses was arrested and tried in the United States court on the charge of murder but was released by the court on the ground that at the time of the killing "a state of war" existed between his tribe and the United States, and that the killing of Lieut. Casey was an incident of the war and not murder under the law.

On the other hand, an unprovoked attack made January 11, 1891, by white citizens upon a hunting party of friendly Sioux Indians, in Mead County, greatly excited the Indians, and had a strong tendency to retard their pacification. Some United States troops, at the instance of the attacking party, joined in pursuit of the Indians and fired upon them. Few Tails was killed and 2 Indian women were wounded. Few Tails was a peaceable Indian, and the attack upon his party was cold-blooded and wanton. For the murder of Few Tails 5 white men were indicted in the State court, Sturgis, S. Dak. Their trial, June 22 last, was ended July 2, with a verdict of "not guilty."

In stating the events which led to this outbreak among the Sioux the endeavor too often has been merely to find some opportunity for locating blame. The causes are complex and many are obscure and remote. Among them may be named the following:

First. A feeling of unrest and apprehension in the mind of the Indians has naturally grown out of the rapid advance in civilization and the great changes which this advance has necessitated in their habtis and mode of life.

Second. Prior to the agreement of 1876 buffalo and deer were the main support of the Sioux. Food, tents, bedding, were the direct outcome of hunting, and with furs and pelts as articles of barter or exchange, it was easy for the Sioux to procure whatever constituted for them the necessaries, the comforts, or even the luxuries of life. Within eight years from the agreement of 1876, the buffalo had gone and the Sioux had left to them alkali land and Government rations.

It is hard to overstate the magnitude of the calamity as they viewed it, which happened to those people by the sudden disappearance of the buffalo and the large diminution in the numbers of deer and other wild animals. Suddenly, almost without warning, they were expected at once and without previous training to settle down to the pursuits of agriculture in a land largely unfitted for such use. The freedom of the chase was to be exchanged for the idleness of the camp. The boundless range was to be abandoned for the circumscribed reservation, and abundance of plenty to be supplanted by limited and decreasing Government subsistence and supplies. Under these circumstances, it is not in human nature not to be discontented and restless, even turbulent and violent.

Third. During a long series of years treaties, agreements, cessions of land and privileges, and removals of bands and agencies have kept many of the Sioux, particularly those at Pine Ridge and Rosebud, in an unsettled condition, especially as some of the promises made them were fulfilled tardily or not at all. (A brief history of negotiations with the Sioux was given in my letter of December 24, 1890, to the Department. . . .)

Fourth, The very large reduction of the Great Sioux Reservation, brought about by the Sioux Commission through the consent of the large majority of the adult males, was bitterly opposed by a large, influential minority. For various reasons they regarded the cession as unwise, and did all in their power to prevent its consummation and afterward were constant in their expressions of dissatisfaction and in their endeavors to awaken a like feeling in the minds of those who signed the agreement.

Fifth. There was diminution and partial failure of the crops for 1889 by reason of their neglect by the Indians, who were congregated in large numbers at the council with the Sioux Commission, and a further diminution of ordinary crops by the drought of 1890. Also, in 1888 the disease of black-leg appeared among the cattle of the Indians.

Sixth. At this time, by delayed and reduced appropriations, the Sioux rations were temporarily cut down. Rations were not diminished to such an extent as to bring the Indians to starvation or even extreme suffering, as has been often reported; but short rations came just after the Sioux Commission had negotiated the agreement for the cession of lands, and as a condition of securing the signatures of the majority, had assured the Indians that their rations would be continued unchanged. To this matter the Sioux Commission called special attention in their report dated December 24, 1889, as follows:

> During our conference at the different agencies we were repeatedly asked whether the acceptance or rejection of the act of Congress would influence the action of the Government with reference to their rations, and in every instance the Indians were assured that subsistence was furnished in accordance with former treaties, and that signing would not affect their rations, and that they would continue to receive them as provided in former treaties. Without our assurances to this effect it would have been impossible to have secured their consent to the cession of their lands. Since our visit to the agencies it appears that large reductions have been made in the amounts of beef furnished for issues, amounting at Rosebud to 2,000,000 pounds and at Pine Ridge to 1,000,000 pounds, and lesser amounts at the other agencies. This action of the Department, following immediately after the successful issue of our negotiations, can not fail to have an injurious effect. It will be impossible to convince the Indians that the reduction is not due to the fact that the Government having obtained their land has less concern in looking after their material interests than before. It will be looked upon as a

breach of faith, and especially as a violation of the express statements of the Commissioners.

Already this action is being used by the Indians opposed to the bill, notably at Pine Ridge, as an argument in support of the wisdom of their opposition.

In forwarding this report to Congress the Department called special attention to the above-quoted statements of the Commission and said:

> The Commission further remarks that as to the quality of rations furnished there seems to be no just cause for complaint, but that it was particularly to be avoided that there should be any diminution of the rations promised under the former treaties *at this time*, as the Indians would not attribute it to their assent to the bill. Such diminution certainly should not be allowed, as the Government is bound in good faith to carry into effect the former treaties where not directly and positively affected by the act, and if under the provisions of the treaty itself the ration is at any time reduced, the Commissioners recommend that the Indian should be notified before spring opens, so that crops may be cultivated. It is desirable that the recent reduction made should be restored, as it is now impossible to convince the Indians that it was not due to the fact that the Government, having obtained their lands, had less concern in looking after their material interests.

Notwithstanding this plea of the Commission and of the Department, the appropriation made for the subsistence and civilization of the Sioux for 1890 was only $950,000, or $50,000 less than the amount estimated and appropriated for 1888 and 1889, and the appropriation not having been made until August 19, rations had to be temporarily purchased and issued in limited quantities pending arrival of new supplies to be secured from that appropriation.

It was not until January, 1891, after the troubles, that an appropriation of $100,000 was made by Congress for additional beef for the Sioux.

Seventh. Other promises made by the Sioux Commission and the agreement were not promptly fulfilled; among them were increase of appropriations for education, for which this office had asked an appropriation of $150,000; the payment of $200,000, in compensation for ponies taken from the Sioux in 1876 and 1877; and the reimbursement of the Crow Creek Indians for a reduction made in their per capita allowance of land as compared with the amount allowed other Sioux, which called for an appropriation of $187,039. The fulfillment of all these promises except the last named, was contained in the act of January 19, 1891.

Eighth. In 1889 and 1890 epidemics of *la grippe*, measles, and whooping cough, followed by many deaths, added to the gloom and misfortune which seemed to surround the Indians.

Ninth. The wording of the agreement changed the boundary line between the Rosebud and Pine Ridge, diminished reservations, and necessitated a removal of a portion of the Rosebud Indians from lands which by the agreement were included in the Pine Ridge Reservation to lands offered them in lieu thereof upon the diminished Rosebud Reserve. This, although involving no great hardship to any considerable number, added to the discontent.

Tenth. Some of the Indians were greatly opposed to the census which Congress ordered should be taken. The census at Rosebud, as reported by Special Agent Lea and confirmed by a special census taken by Agent Wright, revealed the somewhat startling fact that rations had been issued to Indians very largely in excess of the number actually present, and this diminution of numbers as shown by the census necessitated a diminution of the rations, which was based, of course, upon the census.

Eleventh. The Messiah craze, which fostered the belief that "ghost shirts" would be invulnerable to bullets, and that the supremacy of the Indian race was assured, added to discontent the fervor of fanaticism and brought those who accepted the new faith into the attitude of sullen defiance, but defensive rather than aggressive.

Twelfth. The sudden appearance of military upon their reservation gave rise to the wildest rumors among the Indians of danger and disaster, which were eagerly circulated by disaffected Indians and corroborated by exaggerated accounts in the newspapers, and these and other influences connected with and inseparable from military movements frightened many Indians away from their agencies into the bad lands and largely intensified whatever spirit of opposition to the Government existed.

Joseph Kossuth Dixon

"They have moved majestically down the pathway of the ages"

1914

In the two decades after Wounded Knee, the Indian became a relic, a curiosity, a symbol of a vanishing way of life. He had been an enemy, but a noble one, and if he was still exploited by purveyors of popular entertainment, he was also portrayed as a tragic figure whose image was romantic because the reality of his life was remote in time and space. This was nostalgia, and it took many forms. In September, 1909, the Bureau of Indian Affairs organized a "last council" of leaders from various Indian tribes to convene in the Little Big Horn Valley of Montana. Joseph Kossuth Dixon prepared an account of the council, a wistful volume distinguished by striking photographs, interesting oral history, and Dixon's overblown prose. What follows is Dixon's nostalgic memorial to Indian life, a passionate statement marking still another transformation of the Indian myth.

We are exchanging salutations with the uncalendared ages of the red man. We are measuring footsteps with moccasined feet whose trail leads along the receding sands of the western ocean. A bit of red colour set in immemorial time, now a silent sentinel, weeping unshed tears with eyes peering into a pitiless desert.

Life without humour is intolerable. The life of the Indian has been a series of long and bitter tragedies. There is a look in his face of bronze that frightens us, a tone lights up the gamut of his voice that makes it unlike any other voice we have ever heard—a voice

From Joseph K. Dixon, *The Vanishing Race: The Last Great Indian Council* (Garden City, N.Y., Doubleday, Page & Company, 1914), 3–36.

that will echo in the tomb of time—a Spartan courage that shall be regnant a millennium beyond the Thermopylae of his race.

We have come to the day of audit. Annihilation is not a cheerful word, but it is coined from the alphabet of Indian life and heralds the infinite pathos of a vanishing race. We are at the end of historical origins. The impression is profound.

A vision of the past and future confronts us. What we see is more wonderful than a view the points of which can be easily determined. We behold a dead sea of men under the empty and silent morning, a hollow land into which have flowed thousands upon thousands—at last the echo of a child's cry.

The door of the Indian's yesterdays opens to a new world—a world unpeopled with red men, but whose population fills the sky, the plains, with sad and spectre-like memories—with the flutter of unseen eagle pinions. A land without the tall and sombre figure worshipping the Great Mystery; without suns and snows and storms —without the scars of battle, swinging war club, and flashing arrow —a strange, weird world, holding an unconquered race, vanquished before the ruthless tread of superior forces—we call them the agents of civilization. Forces that have in cruel fashion borne down upon the Indian until he had to give up all that was his and all that was dear to him—to make himself over or die. He would not yield. He died. He would not receive his salvation by surrender; rather would he choose oblivion, unknown darkness—the melting fires of extermination. It is hard to think this virile, untamed creation has been swept like hurrying leaves by angry autumn gusts across the sunlit plains into a night without a star.

The white is the conquering race, but every-whither there is a cry in the heart to delve into the mystery of these ancient forerunners. This type of colour holds the eye, rivets and absorbs the interest.

Men are fast coming to recognize the high claim of a moral obligation to study the yesterdays of this imperial and imperious race. The preservation of this record in abiding form is all the more significant because all serious students of Indian life and lore are deeply convinced of the insistent fact that the Indian, as a race, is fast losing its typical characters and is soon destined to pass completely away. So rapidly are the remaining Western tribes putting aside their native customs and costumes, their modes of life and ceremonies, that we belong to the last generation that will be granted the supreme privilege of studying the Indian in anything like his native state. The buffalo has gone from the continent, and now the Indian is following the deserted buffalo trail. All future students and historians, all ethnological researches must turn to the pictures now made and the pages now written for the study of a great race.

It is little short of solemn justice to these vanishing red men that students, explorers, artists, poets, men of letters, genius, generosity, and industry, strive to make known to future generations what manner of men and women were these whom we have displaced and despoiled.

Indisputable figures, the result of more than five years of painstaking research on the part of the Bureau of Ethnology at Washington, place the decrease of Indian population in the United States, north of Mexico, since the coming of the white man, at 65 per cent. They have gone from the forests and plains, from the hills and valleys over which they roamed and reigned for uncounted ages. We have taken their land, blotted out their faith and despoiled their philosophy. It has been the utter extinction of a whole type of humanity. The conquering Anglo-Saxon speech has swept out of existence over a thousand distinct languages. These original Americans *Deserve a Monument*. They have moved majestically down the pathway of the ages, but it culminates in the dead march of Saul.

The record of the North American Indian has naught to do with the tabulation of statistics, the musty folios of custom reports, the conquests of commerce. He has never walked up to the gates of the city and asked entrance to its portals, nor subscribed himself as a contestant in the arena of finance. He has had no share in the lofty ideals of statecraft, nor the spotless ermine of the judiciary. He lived and moved and had his being in the sanctuary of the hills, the high altar-stairs of the mountains, the sublime silences of the stately pines —where birds sung their matins and the "stars became tapers tall"; where the zitkada^{n}to—the blue bird—uttered its ravishing notes. He sought the kat-yi-mo—the "enchanted mesa"—as the place of prayer, the hour in which to register his oath. On the wide extended plain, rolling green, like the billows of the ocean, he listened for wana'gipi tah'upahupi—"the wings of the spirits." In wana'gi ta'ca^{n}ku—the milky way—he saw the footprints of departed warriors. His moccasined feet penetrated wakoniya—"the place where water is born"—the springs that gushed forth to give life, and refreshing to all the earth. Ca^{n}hotka ska—the "white frost"—became the priest's robe as he petitioned at the sacrament of winter. The universe to him became a sounding-board of every emotion that thrilled his being. He found in its phenomena an answer to his longings and the high expression of every fervour of his soul. We cannot understand this, because the Indian chased the ethereal, the weird, the sublime, the mysterious: we chase the dollar. He heard the voice of nature; we listen for the cuckoo clock of commerce.

The camera, the brush, and the chisel have made us familiar with his plumed and hairy crests, but what of the deep fountains of his inner life? What did he think? How did he feel? What riotous impulses, or communion with the Great Mystery, carved his face of bronze? These no scientist, no discoverer, no leader of expeditions have ever borne into the light. No footprints along the trail can spell out for us his majestic mien, his stolid dignity, his triumphant courage, his inscrutable self-poise, and all of these dyed with a blood-red struggle for survival such as crowns no other page of American history.

To gain this close measure of the Indian mind, his friendship and confidence must not suffer eclipse. It is a superlative task, for the inner Indian shrine is crossed by only a favoured few. The Indian is averse to being photographed, for he feels that every picture made of himself by so much shortens his life. He looks at his portrait, then feels of his person; he realizes that he has not lost a hand or a foot, but feels most profoundly that his soul will be that much smaller in the future world. His medicine is sacred, and you may not interrupt the daily tenure of his life without destroying some ceremonial purpose. It is meaningful, therefore, that these red men allowed us daily communion. This story is then simply instinct with the Indian's inner self: how we sat with him in his wigwam, and amid his native haunts, surrounded by every element of the wild life we were to commemorate; how his confidence was gained, and he was led to put aside his war-shirt and eagle feathers, and pull in twain the veil of his superstitious and unexplained reserve and give to the world what the world so much craves to know—what the Indian thinks and how he feels.

Memorable hours these under clear Montana skies, at at the midnight hour by the dim campfire light, the rain beating its tatoo on the tepee above our heads—surrounded by an army of shining tepees, like white ghosts of the plains, while these pathetic figures told the story of their lives. The warrior of other days gave himself up to mirthful tale, to boyhood's transports, to manhood's achievements, to the wild chase of the hunter, to the weaponry and woes of savage warfare, to the hallowed scenes of home life, to the primitive government of the tribe, and the busy and engaging activities of the camp; finally, to the royalty of the Great Council, when the chiefs assembled in solemn conclave to hold communion, to say a long and last farewell.

Months of arduous labour were spent in the effort to make a comprehensive and permanent record of an old-time Indian council. For this purpose eminent Indian chiefs were assembled in the Valley of the Little Big Horn in Montana, from nearly every Indian tribe in the United States. This council involved permission and unstinted aid from the Bureau of Indian Affairs at Washington, the coöperation of the Indian superintendents on all the reservations; the selection of the most distinguished chiefs—chiefs eminent for ability and honourable achievement among their tribes. The council involved the necessity of interpreters from each tribe, for they could only talk in the sign language. It involved the construction of a primitive council lodge along the lines of history and tradition, and again, the reproduction of primitive customs and traditions, both in paraphernalia, costume, and conduct.

These imprints are the trail marks left by this Great Council of Chiefs—the last Great Indian Council that will ever be held on American soil. The story most faithfully records the idiom and phrasing and atmosphere of the Indian's speech as it came from Indian lips. The language of the landscape where the Indian made his home, where he fought his battles and lived his life, where this solemn council was held, is manifest . . . On the Indian trail, we may note as a hint of the many, a few of his imprints.

The life of the Indian is one vast and glittering mosaic of rite and ritual. His warfare, his dress, his medicine, his ceremonies, his wooing, and his dying are all of them expressive of a dominant idea that pervades his life and controls his purpose. He lives constantly and absorbingly in a mystic land. He is beckoned by unseen hands and is lured into the realms of mystery by the challenge of voices silent to all other ears. His dress is studded with resplendent colours significant of the green earth, the blue sky, and the cry of his soul for a place in the great beyond. Like the high priest of old, he wears on his breast the fiery filaments of his faith.

The Indian sits in the tabernacle of the mighty forest or on the heights of some deserted and wind-swept mesa, beats his tomtom or drones song upon song, prays to the Great Mystery, pleads with the fires of the sun to give him strength and life and health, and calls the sun his father. The whispering winds tell his tale to the clouds. He peers into the depths of the stars, watches the aurora as the death dance of the spirits, answers the high call of the thunder as the voice of the Great Mystery, utters the cry of his soul to the lightnings—the arrows of taowity—communes with the rivers and the lakes, the moon, and the legion of wild beasts, and all of it with a pitiful longing that his days of fasting and his vicarious devotion may bring upon his life and his tribe the favour of the gods.

These primitive men hold time and money and ambition as nothing. But a dream, or a cloud in the sky, or a bird flying across the trail from the wrong direction, or a change of the wind will challenge their deepest thoughts. To the Indian mind all signs are symbolic. Their ceremonies are as complicated as any of ancient Hebrew or Greek tradition. The Indian aspires to be a great hunter, he seeks fame as a noble warrior; he struggles for the eagle feathers of distinction, but his greatest longing is to become a Medicine Man and know the Great Mystery. All medicine people of the tribes carry on their necks, or in a pouch at the belt, some sacred thing used in their magic practices—the claw of a bear, the rattle of a snake, a bird's wing, the tooth of an elk, a bit of tobacco. Every Indian carries his individual medicine, and his medicine is good or bad according to his success. If he finds a feather at wrong angle in his path, his medicine is bad for that day. The Indian fasts and dances and chants, using his mind, his spirit, and his body as pliable instruments in the making of his prayer. He finds in the veritable exhaustion of his body the spirit path made clear for his dreams, until the very stars seem as the eyes of the gods, and the sighing of the pines comes to him as the rustle of eagle wings to bear his spirit to loftier realms. Instead of the common acceptation that the Indian has no religion whatever, every single act of his life carries with it some ceremonial function, and his whole being is surrounded by a shining host of ceremonial spirits. The Indian goes with prayer thoughts to the water. His bath is a sacrament. He cuts the long supple willow withes that grow on the banks of the stream, enters the sharpened end into the soil, bends and ties the feathery tops into an arch; over the arches thus made he throws his blankets; meanwhile, gathered stones have been heated in the burning fire. These stones glowing white with heat are placed in a tiny pit underneath the covering of this booth, now to be called his sweat bath. First one stone until four have been counted are placed by the attendant in the pit, and then the fiery pile is thrown in promiscuous fashion on the heap. The Indians enter the closed covering, the ceremonial pipe is smoked, a gourd of cold water is handed to each; they then disrobe, the attending priest lowering the blanket over the entrance. Cold water is then poured over the heated stones, filling the enclosure with steam. In silence they commune with the Great Mystery until one of their number is blessed with a vision; then a call is made and the attendant lifts the blanket, almost immediately lowering it again. This action is repeated until the vision has been vouchsafed four times, when they all come forth and plunge into the river. These sweat baths are always located on the banks of a flowing stream. The Indian sees in every ripple of the flashing water that comes to meet him a shining token of the medicine he has seen in his vision. They then repair to the wigwam and listen in solemn silence to the chanting cadences of the Indian who has been favoured.

The curling smoke from the long-stemmed pipe breathes forth the fumes of war or the pale quiet of peace. With his pipe he pacifies the elements. On festal occasions, or when the camp rejoices at the joys of harvest, the priest smokes his pipe, blowing the smoke first to the earth, then to the sky, to the north, the south, the east, and the west, in token of gratitude for the favour of the gods. With the pipe the Indian also seals his councils.

The Indian buries his dead upon some high elevation, because it is a nearer approach to the spirit world. They bury on scaffolds and in trees that in some mute, sorrowful way they may still hold communion with their loved and their lost. At the grave they go to the four points of the compass and mourn, singing all the while a weird chant. They bury with their dead all of the belongings of the deceased, the playthings of the Indian child, for the Indian boy and girl have dolls and balls and baubles as does the white child: you may see them all pendent from the poles of the scaffold or the boughs of a tree. When the great Chief Spotted Tail died they killed his two ponies, placing the two heads toward the east, fastening the tails on the scaffold toward the west. The war-bonnets and war-shirts are folded away with the silent dead; then follow the desolate days of fasting and mourning. In some instances hired mourners are engaged, and for their compensation they exact oftentimes the entire possessions of the deceased. The habitation in which the death occurs is burned, and many times when death is approaching the sick one is carried out so that the lodge may be occupied after the loved one has been laid to rest. The grief of the sorrowing ones is real and most profound. They will allow no token of the departed to remain within sight or touch. In their paroxysms of sorrow the face and limbs are lacerated, and often the tips of fingers are severed. Until the days of mourning are over, which is for more than a year, they absent themselves from all public gatherings. The bereaved fold themselves in a white blanket, repair to some desolate hillside overlooking the valley, the camp and the distant weird scaffold, and sit, amid cloud, sunshine, and storm, with bowed head, in solemn silence. White blankets are worn by the mourners as they move through the camp, significant of the white trail of the stars whither the Indian feels his loved ones have gone.

The Indian has a sublime idea of creation. He loves the brown earth and calls it his mother, because it has creative power and because it nourishes. And thus we might gather in from the thirty-two points of the compass the forces operant in earth and sky, and each would become a herald of the Indian's life of faith.

The Indian child is nursed on Indian song and story. Tribal traditions are handed down from age to age by enacting in the dance, on the part of the warriors and braves, their deeds of valour in war, their triumphs in the chase, their prowess against all foes. Forest lore is a constant text book. He is taught to observe which side of a tree has the lightest bark—which side the most branches; why the tree reaches forth longer arms on the edge of the wood than in the depths of the forest where his eye is taught to penetrate. The squirrel, the rabbit and the birds all become his little friends: where and how they get their food, their manner of life, their colour, and how they call their mates, who are their enemies, and how they may be protected. His ear is trained to hear sounds ordinarily inaudible, his nostrils are early taught to distinguish the scent of the different wild animals. Then came his ability to imitate the call of this wild life, sometimes by direct vocalization, or by placing two reeds to the lips so dexterously that the timid fawn is led to his feet. This literature the Indian child studies, until his arms are strong enough to bend the bow and send an arrow speeding to its mark. He soon essays the rôle of a warrior. His study of the birds enables him to find the eerie of the eagle, for a victory means that he may add an eagle feather to his war bonnet or coup stick. His study of the hills enables him to find in their vermilion and golden seams the colours for his war paint. In the crimson berries festooning the banks of the stream, when crushed, he finds still another element of decoration. The white man makes a book whose leaves talk. The sunshine bears speech and light to the Indian. He lives by communion with the stars. The Great Bear of the stars is called the great animal of cold weather. When a shadow crosses his mind he watches the clouds that touch the moon when it is new. He reads the stars, for they travel to him in a familiar pathway across the sky. They are bright spirits sent earthward by the Great Mystery, and when thick worlds gather in clusters, there are so many souls of earth people that their trail makes luminous the white way of the sky. The wing of a bird is the symbol of thoughts that fly very high. From the bird that soars nearest the blue he plucks prayer feathers. These he dyes and cherishes with jealous care. The Indian possesses a strange love for growing things, tall grasses with lace-like plumes forming a lattice for the deep green of the slender bushes that bear the rich clusters of crimson buffalo berries. He knows and loves the wild flowers that hang their golden heads along the banks of the purling stream or that in gleaming colours enamel the wide stretches of the plain. There are a thousand leaves in every book, and with every book in nature's library he is familiar to the point of success.

To the casual observer the costume and character of the Indian all look alike. The mind is confused amid a riotous and fantastic display of colours. The fact is that the minor details of Indian dress are an index to Indian character and often tell the story of his position in the tribe, and surely tell the story of his individual conception of the life here, and what he hopes for in the life hereafter, and like the laurel wreath on the brow of the Grecian runner, they spell out for us his exploits and achievements. To the white man all these decorations are construed as a few silly ornaments, the indulgence of a feverish vanity, but they open like a book the life of the Indian. His motive in adornment is to mark individual, tribal, or ceremonial distinction. The use of paint on the face, hair, and body, both in colour and design, generally has reference to individual or clan beliefs, or it indicates relationship, or personal bereavement, or is an act of courtesy. It is always employed in ceremonies, religious and secular, and is an accompaniment of gala dress for the purpose of honouring a guest or to celebrate an occasion. The face of the dead was frequently painted in accordance with tribal or religious symbolism. Paint is also used on the faces of children and adults as a protection from wind and sun. Plucking the hair from the face and body is a part of the daily program. The male Indian never shaves and the beard is a disgrace. A pair of tweezers becomes his razor. Sweet grasses and seeds serve as a perfume. Ear ornaments are a mark of family thrift, wealth or distinction, and indicate honour shown to the wearer by his kindred.

Among the Plains Indians the milk teeth of the elk were the most costly adornments. They were fastened in rows on a woman's tunic and represented the climax of Indian fashion, the garment possessing a value of several hundred dollars. Head bands, armlets, bracelets, belts, necklaces, and garters of metal and seeds and embroidered buckskin were in constant use. They were not only decorative but often symbolic. Archaeological testimony tells of the almost general use of sea shells as necklace ornaments, which found their way into the interior by barter or as ceremonial gifts. The chiefs of the tribe were fond of wearing a disk cut from a conch-shell, and these were also prominent in religious rites, ranking among the modern tribes as did the turquoise among the people of the Southwest. A necklace of bear claws marks the man of distinction, and sometimes was worn as an armlet. In the buffalo country the women seldom ornamented their own robes, but embroidered those worn by the men. Sometimes a man painted his robe in accordance with a dream or pictured upon it a yearly record of his own deeds, or the prominent events of the tribe. Among the southern tribes a prayer rug was made on deer skin, both the buffalo and deer skins having been tanned and softened by the use of the brains taken from the skull of the animal. The skins were painted with intricate ornamentation, symbols and prayer thoughts adorning the skin in ceremonial colours; white clouds and white flowers, the sun god, and the curve of the moon with its germ of life, the morning star, and also a symbol of the messengers from the gods. Above it all zigzag lines ran through the blue of the sky to denote the lightning by which the children above sent their decrees to the earth children who roamed the plains.

Footgear often proclaimed the tribal relation, the peculiar cut and decoration of the moccasin denoting a man's tribe. The war-shirt was frequently ornamented to represent the life story of the man wearing it. The breast contained a prayer for protection, and on the back might be found woven in beaded tapestry the symbols of victory. He had conquered the trail behind him. The shirt was often decorated with a fringe of human hair, the more warlike appending the scalps of the slain. The warrior wore no regalia so imposing as his war-bonnet with its crown of golden eagle feathers. Before the coming of the horse the flap at the back rarely extended below the waist, but when the warriors came to be mounted, the ruff of feathers was so lengthened that when the Indian was dismounted it trailed on the ground. The making of a war-bonnet was accompanied by song and ceremony. Each feather before it was placed in position was held in the hand and had recounted over it the story of some war honour. A bonnet could not be made without the consent of all the warriors and it stood as a record of tribal valour and a special mark of distinction granted to the man by his tribe. Every Indian takes great joy in laying out his colour scheme. It becomes a mosaic of artistic talent. Feathers are gathered from the eagles' flight. Skins are taken from the wild beasts. Bones, beads, sparkling metals, soft-tinted sea shells, and all of them blended with the vari-coloured paints that he has compounded in nature's mortar. The woman enters into the work with intelligent zest, and when completed the whole array of blended colours is beyond the criticism of the tribe. The back of an Indian's war-bonnet and war-shirt is always more gaudy and sumptuous than the front view and this because when Indians pass each other their salutation is brief and formal. They ride right on. But after the meeting they turn in the saddle and look back to take an inventory. The wealth of the Indian, his position in the tribe, his ceremonial attainment are all passed upon and estimate entered. This colour scheme goes on through the entire Indian wardrobe to pipe sack, coup stick and moccasins. The Indian could not have received his suggestion for a colour scheme from the tinted leaves of autumn for they are dull in comparison. He may have had a hint from the glowing sunsets that in that western land fill earth and sky with a glory so transcendent that mere rhetoric is a profanation. More likely is it that when free and unrestrained he roamed over plain and hill his soul became enamoured with the dazzling array of colours, beyond the genius of the proudest palette, to be found in the marvellous formations that surround the great geysers of the Yellowstone, colours more exquisitely beautiful than the supremest refinement of art. Every-whither down the cone-shaped mounds are tiny steam-heated rivulets interlacing each other, edged with gold and vermilion and turquoise and orange and opal. Indian trails have been found also interlacing each other all through this wonderland. Deep furrows in the grassy slopes of these ancient footprints are still plainly visible.

Thither we may believe came the red man imbued with the spirit of reverence and awe before all this majesty and beauty, and from this exhaustless laboratory claimed the vivid colouring for the expression of his life of faith.

The Indian has lived such a life of hazard for long centuries that he has had trained into him a first great instinct to fight. They have a war star in the sky, and when it moves the time to make war is heavy upon them. There are many cogent reasons for the belief that before the coming of the white man there were no general or long-continued wars among the Indians. There was no motive for war. Quarrels ensued when predatory tribes sought to filch women or horses. Strife was engendered on account of the distribution of buffalo, but these disturbances could not be dignified by the name of war. The country was large and the tribes were widely separated. Their war implements were of the crudest sort. A shield would stop a stone-headed arrow, and it necessitated a hand-to-hand conflict for the use of a flint-headed lance and the ponderous war club. The white man came, and for hundreds of years their contest has been waged against a superior force. They have disputed every mile of territory which has been acquired from them. During all that time they could not make a knife, a rifle or a round of ammunition. Their method of communication was confined to the smoke signal, signal fires and scouts. They had no telegraph, no heliograph, no arsenal. Modern implements of war they have been able to obtain only in late years and then in meagre quantities, even then only by capture or at exorbitant rates. The Indian has proved himself a redoubtable and masterful foe. For more than three hundred years millions of civilized white people have fought a bitter battle with three hundred thousand red men. During all these tragic years the nations of the world have moved on to discovery, subjugation, and conquest. Nation has taken up arms against nation. England, France, and Spain have put a rim of colonies about the globe. Our own great civil struggle has been written down on the pages of history with letters of blood. England, France, Spain, and the United States have during this period tried their prowess with these less than three hundred thousand braves and only now has the decimation become complete. No such striking example of endurance, power of resistance, and consummate generalship has been recorded in the annals of time. Sitting-Bull, Red Cloud, Looking-Glass, Chief Joseph, Two Moons, Grass, Rain-in-the-Face, American Horse, Spotted Tail, and Chief Gall are names that would add lustre to any military page in the world's history. Had they been leaders in any one of the great armies of the nation they would have ranked conspicuously as master captains. The Indian, deprived of the effectiveness of supplies and modern armament, found his strongest weapon in the oratory of the council lodge. Here, without any written or established code of laws, without the power of the press and the support of public sentiment, absolutely exiled from all communication with civilized resources, unaided and alone, their orators presented the affairs of the moment to the assembled tribe, swaying the minds and wills of their fellows into concerted and heroic action.

The wonderful imagery of the Indian orator—an imagery born of his baptism into the spirit of nature—his love of his kind, and the deathless consciousness of the justice of his cause made his oratory more resistless than the rattle of Gatling guns, and also formed a model for civilized speech. It was an oratory that enabled a few scattering tribes to withstand the aggressions of four great nations of the world for a period of several centuries, and to successfully withstand the tramping columns of civilization.

The science and art of Indian warfare would take volumes to compass. His strategy and statesmanship compelled victory. He was almost always assured of victory before he proceeded to battle. He knew no fear. A thousand lives would have been a small gift had he the power to lay them on the altar of his cause. He pitted the perfection of details against the wily strategy of his own colour and the pompous superiority of the white man's tactics. On the trail care was taken to cover up or obliterate his footprints. When a fire became necessary he burned fine dry twigs so that the burning of green boughs would not lift to the wind an odour of fire, nor carry a trail of smoke. He conceived and carried out a wonderful deception in dress. In winter a band of warriors were painted white. They rode white horses and their war dress was all of it made of the plainest white so that a group of warriors, stationed on the brow of a hill, would appear in the distance like a statuesque boulder clad in snow. This disguise also enabled them to come with stealthy step upon wild game. In autumn their horses were painted yellow and they wore a garb of yellow so that fringing the edge of the forest they could not be distinguished from the leaves of the dying year. The blue-green of the sagebrush, so conspicuously omnipresent on the prairies, furnished the Indian with another helpful form of disguise. He would almost completely disrobe and paint his face, his arms, and his hair, as well as the body of his horse, exactly the colour of the sagebrush; and when scouting, after their crouching fashion, among the clusters of sagebrush, or riding in the distance along the verdure-covered banks of a stream, the disguise would be so absolutely complete that detection became a difficult task. It was an ingenious and artistic display of war talent.

We are led to wonder often concerning the Indian's passion for his coup stick (pronounced coo). This rod, bedecked with eagle feathers and his own colour scheme, is the Indian's badge of empire. It is the "Victoria Cross" of his deeds of valour. In battle he rushes amid his foes, touches the enemy with his coup stick—that man is his prisoner, and he has counted a coup. He slays an enemy, then rushes up and touches him with the stick, takes his scalp; another coup is counted. The credit of victory was taken for three brave deeds: killing an enemy, scalping an enemy, or being the first to strike an enemy, alive or dead; any one of these entitles a man to rank as a warrior and to recount his exploit in public; but to be the first to touch an enemy is regarded as the bravest deed of all, as it implied close approach in battle. In the last Great Indian Council and on the journey home the attention of the writer was called to the prominence given to the coup stick. They are present at all ceremonial functions and are carried on all ceremonial parades. The warrior who can strike a tepee of the enemy in a charge upon a home camp thus counted coup upon it and is entitled to reproduce its particular design in the next new tepee which he made for his own use, and to perpetuate the pattern in his family. The eagle feathers on the stick can only be placed there after the warrior has counted his coup, recounted it in public, and the deed has met with the approval of all the warriors. The eagle, the proudest and most victorious of birds, then yielded a feather, which is deftly fastened with a circle of shining beads to the stick, and the proud victor flaunts another emblem of his bravery.

The buffalo, once the king of the prairies, has been practically exterminated. Perhaps no greater grief has ever entered into the life of the Indian than this wilful waste and irreparable loss. To this hour the Indian mourns the going away of the buffalo. He cannot be reconciled. He dates every joyful and profitable event in his life to the days of the buffalo. In the assembly of chiefs at the last Great Council the buffalo was the burden of every reminiscence. These veteran chiefs studied with melancholy eyes the old buffalo trails, and in contemplation of the days of the chase they said, as they thought backward, "My heart is lonely and my spirit cries." So much did they love the buffalo that the Indian children played hunting the buffalo. The animal furnished food and clothing, and many parts of the stalwart frame they counted as sacred. The annihilation of these vast herds aroused the darkest passions in the heart of the Indian, and many times stirred his war spirit and sent him forth to do battle against the aggressors. Within the nine years between 1874 and 1883 over eight millions of buffalo were ruthlessly slain. But the war curtain of the Indian has been rung down, and the vast area which twoscore years ago supported these vast herds of wild game is covered to-day with domestic animals and teems with agricultural life, furnishing food supplies for millions upon millions all over the civilized world.

Far stretches of prairie, winding watercourses, leagues of white desert with only the clouds in the sky and the shadow of the clouds on the blistering sand, an army of buttes and crags, storm carved, forests whose primeval stillness mocks the calendar of man, the haunts of the eagle, the antelope, the deer and the buffalo—and the edge of the curtain is lifted on the land where the Indian roamed and where he made his home.

Game has been found, a semi-circle of cone-shaped tepees dot the green of the plain; a stream, tree-fringed, fresh from the mountains, flows by the camp—a camp that in earlier times was pitched upon some tableland as an outlook for the enemy, white or red. Horses are browsing near at hand or far afield; old warriors and medicine men sit in the shade and smoke the long-stemmed, red sandstone pipe, and tell of the days of yore. Gayly clad figures dart hither and yon as the women are bent upon their tasks. Great loads of wood are brought into camp on an Indian woman's back. She carries water from the river, bakes the cake, upturned against the fire, boils the coffee and then all are seated on the ground when they partake of jerked beef, coffee, bread, and berries. Hands are better than knives and forks, one cup answers for many, and the strip of dried beef is passed along that all may cut off his desired portion. A noisy, gleeful group of children play with their dolls and their dogs—dogs that are made to serve as beasts of burden and instruments of torture. At night beds are made on the ground around the interior circle of the tepee and the chill of frost is driven out by a fire in the very centre—the most perfectly ventilated structure in the world—the air passing underneath the edge of the tepee in the loop where it is tied at the bottom of the poles, then passing on out through the opening at the top, carrying with it all dust and smoke. The Indian never knew anything about tuberculosis until the white man confined him in log cabins where a score of people live in one room, the cracks and keyhole entirely filled, and where they breath each other over times without number. Within the tepee the chief has the place of honour. A rest is made with supports like an easel. A lattice-work of slender willow rods passed down the front, which is covered by a long strip of buffalo hide. Against this the chief rests. Each member of the family has his allotted place inside the lodge and he may decorate his own section according to ability or fancy. Here the warrior hangs his war-bonnet and sometimes records his achievements in the chase or on the warpath. Lying all about the circle are many highly coloured parflesche bags containing the minor details of dress or any personal possession. Many of the tepees in an Indian village are embellished with Indian paintings setting forth the heroic deeds of the warriors who abide in the lodge. The figures are often grotesque and without parallel in the realm of art. The medicine is given a conspicuous place in the lodge. No one sits or lies down on the side of the tepee where they have placed the medicine of the household, and when they pass it on entering or leaving the lodge all heads are bowed. The medicine tepee is distinct from all others. It is painted a maroon, with a moon in green surrounded by a yellow circle. The medicine of the ordinary family is hung over the entrance of the doorway or suspended on a pole, and may consist of a wolf skin or a dark blanket rolled in oblong fashion containing the sacred tokens of the family. Every Indian family takes pride in the ownership of a bevy of dogs. They are rich in dogs. In our camp of about thirty tepees a reliable Indian estimated that there were over three hundred dogs. These canines have free run of the lodge, and at night they crawl in under the edge of the canvas and sleep by their Indian master. Let an intruder enter the camp during the hours of darkness and they rush out simultaneously, howling like a pack of wolves until one might think the bowels of the earth had given forth an eruption of dogs. The Indian warrior makes a companion of his dog, and he can show no greater hospitality to a guest than to kill his favourite friend and serve his visitor with dog soup. To refuse this diet is an insult most vital.

The Indian woman is master of the lodge. She carries the purse. Any money that comes into the hands of the husband is immediately handed over. The servile tasks of the camp are performed by the women. Herein we have an expression of the law of equality. The husband has to perform the exhausting and dangerous task of hunting wild game for food and the skins for clothing. He had to protect the camp against hostile attacks, and the woman felt that her task was easy in comparison. The Indian child rules the family. They are rarely, if ever, corrected. No Indian mother was ever known to strike her child. If they want anything they cry until they get it—and they know how to cry. In play they are as mirthful and boisterous as any white child. They ride mock horses, and play mud ball. The Indian boy prepares willow sticks, peels off the bark, then rolls the wet clay into balls, and, sticking the ball on the end of the twig, he throws it at a mark with great speed and accuracy. Perhaps the most popular sport among the children is what they term the stick game. Again willow rods are used without the bark, only this time they are cut short enough to be rigid, and they drive them with great velocity up an inclined board. When the stick leaves the board it speeds like an arrow far in the distance. Every Indian boy and girl owns a pony, from which they are almost inseparable, and which they ride with fearless abandon.

While men are off in search of game the women make bead work of a most bewitching order, meanwhile watching the pappoose, fastened completely in its wooden bead-covered cradle, only the head protruding. The cradle is hung from a lodge or the bough of a tree, rattles and bells playing in the breeze. Other women gather in the shade and play the game of plum stone, a gambling game. They use the stones of the wild plum, which they colour with fanciful devices, and toss them up in a wooden bowl.

The wooing of Indian lovers varies with the tribes. One pair of lovers seal their vows by standing a little removed from the parental lodge, with a blanket covering their heads. In another tribe the negotiations are made entirely through the parents, when the transaction resolves itself into a barter, so many ponies for a bride; while in still another tribe, when a love fancy strikes a young man, he arranges to meet the young woman who has attracted him as she goes to the river for water. They pass each other in the path without any recognition. This occurs two or three times. Finally if the young girl welcomes these attentions she looks toward him as they pass. That night he comes to the lodge of her parents, remains outside, beating a tomtom and singing the love song. The young girl then goes out to meet him and they sit outside and talk. The next morning the mother asks her daughter about the affair, and then the mother invites the young man to come and dine with them and sit around the campfire. Thus the courtship proceeds until he finally says, "I will take this girl for my wife," and the two go to their own lodge.

The Indian has an unwritten code of family morals to which he most rigidly adheres. In some tribes no Indian will cross the threshold of another if the wife of that man is alone, and in others no brother goes into the house where his sister is unless she has a companion. This is an ancient law and belongs to many tribes. The Crows have an eccentric custom that a sister after marriage is not allowed to be seen in public with her brother. Should an Indian alienate the affections of the wife of another Indian or steal his horse the injured one would be justified in taking his rifle and killing the offender. The whole camp would sanction the action on the ground that it would rid the camp of bad blood.

The Indian's civility and hospitality, both to his own kind and to strangers, has been a marked feature of his character from the coming of the white man to the present day. When Columbus touched the shores of the New World the friendly Caribs gave him hearty welcome. The heart's right hand of fellowship was stretched out in welcome and hospitality as explorers and settlers landed on American soil. Dignity, generosity, and courtesy marked the attitude of the Indian toward these new white strangers. The character generally attributed to the Indian is that of a savage, but this blemish came upon him through contact with the white man. Their ingenuous and trustful nature quickly degenerated as they were enslaved, betrayed, and slain. Advantage was taken of their ignorance and kindness. Then came on a race war unparalleled in ferocity and barbarism. The inexorable march of civilization regardless of ethics swept on until we heard the Indians' war cry and failed to see the diviner grace of friendship. The Indian returned with interest every injury and hardship, every bitter assault and wicked aggression. He paid in full all accounts in the coin of pitiless revenge. These shadows obliterate our thought of him as courtier and hospitable host. The Indian will divide his last crust and then go hungry himself that you may have his half of the crust. Had it not been for Indian generosity in furnishing supplies of food, the early settlers in both New England and Virginia must have perished with hunger. Every guest entering an Indian wigwam is met by all the graces of hospitality—in cordial greeting—in a splendid home feeling.

Indian trails are no longer worn deep through the prairie sod, they have been growing ever more dim and indistinct. It is to-day, the "thin red line," a swift gathering of all that is left, in the gloaming, after the sunset.